HISTORY

OF

TENNESSEE

From the Earliest Time to the Present; Together with an Historical and a Biographical Sketch of Lawrence, Wayne, Perry, Hickman and Lewis Counties; Besides a Valuable Fund of Notes, Reminiscences, Observations, Etc., Etc.

ILLUSTRATED.

NASHVILLE:
THE GOODSPEED PUBLISHING CO.,
1886.

New Material Copyright © 1979 by:

The Rev. Silas Emmett Lucas, Jr.

All rights reserved. No part of this publication may be reproduced, stored in a retrieval system or transmitted in any form or by any means without the prior written permission of the publisher.

Please Direct All Correspondence and Book Orders to:

Southern Historical Press, Inc.
PO Box 1267
375 West Broad Street
Greenville, SC 29602-1267
----
southernhistoricalpress@gmail.com

ISBN #0-89308-113-2

PREFACE.

THIS volume has been prepared in response to the prevailing and popular demand for the preservation of local history and biography. The method of preparation followed is the most successful and the most satisfactory yet devised—the most successful in the enormous number of volumes circulated, and the most satisfactory in the general preservation of personal biography and family record conjointly with local history. The number of volumes now being distributed appears fabulous. Within the last four years not less than 20,000 volumes of this class of works have been distributed in Kentucky, and the demand is not half satisfied. Careful estimates place the number circulated in Ohio at 50,000; Pennsylvania, 60,000; New York, 75,000; Indiana, 35,000; Illinois, 40,000; Iowa, 35,000, and every other Northern State at the same proportionate rate. The Southern States, with the exception of Kentucky, Virginia and Georgia, owing mainly to the disorganization succeeding the civil war, yet retain, ready for the publisher, their stores of history and biography. Within the next five years the vast and valuable fund of perishing event in all the Southern States will be rescued from decay, and be recorded and preserved—to be reviewed, studied and compared for the benefit of future generations. The design of the present extensive historical and biographical research is more to gather and preserve in attractive form, while fresh with the evidences of truth, the enormous fund of perishing occurrence, than to abstract from insufficient contemporaneous data remote, doubtful or incorrect conclusions. The true perspective of the landscape of life can only be seen from the distance that lends enchantment to the view. It is asserted that no person is competent to write a philosophical history of his own time—that, owing to conflicting circumstantial evidence that yet conceals the truth, he can not take that luminous, correct, comprehensive, logical and unprejudiced view of passing events, that will enable him to draw accurate and enduring conclusions. The duty, then, of a historian of his own time is to collect, classify and preserve the material for the final historian of the future. The present historian deals in fact, the future historian, in conclusion; the work of the former is statistical, of the latter, philosophical.

To him who has not attempted the collection of historical data, the obstacles to be surmounted are unknown. Doubtful traditions, conflicting statements, imperfect records, inaccurate private correspondence, the bias or untruthfulness of informers, and the general obscurity which envelopes all passing events, combine to bewilder and mislead. On the contrary, the preparation of statistical history by experienced, unprejudiced and competent workers in specialties; the accomplishment by a union of labor of a vast result that would cost one person the best years of his life and transfer the collection of perishing event beyond the hope of research; the judicious selection of important matter from the general rubbish; and the careful and intelligent revision of all final manuscript by an editor-in-chief, yield a degree of celerity, system, accuracy, comprehensiveness and value unattainable by any other method. The publishers of this volume, fully aware of their inability to furnish a perfect history, an accomplishment vouchsafed only to the imagination of the dreamer or the theorist, make no pretension of having prepared a work devoid of blemish. They feel assured that all thoughtful people, at present and in future, will recognize and appreciate the importance of their undertaking and the great public benefit that has been accomplished.

In the preparation of this volume the publishers have met with nothing but courtesy and assistance. They acknowledge their indebtedness for valuable favors to the Governor, the State Librarian, the Secretary of the State Historical Society and to more than a hundred of other prominent citizens of Nashville, Memphis, Knoxville, Chattanooga, Jackson, Clarksville, Columbia and the smaller cities of the State. It is the design of the publishers to compile and issue, in connection with the State history, a brief yet comprehensive historical account of every county in the State, copies of which will be placed in the State Library. In the prosecution of this work they hope to meet with the same cordial assistance extended to them during the compilation of this volume.

THE PUBLISHERS.

NASHVILLE, November, 1886.

CONTENTS.

LAWRENCE COUNTY.

	PAGE.
LAWRENCE COUNTY	749
Courts, The	752 to 756
Churches, The	762
Geology and Drainage	749
Lawrenceburg	757
Military Matters	760
Mills, etc	749
Organization of the County	752
Public Buildings	752, 753
Poor, The	753
Railroad, The	754
Settlers, The Early	750
Schools	761

WAYNE COUNTY.

WAYNE COUNTY	763
Buildings	766
Court Trials	767 to 769
County Formation, etc	765
Education	775
Miscellany	765
Religion	776
Settlement	764
Streams	763
Villages	771 to 773
War Record	773
Waynesboro	770

PERRY COUNTY.

PERRY COUNTY	777
County Officers	783
Churches	788
Formation of the County	781
Geology, etc	777, 778
Industries, The Early	780, 781
Linden	784
Military Affairs	785, 786
Other Towns	785
Pioneers, The	779, 780
Schools	787

HICKMAN COUNTY.

HICKMAN COUNTY	801
Centerville	795
County Seat, The	793
County Officers	793, 794
Education	798
Iron Ore, etc	789
Milling Interests	791
Productions	792
Religion	799
Settlement	790
Small Villages	797
Wars, The	793

LEWIS COUNTY.

	PAGE.
LEWIS COUNTY	801
Boundary and Drainage	801
Courts	804, 805
County Officers	805
Churches	807
Military	806
Merriwether Lewis	803
Organization of the County	803
Schools	806
Settlement	802
Towns	806
Water-Mills	802

BIOGRAPHICAL APPENDIX.

Hickman County	910
Lawrence County	807
Lewis County	923
Perry County	889
Wayne County	849

LAWRENCE COUNTY.

LAWRENCE COUNTY belongs to the natural division known as the Highland Rim, the higher lands lying from the northeast to the southwest. From the general level there rises occasional bluffs 300 feet in height. The elevation above the sea level is about 700 or 800 feet. The general surface, however, is sufficiently level to admit of agricultural pursuits. The principal streams of the county are Shoal Creek, Factory Fork, Beeler Fork, Chisholm Creek, Knob Creek, Sugar Creek, Blue Water, Little and Big Buffalo Rivers, and many other smaller streams. These streams have their source in the numerous large springs that burst from the hill-sides and flow pure as crystal over beds of shale, limestone, chert or pebbles. These streams abound in fine trout and other fish that furnish pastime for not a few Izaak Waltons. The streams furnish fine water power for machinery, such as saw-mills, flouring-mills and cotton and woolen factories. The Shoal Mills, two and a half miles from Lawrenceburg, are owned by Wm. Parker, and have 1,068 spindles, 30 looms, and manufacture sheetings, drills, carpet-chain, etc. These mills have a 35-horse power turbine wheel, also a 25-horse power engine. The Crowson Mills, on Crowson Fork of Shoal Creek, were built in 1856. The mills are owned by W. H. Sykes & Bro., and have 576 spindles. The machinery is moved by a 35-horse power turbine wheel. The Crescent Mills, on Simonton Fork of Shoal Creek, were built in 1852. These mills have 32 looms, 1,152 spindles and a 40-horse power wheel. The Hope Mills have a 35-horse power wheel and 768 spindles. The Eagle Mills of McCrea & Co. have 1,176 spindles and a wheel of 40-horse power. The Laurel Hill Mills, on Buffalo River, have 1,570 spindles and 56 looms. The Marcella Falls Woolen Mills were built in 1882 by I. B. Rains, J. M. Mays, G. T. Hughes, A. B. Rains and L. E. Frierson, with the above name.

Lawrence has some excellent farming lands, that produce fine corn, wheat, cotton, tobacco and fruits. Only about eighteen per cent of the lands in the county is cleared. The principal wealth lies in the beds of iron ore and fine timber. The valuable timbers are the walnut, oak, ash and poplar, of which there are vast quantities.

The first settlements made in the county were on Big Buffalo River, near Pennington's old mill site, near the crossing of that stream by the Columbia & Waynesboro Turnpike, in 1815. The settlers came chiefly from North Carolina. Among them were Jacob Pennington and sons (Moses, Absalom, William, Isaac and David), Archibald Coulert, Joshua Ashmore, Drury Chambers, John Voorhees, David Matthews, James McMillan, George Kitchen, Phillip Chromister, Absalom Murphy, Daniel Pennington, John and Wm. Voss, Joe Reynolds, Aquila Brown, John Lockhart, Wm. Williams, Miles Parsons, Wm. Leahorn, Wm. Burlesson, John Bromley, C. Hutchinson, John Ray, Adam Chromister, Jesse Hutchinson, Daniel Simms, Daniel Smith, John Garrison, Geo. Isham, Wm. Long, Joseph Teas, James Teas, James Horton, Thomas and James Christy, John McChish, Thos. Mitchell, the Fosters, Steels, Bryants, Duckworths, Hurleys, Williamses, Bennets, Garrets, Pollocks, Perkinses, Cunninghams, Kennedys and McBrides. At Pennington's the first water-mill in the county was built in 1816 by Moses Pennington; a distillery was also built near the mill—the first in the county. The Primitive Baptists built the first church in 1817, near where Henryville was afterward built, of which church the Rev. John Hunter was the first minister. The first school was taught in the above church in 1817. The pioneers on Beeler Fork were John Beeler, M. Duncan, Robert Hayne, Josephus Irvine, Samuel Thomas and Thomas Paine. On Middle Fork were Bailey Alford, Samuel McLean, William Thomas, John Welch, John Chambers, J. E. Edmiston, Warren Mason, David Crockett, Daniel Levi, Jacob and William Matthews, William and Nehemiah Reynolds, John, William and John (Jr.) McAnally, Solomon, Wm. and Noble Stone, John Crisp, John King, Wm. Cannon, James Bumpass, Willis Lucas, Martin Prewett, Aaron Cheat, Moses Holliday, Stephen Holliday, Richard Cheat, George Lucas, Patterson Crockett, Abner and Gabriel Bumpass, Jacob Adair, John Poley, Ebenezer Thompson, James and Joseph Halford, W. S. Dalton, John Shirley, Levi Blackard, James Bradstreet, James Birgen, George Rodgers, Wm. Worten, Stephen Roland, John Smith, John Sullivan, John M. Hughes, Charles, James and Nathan Armstrong, William and O. N. Green, John Henson, John Talby, Samuel Akin and Green Depoint. On Shoal Creek and vicinity were Harlan Paine, John Buchanan, George Lucas, Archibald Morrow, Green D. Priest, Samuel Armstrong, David McIntyre, Wm. Melton, A. McLaren, David Stewart, Jacob Blythe, David Adkison, Benjamin Smith, Beasley Ingraham, John Miller, James Brooks, Wiley Brown, Robert Carr, Edward Denton, John Gest, Barney Gabill, Thomas Dollane, Henry Wellington, James and William Hearlson, Robert Hillhouse, John and Daniel McIntyre, Elisha and Elijah Milton, John Null, Andrew McLaren, Andrew Pickens, Spencer Pearce, William Smith, Nathan Spear, Thomas Spencer, Horace Strawn, Wm. Simmons, Abraham Sizemore, Jacob Turnbow, Elijah Welker, Moses Williams, Wm. Jackson (Sr.) and William Jackson (Jr.) On Sugar Creek and vicinity there settled Jacob Brashers, John Miller, John and William Brashers, George Brenn, Joseph Baldwin, and others. On Chism Fork of Shoal Creek were Wm. Tucker, Jesse Tucker and James Welch. On Knob Creek were Pollard Wisdom, Solomon Azbell, Thomas Ethridge, John Ethridge, and others. In different parts of the county there were the Alexanders, Gaswells, Higgs, Phenixes, Lindseys, McConnells, Kilburns, Cunninghams, Stringhams, McClindens, Davises, Joneses, Grays, Tutnells, Alcorns, Hills, Haynes, Gambells, McCains, Sharps, McKinneys, Mitchells, Walkers, Whartons, Campbells, Fosters, Stricklands, Morgans, Oxfords, Fallses, Allsops, Poteets and Pennicuffs.

All the families had settled in the county previous to 1818. By actual enumeration in 1818 the enrollment shows a voting population of 458. This shows a very rapid immigration when it is considered the first permanent settlers came in 1815. The first settled mainly on the larger streams, which furnished fish for food, power to run mills, cotton-gins and other machinery, but, also, in the absence of roads, they furnished outlets to other parts of the county. Jesse Helton built the first cotton-gin in the county in 1817, on Middle Fork. James Scott erected a mill on Shoal Creek in 1820. Many deer, wolves, bears, wildcats and turkeys were found in the county, and the food of the pioneer consisted largely of game. Among the most noted hunters of his day was the celebrated David Crockett, who was one of the justices chosen for the county at its organization. He resigned his office on November 1, 1819, and soon became involved in numerous lawsuits for debt. At one time he owned nearly 400 acres of land in the county, but in 1822 he gave away what property he had left, by his "free will," to Nancy Musgrave, and moved to Gibson County, W. Tenn. From this section he was a representative and afterward congressman. About 1835, having been defeated for Congress, he left the State and went to Texas, where he assisted the Texans in their struggle for independence. He fell bravely fighting at the Alamo. The following persons received either military grants or occupants' grants about 1820: James Scott, James Appleton, James Byter, Stephen Bushby, John Crosthwait, Andrew Fugate, John Garner, Thomas Holland, Daniel Williams, Willis Lucas, Martin Prewett, John Ray, W. E. Tipton, Enoch and William Tucker, Thomas Welch and Wisdom. In 1870 J. B. Juep, editor of *Volksfreund*, of Cincinnati, and president of the "German Catholic Homestead Association," purchased at one time 15,000 acres of land in this county, the whole amounting to about 25,000 acres, and large numbers of those industrious and thrifty people found homes here, and thus added materially to the wealth of the county.

Lawrence County was established by an act of the General Assembly in 1817, but was not formally organized until the first Monday in May, 1818. The county was cut off from "the territory south of Maury and west of Giles," and embraced a much larger area formerly than now. It has been reduced from time to time. The same act which ordered the new county, also ordered that it should be called Lawrence, in honor, it is supposed, of Commodore Lawrence, of the United States Navy. The act further provided for the laying out of a county seat. David Crockett, Henry Sharp, Maxmilian H. Buchanan, and John Beeler were selected to lay out the county and to select a county seat. Duncan McIntyre surveyed and marked the county boundaries, for which he was allowed the sum $35. The justices selected by the Legislature were Henson Day, Mansil Crisp, John Hillhouse, Pollard Wisdom, Richard Hill, Thomas Welch, Willis Hammond, Daniel Beeler, Samuel D. Poteet, Henry Sharp, Philip Chromister, Nathan McClendon, David Crockett, Robert Chaffin, Robert Newton and Thomas Archer. The other officers appointed were Daniel Beeler, chairman; M. H. Buchanan, clerk; Luke Grimes, sheriff; Alexander Miller, register; George Gresham, ranger; Solomon P. Cunningham, coroner.

The first court was held at the house owned by Dr. Joseph Farmer, but occupied afterward by Josephus Irvine. In 1819 the court gave an order to Irvine "to build a temporary court house for the county on such spot of ground as he may think proper, about twenty-five feet square, and he wait the future generosity of the court for compensation for the same; to which the said Irvine agreed." The reason for building a temporary court house was, that the county seat had not yet been established. Irvine was allowed $25 per year for his court house, but the seat having been established in 1819, orders were given for the erection of a new court house in Lawrenceburg. The new building was of brick—the old one was of logs—and two-stories in height, but about the same dimensions otherwise as the old one. This building was ready for occupancy at the April term of 1821. No record of the cost or contract of this building is to be found. This building is a part of the present court house. On January 4, 1847, S. E. Rose, J. O. Tarkington, Wm. A. Edmiston, Francis H. Kennedy, Robert Brashers, W. T. Stewart and John McCracken were appointed a committee to examine into the finances of the county, to ascertain the probable cost of a new court house and the feasibility of repairing the old house. It was decided to repair the old house by building around it, and by increasing its height two feet. The contract was let to Wm. A. Edmiston, Thomas D. Deavenport and J. W. Tarkington for $2,350. On January 4, 1850, an order was passed allowing the Freemasons and Odd Fellows to erect an additional story to the building at their own expense. This was done at a cost of $1,500. This building is still in use, but is considerably out of repair; however, it is under contract for repairs.

Under the law for imprisonment for debt, the following prison bounds were established in October, 1820: "Beginning at the most northern part of Jenkins' blacksmith shop; thence to the most northern part of the Widow Irvine's house; thence to the most northern corner of the old schoolhouse near the jail; thence to the southeast corner of Col. Irvine's plantation; thence, with the fence of the same, to the place of beginning, to include all the plantation." Alexander Miller was awarded, on November 3, 1819, $277.50 for furnishing a temporary jail. This was repaired from time to time till 1839, when the sheriff entered his protest against the further use of the old jail. A new lot was purchased, and, on April 9, Wm. Chaffin, Wm. A. Edmiston, P. G. Austin, L. M. Bently and C. B. Davis were appointed a committee to draw plans and specifications for a new jail and to let the building of the same to the lowest bidder. This was let in October, 1859, to be completed by March, 1860, at a cost of $3,999, in three equal installments. The dungeons were ten feet square and built of hewn timber, having double walls, with the space between filled with rocks, etc. This jail was burned in 1863 by some conscript soldiers, who had been confined therein, but was not rebuilt till 1870. It was rebuilt by a committee—C. B. Davis, P. A. Austin, S. A. Carrell, S. Bushby and G. O. White, at a total cost of $3,056.95. In 1871 an order was passed by the county court allowing Lawrenceburg the use of the upper cells for city prisoners.

The first commissioners of the poor were Robert Hill, George Lucas and Robert Chaffin, who were appointed in 1820. In 1824 Mr. Lucas, James Burns and Hardin Payne distributed $62 to the poor. Previous to the purchase of the poor farm in 1837, paupers were cared for by private individuals; in fact they were farmed out to the lowest responsible bidder. In that year George Lucas, A. W. Bumpass, Wm. Davis, A. Hill and C. J. Henson were ordered to select a site for a poor farm. A purchase of 200 acres of land was made, twenty-five acres of wild land and 175 acres of "occupant land" of the place where "Needham Tutnell now lives." The cost of the whole was only $245. On the purchase of the above, which included a house, all paupers were ordered thither, and Mrs. C. C. Brown was appointed poorhouse keeper. This site was afterward sold, and Lewis Miller and W. C. Craig were chosen to sell the same and to purchase a new site. This was done in 1847, and a new farm purchased. The county now owns 196 acres of land, and the poor are kept at a nominal expense to the county.

The first divisions into districts were only two, viz.: Lawrenceburg and Pennington. In 1823 there were divisions by companies of Capts. Gresham, McCauley, Welch, Prewett, Segmore, Wisdom, Seahorn and Wharton. In 1835, the last division before they became permanently fixed by number, the divisions were Capts. Roberts, Lucas, Hunt, Green, Abel Hill, W. Hill, Wm. K. Hill, Price, Alton, McClintock, Keys, White, Warren, Tally and Steen. Under the constitution of 1836 the county was divided into twelve civil districts. Beginning in the southwest corner of the county they were numbered First, Second and Third to the East, and then Fourth, Fifth and Sixth to the West, and so on through the whole county. The most of those divisions have been changed somewhat, and the number increased to fifteen, so that they are no longer in regular order as they were at first. John Warren, Hugh C. McIntyre, Rob. Brashers and Wm. McCallister were appointed to make these divisions in 1836. The place for elections in No. 1, was at Alex Stewart's; No. 2, at Benjamin Powell's; No. 3, at Rob Brasher's; No. 4, at Thomas Frank's; No. 5, at Jacob Bryant's; No. 6, at Col. Hail's; No. 7, at Wm. Monday's; No. 8, at Lawrenceburg; No. 9, at James Helton's; No. 10, at Wm. Wasson's; No. 11, at John Fisher's; No. 12, at John Kennedy's.

On April 7, 1879, the Columbia, Lawrenceburg & Florence Railroad Company filed a petition with the county court asking $50,000 to be given in aid of building said road. The road was to start at Columbia, Maury County, and pass through Mount Pleasant, Lawrenceburg, and to the Alabama line. Said aid was to be voted in bonds to run thirty years at 6 per cent interest, $25,000 to be given if the road was completed to Lawrenceburg only, and the remaining $25,000 to be payable if the road was completed through the county. The bonds were voted on May 13, 1879, and the road completed to Lawrenceburg in due time, and the remaining part south of Lawrenceburg has since been completed. The parties comprising the company were G. H. Nixon, M. M. Powell, J. W. Stewart, Wm. Parkes, J. T. Ellis and W. P. H. Garner, of Lawrence, and Ed. Hughes and G. T. Hughes, of Maury County. The chief engineer's estimate of the cost of the road though the two counties was $73,358, the cost in Lawrenceburg $44,728. The Columbia & Waynesboro Turnpike was completed through the county about 1847, but the same is not now kept up.

The county court was organized at the house of Dr. Joseph Farmer, then occupied by Josephus Irvine. The court met on the first Monday in May, 1818, and there were present the Worshipful Duncan McIntyre, Joseph Gest, James Forbes, John Hillhouse and Henson Day, justices. The court promptly organized by choosing Daniel Beeler, chairman, Maxmilian A. Buchanan, clerk, and Richard Farmer, sheriff, instead of Luke Grimes as appointed by the Legislature. The first official acts were the approval of the bonds of the county officers. The court next levied a county tax equal to the State tax for county purposes, and granted tavern license to Wm. McGaw and Wm. Strawn, "agreeably to the late law to suppress gambling." The first jury consisted of Henry Ross, Gabriel Bumpass, Daniel Matthews, James McConnell, Jesse Helton, George Rogers, Robert Chaffin, James Helton, Alex Miller, Andrew Allison, Thomas Hays, John Anthony, Aaron Choat, Isaac Pennington, George Sanders, John Branden, James Welch, James Bradstreet and Thomas Keys; of these, Henry Ross was chosen foreman. Fines for "affrays," making allowances for wolf scalps, and ordering new roads occupied the principal attention of the court. At the first term of this court James Helton was fined $1.50 for profane swearing, and a suit between David Beeler and John Welch was referred to David Crockett and John White as arbitrators, in which suit John Welch was allowed $5.40 for 108 pounds of pork.

The first term of circuit court was held in November of 1818, at the house of Dr. Farmer, as above. Thomas Stewart, of Franklin, appeared as judge, Charles Hicks as clerk, and Thomas Chadwick as solicitor-general. Judge Stewart became circuit judge of what was then the Fourth Circuit at its organization, in 1810, and continued to sit till his death, in 1842. Men have left more brilliant records than Thomas Stewart, but few had a higher literary taste or left a more spotless name. The first circuit jury was composed of John Simonton, Thomas Parker, Thomas Welch, George Lucas, John Hillhouse, Pollard Wisdom, Henson Day, David Crockett, Joseph Gest, Nelson McIntyre, James McConnell, James Forbes, Nathan Mason, Henry Sharp, George Hanks, Wm. Wisdom, James Brooks and William Straughn. Wm. Mackey was tried before this jury for petit larceny, but was found "not guilty." The court, however, thought there was strong grounds for belief in his guilt, and, therefore, taxed him with the cost of his prosecution. Wm. Cash brought suit for slander against James Hill, but in November, 1819, withdrew the suit and paid costs. Wm. Higgs, Thomas Keys, Daniel Adams and James Helton were each fined $5 and costs for gambling, August 4, 1819. November 1 David Crockett resigned as justice of the peace, and Rob. L. Cobbs was allowed $32 for *ex officio* services as solicitor-general for

1819. The court granted James Scott permission to build a mill-dam on Shoal Creek, near Lawrenceburg, in October, 1820. In 1821 the court met for the first time in the court house in Lawrenceburg, with R. L. Cobbs again as solicitor-general. For 1821 the county court appointed George Isom, David Steel and A. F. Larney judges of election at Pennington; Chas. Anderson and Chas. Thomas at Johnson's Mill, and Rob. Chaffin, Maurice Crisp and Richard Hill at Lawrenceburg. At the January term of 1821 the justices of the county were divided into four divisions: Pollard Wisdom, George Archer, John Hillhouse, Andrew Brown and Henry Sharp being of the first; George Lucas, M. Crisp, Jesse Jackson, Sam D. Poteet and Phillip Chromister being of the second; Richard Hill, Robt. Chaffin, John Welch and Lazarus Stewart of the third, and Daniel A. Flannery, Jacob Pennicuff, Maurice Crisp, Henson Day and Henry Sharp of the fourth. In the same year five judgments for debt were rendered against David Crockett, all of which were allowed to go by default. July 5, 1822, a standard of weights and measures was ordered and a county seal adopted. Judgment was rendered against Patrick Gillespie, on October 6, 1825, for petit larceny, and for punishment he received twenty-five lashes upon the bare back. In 1832 Patrick Dyal got a $5 fine for gaming and foot-racing. Because T. J. Lindsey had gone to White County, Ill., and married Lucinda Hinton, his wife, Nancy, was granted a divorce from him. The first case for the penitentiary was John Branden, for horse-stealing. He was prosecuted by Judge Dillahunty and defended by Amos F. Goff and T. H. Cahal. He was sentenced to the penitentiary for three years, on August 28, 1833. In 1835, at the February term, there were thirteen cases of gaming, amounting in each case to a fine of about $5. In 1837 Isaac Hamilton received the long sentence of seven years and six months for an assault with intent to commit a rape. November 14, 1837, Margaret C. Parrott, on *ex parte* testimony, was granted a divorce from James Parrott, and she was entitled to all the rights and privileges of a *femme sole*. In 1839 T. J. Deavenport was fined $5 for betting on elections. Nicholas Perkins was allowed 3,000 acres of land in the Seventh District, Range 4, Town 5, according to the law to "Incorporate Iron Works," passed October 25, 1824.

The first term of chancery court was held May 24, 1840, with L. M. Bramlett as chancellor of the middle division. There appearing no candidate for clerk and master, no business was done till the November term, when Augustine W. Bumpass was appointed clerk and master. Chancellor Bramlett served till May, 1844 when he was succeeded by T. H. Cahal, the well known lawyer and statesman of Columbia. Chancellor Cahal was succeeded by Hon. A. O. P. Nicholson, of the same place, in 1851, and he by J. L. Brine, in 1852. Stephen C. Pavatt became chancellor in February, 1855, and served till the courts were closed by the war. In 1870 this court was reorganized and Hon. G. H. Nixon became chancellor, which position he held with credit to himself and satisfaction to all to the present time. On February 7, 1859, the State found an indictment for murder in the first degree against Lewis M. Kirk for the murder of Thomas J. Westmore, on November 9, 1858. The case was continued from court to court till in 1860, when the death of the defendant stopped proceedings, after having incurred a cost of $858.95, besides lawyers' fees. In December, 1878, Bob Bently (colored) was indicted for the murder of Morgan McLaren (colored), and on the 21st of December was sentenced to a term of twenty years in the penitentiary, while Sam Swinton, an accomplice, received a fifteen-year sentence for the same offense. The Lawrence County Courts have had, comparatively, little litigation, yet they have been represented by very able men.

The city of Lawrenceburg is situated on a 400-acre tract of land that was granted to John Thompson by the Legislature of North Carolina on April 14, 1792, for services rendered in a battalion raised for the defense of Davidson County. This claim was confirmed by an act of the General Assembly of Tennessee, passed November 23, 1819. This land was surveyed on August 10, 1821, and was found to lie in Range 4, Section 4. The site was selected by David Crockett, Henry Sharp, John Beeler, M. H. Buchanan, Henry Phenix, Enoch Tucker and Josephus Irvine, to whom the State of Tennessee gave the 400 acres for the use of the town to be called Lawrenceburg. The place was selected on November 14, 1819, as above, and purchased by the State from M. H. Buchanan and George Gresham. The location was four miles southeast of the geographical center of the county, about seventy-five miles west of south from Nashville on the old United States Military road. The first settler where Lawrenceburg stands, was Maximilian H. Buchanan, who erected a house some years previous to the laying out of the town. The first merchant in the place was Joshua Borders, who began business in the place in 1820. The first hotel was opened in 1825, by Col. Joseph Terrell. Dr. Obediah Stribling, who was the first practicing physician, began practice there in 1821. A school was opened in the place in 1819, by Ebenezer Evans. A postoffice was established in Lawrenceburg in 1822, with John Stribling as postmaster. William Davis was the first resident lawyer of the place, he having opened an office in Lawrenceburg in 1822. A Methodist Church was erected in the place in 1826, with the Rev. John Manley as the first pastor. James K. Polk was admitted to the bar at Lawrenceburg October 2, 1820, and it is claimed he made his maiden speech at this place, but as other places claim that honor, it is doubtless somewhat as the poet said of Homer:

> "Ten cities claimed the Homer dead,
> Through which the living Homer begged his bread."

In the sale of lots, Robert Orr bought Lots 1, 2, 17 and 25; Nathan McClenden, Lots 14, 21 and 13; Thomas Deavenport, Lot 22; Deavenport & Lucas, Lot 60; Tom Holland, Lot 6; A. W. Bumpass, Lots 70 and 73; Jacob Hueler, Lot 38; Robert Hay, Lot 41; Matthew Love, Lot 42; Daniel Brentley, Lot 29; Thomas Blair, Lot 51; R. L. Cobb, Lots 65 and 72; and I. S. W. Cook ten acres of the original 400 acres. The prices ranged from $50 to $300 per lot. The lands lying adjacent to the town were owned by James Scott, Josephus Irvine, Daniel Beeler and Samuel H. Williams. The halcyon days of Lawrenceburg were about 1850. It was then a place of great industrial activity. Various causes have brought about business changes. The present business of the place is as follows: General stores—Simms & Stewart, Dustin & Dunn, M. J. Richardson, George Goedeker, Henry Cook, and Mrs. Mary Fath. Grocery stores—Springer & Busby, C. E. Barnett, Mrs. S. D. Luker; Harvey & Bro., grocery and furniture. Drug store—W. W. Neal. Professions, attorneys—R. H. Rose, T. D. Deavenport, W. A. Stewart, S. A. Carrell, H. B. Sowell, J. B. Simms, J. B. Parker and H. Nixon. Physicians—W. W. & P. A. Neal, E. McClain and Dr. R. Harvey. Hotels—Lawrenceburg House, Collins House. Livery stable—Thomas Meredith.

The first newspaper published in Lawrenceburg was in 1846, and was called the *Academist*, and edited by Dr. William P. Rowels. This paper was purchased in September by Horne & Harrison; the latter sold his interest to A. Stribling in a short time. About 1853–54, the paper was bought by Hatcher & Jarrett. It soon passed into the hands of a man named Anderson, and the whole was destroyed by fire about 1857 or 1858. In 1872, a paper called the Lawrenceburg *Journal* was started; connected with this paper have been H. C. Bate, W. T. Nixon, Malone & Buchanan, Mr. Leman and John Schade. The paper has been changed in politics and name. It is now a stanch Republican paper, and is called the Lawrence *Union*. It is owned and managed by John Schade. The Lawrence *Journal* is the Democratic organ for Lawrence County. It is owned by the Lawrenceburg Publishing Company, formed in October, 1884. It is composed of W. J. Nixon, W. H. Dustin, J. T. Stribling, W. A. Stewart and S. A. Carrell.

West Point was formerly called Blountsville, and was established in 1844 on a bank of Shoal Creek, fifteen miles southwest from the county seat. It now contains one store with several saw-mills in the vicinity.

Wayland Springs is situated on the west bank of Shoal Creek, twenty miles southwest from Lawrenceburg. It was founded in 1846 on land owned by Simeon H. Wayland, in honor of whom it was named. This was a place of some note before the war as a health resort, but the place was destroyed during that time, and has never since regained its former prestige. It now contains one store. Summertown lies thirteen miles north of Lawrenceburg, on the Columbia & Waynesboro Pike, and near the Nashville & Florence Railroad. It is more a camping place or summer resort than a place of business. It has excellent water and is considered a very pleasant summer resort. It is very largely patronized by the people of Maury County.

Henryville is on the Columbia & Waynesboro Pike, twenty-six miles from either place and twelve miles north of Lawrenceburg. It was founded in 1844, and took its name from Henry, the original postoffice at that point. It was located on the land of Daniel McIntyre, near the site of "Old Town," an old Indian village, which stood on the west bank of Buffalo River. The first dwelling in the place was built by Leroy Burns. It now contains one store and a blacksmith shop. Loretto is a small village on the old military road, fourteen miles south of Lawrenceburg. It was founded in 1872 by Rev. John H. Hueser, of the Catholic Church. This was the outgrowth of the Homestead Association. The place contains about twenty-five houses, a Catholic Church, priest's residence, a convent and school. St. Joseph is about twenty miles southwest of Lawrenceburg and was founded in 1873. Alois Sandroell was the first citizen and merchant. The village now contains about twenty-five houses, a school, a fine store and a very fine Catholic Church, built at an actual cost of about $17,000 besides the labor that was donated.

The military history of this county begins properly with the Mexican war, although eight or ten Revolutionary veterans were buried in the county and a few of the later wars. In 1846 a company was raised for the Mexican war by Capt. William B. Allen, with the Hon. George H. Nixon as first lieutenant. A detail of the movements of the regiment, First Tennessee, Col. W. B. Campbell, is given in the State history. In the Public Square is a fine monument erected to the fallen of Capt. Allen's company. The structure is about ten feet square at the base and forty feet in height. On the north face of the shaft is inscribed: "Erected to the Memory of Capt. William B. Allen, J. R. Burkett, G. W. Wilson, A. J. Eaton, J. A. Hill, E. W. Thomas, B. H. Dalton, B. Soaper, W. Rhodes, A. J. Gibson, G. B. Porter, J. B. Turner, J. H. Elliott, H. Collins, F. Glover, A. J. Pratt, Lieut. L. M. Putnam, W. H. Robinson, R. D. Willis, P. H. Martin, W. M. Alford, J. M. L. Campbell, J. H. Sanders, J. F. Coffee, J. H. Johnson, E. Prior, of the First Regiment Tennessee Volunteers, who fell on the 21st of September, 1846, at the capture of Monterey by the Americans, under command of Maj.-Gen. Z. Taylor." On the east side is "Died of disease: S. H. Allen, J. Billingsby, L. Garrett, J. M. Gray, W. W. Lindsey, E. Tucker, A. Boswell, J. Farris, J. Goodman, S. G. Keltner, A. J. Lindsey, J. W. Walker." The venerable Col. George. H. Dixon, of Lawrenceburg, is believed to be the only one of that company left living.

The first troops for the late war were Capt. B. F. Matthews' company of the Third Tennessee. This company was recruited at Lawrenceburg in May, 1861. The company officers at first were B. F. Matthews, captain; J. C. Chaffin, first lieutenant; J. L. Chaffin, second lieutenant, and Alonzo Lindsey, third lieutenant. The regimental officers were J. C. Brown, colonel; Thomas Gordon, lieutenant-colonel, and N. G. Cheairs, major. There were also Capt. Lewis Miller's company, Capt. A. J. Powell's company and Capt. William P. Moore's company. On the organization of the Thirty-second Regiment, to which Capt. Moore's company belonged, Ed Cook was chosen colonel; W. P. Moore, lieutenant-colonel, and W. J. Brownlow, major. On the promotion of W. P. Moore, T. D. Deavenport became captain; J. M. White, first lieutenant; W. C. Anderson, second lieutenant, and R. L. Bassham, third lieutenant. The regiment encamped at Lake Springs, near Pulaski, and was mustered into the service June 3, 1861, and October 7. left Pulaski, by train, for Nashville, and were sent to Camp Trousdale. A portion of the regiment was sent to Chattanooga, and 200 men were ordered up the Sequatchie Valley, where they remained one week. The regiment was then sent to Bowling Green, Ky., under command of Gen. A. S. Johnson, and placed in S. B. Buckner's brigade, where they were inspected by Gen. Hardee. They were ordered to Russellville, Clarksville and Donelson, where they arrived February 11. They experienced cold weather and hard fighting there, and were captured. Among the killed was Col. Moore. The men were sent to Camp Morton, Indianapolis, were there held as prisoners of war till the last of August, when they were taken to Vicksburg and exchanged. The regiment was reorganized September 13 by electing Ed Cook, colonel; J. P. McGown, lieutenant-colonel, and W. P. Neal, major. The Thirty-second was at Chickamauga September 19 and 20, and at Missionary Ridge November 25. The regiment took part in the Georgia Campaign, and was on the right at the fall of Atlanta. It followed Hood into Tennessee, almost without food or clothing; crossed the Tennessee at Florence, and passed up by way of Wayland Springs, Mount Pleasant, Columbia, and reached

Franklin at 11 o'clock on November 30, and was placed in position for assault. It followed the Federals to Nashville and drove in their pickets. It was then sent to Murfreesboro and skirmished a few days with the enemy, when they came out and gave battle. After the defeat of Hood at Nashville, the regiment retreated by way of Columbia, Pulaski, and crossed the river at Lamb's Ferry. In the retreat the regiment was reduced to little more than a good company. The forces retired to Tupelo, Miss., where they encamped for a time. They were sent into South Carolina. They were at Branchville, Columbia, and in North Carolina. They were placed in D. H. Hill's corps of J. E. Johnson's command. In the retreat the regiment, by mistake, fell in behind the Federals, where they marched several days. The regiment surrendered at Greenboro, in 1865. They returned by way of Ashville, N. C., to Greenville, E. Tenn.; thence, by rail to Tullahoma, home. There were also the companies of Capts. Lewis Kirk (J. H. Hogan, lieutenant) and Thomas Paine in the cavalry service under Forrest. Besides these there were companies of Deering's Fifty-fourth, but on the disbanding of that regiment they were put into Dixon's Forty-eighth.

Schools are contemporaneous with the county, but uniformity in the system is of modern growth. October 31, 1839, deeds to lots No. 52 and 53 were issued to George Lucas, William McKnight, T. D. Deavenport, Ezekiel Lindsey, Daniel Bentley, John Stephenson, A. W. Bumpass and Joseph Miller, as trustees of the Lawrenceburg Academy. September 11, 1848, a similar deed was made to Lots 64 and 78 for Jackson Academy, to the trustees of said academy. These were built out of the seminary fund, and the appointment of trustees was under the control of the county court. It thus remained until since the war.

In March, 1883, Jackson Academy was incorporated as the Lawrenceburg Academy, by Wm. Parkes, Wm. H. Dustin, J. B. Simms, R. H. Harvey, W. C. Spence, W. F. Nixon and J. M. Gilmore, with a capital stock of $1,500, with the usual power granted such corporations. This building is now used as the public school building. An excellent school is maintained ten months in the year.

The amount of expenditure for public schools and the scholastic population, as far as shown by the reports since 1853, are as follows: In 1853, $2,476.44; 1854, $2,350.87; 1855, $1,991.43; 1856, $3,643.19; 1857, $3,777.35; 1858, $4,641.89; 1859, $4,596.31; 1860, $2,564.80; 1861, $4,433.61; 1862, $2,035.80; 1866, $3,049.61; 1869, $3,602.20; 1871, $3,566.45; 1872, $3,164.38; 1880, $2,989.25; 1881, $3,146.82; 1882, $3,042.82; 1883, $5,032.80; 1886, $5,201.82. The scholastic population for 1860 (the first shown) was 3,206; 1861, 3,132; 1866, 3,476;

1880, 3,042; 1885, 3,580. The report of 1885 shows an attendance of 2,385. It further shows fifteen school districts, one graded school, six consolidated schools, one under the management of a town school board, and three incorporated under "four mile law." The length of a school term is about sixty days.

The Cumberland Presbyterian Church in Lawrenceburg was begun in 1851. It was erected by the New School Presbyterians, the trustees at the time being J. A. Bradshaw, R. G. Ramsey, Phillip G. Austin, W. A. Edmiston and George W. Richardson. The trustees borrowed $500 of the "erection fund" of the church for its construction. The church becoming weakened by the war and financially embarrassed, the building was sold, about 1878, to Wm. Parkes, as trustee of the Cumberland Presbyterian Church. The congregation at this place now numbers about sixty members. The membership of this congregation was originally at Mount Ararat, but that was divided as a matter of convenience in worship. The church at Mount Nebo was built in 1857. The trustees at that time were Ruben McLaren, Thomas Gabel and Samuel Pierce.

The first Methodist Church built in Lawrenceburg was in 1826, with Rev. John Manley as pastor. This popular branch of the church has always kept a house of worship here. A new house of worship is now in course of construction.

The church at Pleasant Point was built in conjunction with the Masonic Hall in 1857. The trustees at that time were Thomas Kelsey, William L. McBride and J. J. Pennington. Another church was built in 1859, the trustees at that time being Alex. Stewart, Thomas Archer, William B. Hall, D. H. Adkison and Ambrose Goodman. The Sugar Creek Church was built in 1885, the trustees being J. M. Bassham, J. J. Miller, J. M. Shelton, T. N. Hagan and W. C. Sills. The church in the Fifteenth District was built in 1881; the trustees at that time were David Gabel, Albert Kelly and Henry Welch. There were also churches at Wayland Springs and Chinnuby.

The Christian Church on Buffalo Creek was built in 1854 on the land of J. A. Cavender. The Christians have churches at Liberty, Cherry Hill, Henryville, West Point, and at Wade's Chapel.

The Primitive Baptists built their first church near Henryville, in 1817, of which the Rev. John Hunter was pastor. This popular branch of the church is now not very numerous in the county. An organization has been maintained on Blue Water almost since the organization of the county.

The Catholic Church at Lawrenceburg was built in 1871. There is also in connection therewith two priests, a convent with seventeen or eighteen nuns and six or seven brothers. A Catholic Church also stands about twelve miles west of Lawrenceburg, which is attended by the priests from Lawrenceburg twice a month. There is a church and convent about eleven miles north of Lawrenceburg, with one priest and four or five nuns. The Catholics have churches at Loretto and St. Joseph, mentioned elsewhere.

The only church house of Missionary Baptists is the Bethel Baptist Church, about four miles north of Lawrenceburg. This house was built in 1846, with Thomas Pullen, J. J. Foster and J. C. Sparkman as trustees.

WAYNE COUNTY.

WAYNE COUNTY is on the extreme western side of the Highland Rim, with its northwestern corner extending into the valley of the Tennessee. The county presents a generally broken surface, with parallel and transverse ridges and intervening hollows, the ridges usually radiating from the center in all directions, except to the east, the general surface of the county being a plateau of about 800 feet elevation.

The principal streams are Indian Creek, Hardin Creek, Shoal Creek, Buffalo River, Bush Creek and Second Creek. Mill Creek is a tributary of Hardin Creek. Butler Creek, Big, Middle and Little Cypress and Factor Fork are all tributaries of Shoal Creek. Forty-eight Creek, Moccasin, Rock House, Mill, Opossum, Chapel Creeks and Green River are all tributaries of Buffalo River. Wayne has lands particularly suited for farming and grazing, and the remainder for minerals. Of the 700 square miles of land in the county, about 200 square miles of it are mineral lands of iron ore. This seems to lie in inexhaustible beds of fine quality, the yield at the furnace being forty-four per cent. For working this ore the Wayne Furnace was built about 1835, and in 1868 the Gaylord Iron & Pipe Company bought the old Wayne Furnace and 21,000 acres of land for $40,000. They increased the capacity of the furnace to twenty-four tons per day. The agricultural land is found in the river and creek bottoms, and covers about ninety square miles of fine lands. These lands yield heavy crops of all the cereals, cotton, peanuts, and the other lands are suited for grazing. From the extensive ranges, stock-raising can be carried on at little expense and at immense profit. Wayne County affords an immense growth of valuable timber. In the southern portion of the county are immense growths of yellow pine. The ridges furnish oak, chestnut and poplar, and the glades furnish cedar. Large quantities of the chestnut oak bark is used in the various tanneries in the county. Great quantities of timber are used at the furnaces for wood and charcoal in smelting.

The first settlers of Wayne County were mainly from the older counties of Middle Tennessee and from North and South Carolina. The early settlements were made on North Carolina military grants, occupants' claims and warrants. The first settlement was made by Frederick Meredith, Mark F. Edwards, William Henton, Lovick Rasbury, Richard Churchwell and Craig W. Pope, on Buffalo River in 1815. On Hardin Creek were Isaac G. Grimes, Henry Grimes, Peter Renfrow and John Johnson, in 1816. Thomas G. Harvey, Charles Burns, James Reeves, Samuel Loggans and William Scott settled on Green River in 1816 and 1817. On Indian Creek Henry and John Rayburn, Jesse and Baker Cypert, Benjamin and David Schull settled in 1818. James Surrett settled on the east fork of Hardin Creek in 1819. David Gallaher and John Dixon settled on Shoal Creek in 1818. William B. Payne, William B. Walker, Joseph Staggs, Nathan Biffle and Isaac Robertson settled on Forty-eight Mile Creek in 1818. Other settlers in different parts of the county before 1820 were Jacob Biffle in the Eighth District, where land was entered in 1812; David Carter, assignee of Elizabeth Walker, also in the Eighth District; also William B. Ross, Joseph Denton, Wiley Harrington, Thomas Reeves, J. W. Nunley, T. Gambel, Daniel Cherry, Jacob Fraley, J. R. Russell, John Gibson and J. P. Walker. John Watson settled on Hardin Creek in 1820, and Lewis Johnson and Henry Colston on Beech Creek about the same time. The following entered lands before 1820: Michael Robertson, Henson Grove, Mark F. Edwards, Isaac Rice, William Williams, Thomas G. Harvey, James H. Gambel, Alexander Steele, James R. Russell, Daniel Voorhees, Samuel Mayfield, John Meredith, John Duke, R. P. Scott, John McCulley, David Carter, John Welch, Allen Brown, James Davis, James Collins, John Mitchell, G. H. Garrett, R. C. Harris, John Akin, S. Read, J. L. Smith, James Davis, James Elliott, John Brown, James Staggs, W. B. and James P. Walker, Jesse Thompson and the Morris family.

The first water and tub-mills in the county were built on Moccasin Creek, in 1818, by John Meredith; the first horse-mill was built by John O. Roberts, on Beech Creek, in 1820. The first cotton-gin was built near where old Carrollville stood, by William B. Ross, in 1819. The first ferry across the Tennessee River, within the limits of the county, was established in 1818 at Carrollville, but the owner of the ferry is unknown.

The first church erected in the county was built on Green River, just east of the site of Waynesboro, at the grave-yard, in 1820, by the Methodists. The Rev. James English was the first preacher. At the mouth of Forty-eight Mile Creek the Primitive Baptists also built a church in 1820, the Rev. Willis Dodson was the first pastor of it. The first merchants in the county were Malachi Wimberly and Anderson Stoneball, near Ashland, in 1819. A mill was built on Buffalo, near Ashland, by John Biffle, about 1830. The first tan-yard was built on Eagle Creek, by James Elliott, in 1819.

The first boat up the Tennessee for business was a keel boat owned by Samuel Cade. This was loaded with salt and other supplies. Wesley Warrington kept the first wood-yard for steam-boats, about 1823–25. The first camp-meeting was held on Eagle Creek about 1823.

Near Ashland may be seen many relics of the Mound-Builders. These mounds are of the usual shape, but arranged in a somewhat circular outline, with the larger mounds in the center. The whole cluster numbers perhaps forty or fifty. Surrounding these is an old earth-work of very distinct outline, having a moat and embankment of considerable height. In the hollow below is an old Indian burying-ground, where numerous skeletons have been found, some in a very perfect state of preservation. The graves are marked by stones above ground, with the graves walled and covered by the same material. In all or nearly all are found charcoal or charred remains. This burying-ground was discovered by Prof. Smith, of the Columbia Atheneum, in 1877, where may be seen an excellent specimen of skeleton remains. On a tributary of Forty-eight Creek, called Court House Creek, are two fine natural bridges. Passing beneath the first at a sharp angle in the little stream there appears an open court which rivals almost any of the natural curiosities of the world. Here, according to tradition, the dusky savage once held his council fires. A little further down the stream the water passes under the second archway and dome of splendid beauty and symmetry.

Wayne County was created by an act of the Legislature in 1817, but on failure to have it engrossed it had to be repassed in 1819. It was named in honor of Gen. Wayne, "Mad Anthony," of Revolutionary fame, and embraces an area of 338,291 acres. The court for organization met at Factor Fork, where the old Natchez trace crosses that stream. The next meeting was at William Barnett's, on old Town Branch, where it continued to meet till 1822. The following justices were present, holding commissions from the governor: Benjamin Hardin, Henry Rayburn, Jesse Cypert, Wm. Burns, C. A. Pope, Wm. B. Walker, John Meredith, Reuben Kyle, Wm. B. Curtis, Wm. B. Ross, S. Perley and David N. Gallaher. The officers chosen were Wm. Barnett, clerk; Benjamin Hardin, sheriff; J. M. Barnett, circuit clerk; John McClure, register; John Meredith, trustee; John Hill, ranger; and Wm. B. Payne, coroner.

The first court house was built, it is supposed, by Wm. Barnett in 1819 or 1820. This was a small log house, with a dirt floor, board roof, and large openings in the sides for windows. This house was in use about two years. On the location of Waynesboro as the county seat, in 1822, a new log court house was erected the same year. This house was built at a cost of $800 on the Square, and differed not greatly in size or construction. The third house was built in 1827, and was a frame building. This building was two stories high, and was about 24x30 feet. The upper floor was used as the court room, with the offices below, and had two entrances as the present house.

The present court house was built by Nathaniel Thomas. It was begun in 1843 and completed in 1844. It is a good brick building, in excellent state of preservation, and is two stories in height. The upper floor is used as the court-room, while the offices are below. The building is about 35x40 feet, and was erected at a cost of about $4,000.

The first jail was built at Old Town, and was a very rude structure. It was in use only about two years. The second jail was built of round logs at Waynesboro in 1822. The third jail was built of hewn logs. It stood till some time between 1830 and 1840, when it was replaced by a brick jail. This jail stood just north of the Eureka Building, and was erected at a cost of about $700. The elements, time and war unfitted this as a place of safety. In 1873 J. G. Berry, A. T. Hassell, M. Collier, G. W. Boyd and J. R. Hughes were appointed a committee for the construction of a new jail. The material of the old one was sold to the Methodists, Masons and others, and a new lot purchased east of the Square. The contract was let to Wm. A. Fowler. The new jail was built at a cost of $1,664.25, less $148.95 realized on the old jail.

The poor at first were farmed out to the lowest bidder. The first farm was on Green River, two and three-fourths miles below Waynesboro. This was a small place, and little improvements were made upon it. In 1849 a farm was purchased by Washington Carter, D. J. Jones and Jonathan Morris for $400. In 1866 the present farm was purchased of J. L. Fowler by A. Montague, G. W. Barker and J. A. Grimes, as poor-house commissioners, for $700. The county now owns about 145 acres of good land and maintains its paupers at a small cost.

Although Wayne has neither turnpike nor railroad, the Columbia Central Turnpike formerly passed through the county from Columbia to

Clifton. This road was completed about 1844, but has been suffered to fall into disuse since the war. In 1880 the charter of the Nashville & Tennessee River Railroad was spread upon record. This road is intended to connect the Nashville & Tallapoosa Road with the Memphis & Knoxville Road, at or near Clifton.

The meeting of the first county court is elsewhere stated, both as to place and members. The first circuit court was held at the log court house on old Town Branch, north of Waynesboro, in the spring of 1820, with J. M. Barnett as circuit clerk, Benjamin Hardin as sheriff and Wm. F. Doherty as solicitor-general. A loss of all the county court records to 1848, the circuit court records to 1851, and those in the chancery court to 1861, renders it impossible to follow the courts fully. One of the longest cases ever tried in Wayne County was the case of Meredith against Renfro, which vexed the courts for sixteen years. The first murder case is believed to be the case wherein Haggard killed Busby. The case grew out of a quarrel between two little boys, sons of the two men. The case was tried in Dixon County on change of venue, and Haggard was acquitted. Another case was the "State *vs.* Choat," for the killing of Mosby. This case resulted in acquittal, on the plea of self-defense. In 1828, Wm. Venable and James McDool, the former a gray-bearded old man and the latter a boy of sixteen, were convicted of passing counterfeit money. They received for punishment, on the bare back, twenty-five lashes. About this time the officers of the law were compelled to contend with a gang of counterfeiters, horse-thieves and murderers, under John A. Murrell, whose life and adventures were written many years ago, and whose exploits extended over a large portion of the State. About 1830, occurred several damage suits, one, "Miller *vs.* Robertson," for false imprisonment, in which the plaintiff got judgment for $10,000. Another was the case of Chas. Teas against W. B. Ross, for swearing to a lie. This suit resulted in a verdict for $10,000 for the plaintiff, but was afterward compromised for $900. Charles Reeves brought a suit for slander against John O. Roberts, for saying that Reeves "stole horses, cattle and hogs." The plaintiff was awarded damage to the amount of $2.50. All cases previous to the passage of the "penitentiary law," in 1832, were punished by imprisonment, fines, whipping, standing in the stocks, branding—any or all of these. The first person sent to the State's prison was Mathew Murphy, who was sentenced on March 23, 1839, for a term of three years, and the second case was David Staggs, who was sentenced for one year from October, 1842. The offense in neither case is given, but it is presumed it was larceny. The first divorce suit was the wife of Henry Mahon against her husband. The suit was brought in

1829, on the plea of inhuman treatment, and granted. The first of the circuit court records began with May 26, 1851. The usual number of cases of gaming, peace warrants, wearing bowie knives, larceny, *vi et armis*, and other minor misdemeanors occur. In 1852, Moses Page, "without the fear of God before his eyes, and being moved and seduced by the instigation of the devil," assaulted Thomas H. Short and killed him with a gun. Page was tried, convicted, and sentenced to the penitentiary for a term of three years. One of the heaviest suits for damage, in former years, was the suit of Sanders and Martin against Gallaher, King, McDougal and East, in which the plaintiffs got judgment for $1,126.95. This case was decided at the March term, 1840.

The case of the State against Daniel G. McCarn, on a change of venue from Hardin County, came up for trial in the Wayne County Circuit Court. He was tried for being accessory before the fact for an assault and battery with intent to commit murder. The trial was begun in 1850, and ended October 9, 1852, in conviction and sentence to the penitentiary for seven years. An appeal to the supreme court was taken, and the case reversed and ordered begun *de novo*. The case was tried again with the singular result of conviction and sentence for twelve years instead of seven. A very hotly contested suit was the case of Dr. Wm. G. Childress against John Morrow, for slander. The case was begun in 1857, and ended in February, 1860 in judgment for $5,000 for plaintiff. Dr. Childress had treated a son of Morrow, who died. The latter accused the former of malpractice, hence the suit. The jury in the case were Andrew Jackson, W. T. Bryant, J. M. Moore, Little Choat, J. I. Biffle, John Stockard, J. W. Howard, Jasper Davis, J. L. Kyle, J. Scott, J. N. Hollis and J. C. Whitton. Judgment was rendered, and it was ordered that execution issue, when the plaintiff in open court remitted all the fine except one cent. A very hotly contested case was begun January 3, 1876, entitled State *vs.* John W. Bundrant and Peter Bundrant. They were tried for the murder of S. R. Dicus. The case was continued from January 3, 1876, till November, 1879, and ended in the conviction of John Bundrant and sentence to the penitentiary for five years,

Another case of note was the case of the State against T. G. Brown, D. E. Holt, Wm. Holt, Wallace Hays, Austin Hays, Wm. A. Fowler and Jesse Atkisson. They were tried for the murder of Wm. H. Hays in October, 1878. Atkisson died before trial. The suit ended August 20, 1879, in a sentence of Thomas G. Brown and D. E. Holt for a term of several years in the penitentiary; Wm. Holt, Austin Hays and Wallace Hays to six months in the county jail. The circuit courts were closed from January 29, 1862, to September 23, 1865. The last jury before the war consisted of L. M. Morgan, Little Choat, S. R. Denny, J. H. McClure, Wm. Eads, A. G. Clay, Wm. Pollard, J. H. Rutledge, Jas. Durham, J. C. Walker, Wm. Sinclair, J. J. Porter, J. N. Hollis, J. A. Gibbs, John L. Smith, Isaac Robinson and F. Churchwell. Many very bitter suits grew out of offenses committed during the war. On January 23, 1874, was spread upon the minutes a tribute of respect to the memory of Judge Elijah Walker, of Savannah, who died December 31, 1873. Judge Walker was doubtless the ablest judge ever upon the Wayne County bench.

The chancery court for the District of Wayne, Hardin, Lewis and Lawrence was established by the Legislature February 5, 1847, with Jerry H. Cahal as chancellor, who served till 1852, when J. L. Brine was chosen to fill his place. Judge Brine was succeeded by Stephen C. Pavatt in 1855, who in turn was succeeded by R. H. Rose on February 28, 1866. Judge J. W. Doherty served from 1868 to 1870, when he was succeeded by Hon. Geo. H. Nixon, who served till 1886. The clerks and masters have been Col. McLean, A. T. Hassell, J. W. Helton and Capt. P. H. Craig since 1873. One of the longest and most peculiar cases ever tried in the chancery court was the case of Sarah C. Smotherman against James Smotherman, for divorce and alimony, alleging, as a plea, brutal and inhuman treatment. The case was in the courts for about sixteen years. A judgment was rendered by Judge Hughes in favor of the plaintiff in April, 1868, and the same confirmed by Judge Nixon in September, 1871. The divorce, custody of their child and alimony in lands were granted to plaintiff. The case was taken to the supreme court on a writ of error by the defendant. Whereupon said court found error, not only in the point at issue, but the whole proceedings. The whole case was accordingly referred. Pending this decision the defendant had married a second time and the plaintiff had been confirmed in possession of her lands. The curious case was then presented, of two legal owners of the same property and a man having two legal wives.

In 1861 the case of Mary J. Ricketts, administratrix, *vs.* C. B. McCulley *et al.*, involving the right of title, was begun. McCulley was the legal owner of two tracts of land. On March 2, 1861, he conveyed to his wife and children one of his tracts of land. He was owing Ricketts $1,260. Although it was proved McCulley was owner of other real estate valued at $1,500 and personal property to the amount of $1,000, he subsequently failed. S. S. Ricketts died in 1863, intestate, and the plaintiff, as administratrix, revived the debt in her own name, and got judgment against the land conveyed, and had it sold on execution. The case was taken to the supreme court in 1865, and the conveyance made by Mc-

Culley was confirmed from the fact that at the time of the conveyance he had ample property to pay his debts and the conveyance at the time indicated no fraud. The case of Carr *vs.* Grimes, executor, in 1877, involved the mental capacity of the decedent to make a will. In this suit about $10,000 worth of property was involved. The supreme court confirmed the action of the defendant. W. P. Kendrick and Rob A. Hill were, doubtless, the ablest resident lawyers of the Wayne County bar. The latter is now United States district judge, with headquarters at Oxford, Miss. The present bar is represented by Robert Cypert, Boyd & Haggard and John F. Montague.

Waynesboro was founded in 1821, on lands owned by Wm. Burns. A deed was made for 40 acres to James Hollis, John Hill, Nathan Biffle and Chas. Burns for $300. These men were the commissioners appointed by the General Assembly to establish a county seat for Wayne County. The transfer was made March 1, 1823. The commissioners were empowered to sell lots, and with the proceeds to build a court house, jail, stocks, etc. Among the first purchasers of lots were James Blair, Chas. Burns, Wm. Barnett, Wm. Copeland, Wm. Burns, Willis Copeland, H. W. Mahon, Wiley Simmons, J. W. Lemaster, Jordan Morris, John Hill, Obedience Hill and James Anderson. The first dwelling-house was erected by Wm. Burns in 1821. Wm. Meredith began merchandising in 1821; and Wm. Barnett opened the first hotel in the place, also in 1821. A postoffice was established in 1821, with Wm. Barnett as postmaster. The first practicing physician was Dr. Martin Mahon, who began practice in 1822-23. The first local attorney was Thomas F. Edwards, who began practice about the time of Dr. Mahon. The first school was opened in the town in 1821-22. The first church was built at the grave-yard just east of town, across Green River, with the Rev. James English as pastor. The house of Burns, above mentioned, stood some distance from town near where Mr. Whitby now lives. Wm. Barnett's stood where Mr. Hassell's house now stands; John Hill's was near. These were the first houses in Waynesboro proper, and were small round-log houses.

The business of Waynesboro was about such as is seen in a small inland town till about 1844-45, at the completion of the old Central Turnpike, when the business gradually increased, reaching its maximum activity about 1855, but remained good until the war. Since that period the place has suffered some loss of trade from the sale of goods at many country stores throughout the county. The principal business for one or two decades before the war was done by A. T. Hassell, James Anderson, and Wm. West & Co. The former of these has done an extensive business since 1844. The present business firms are A. T. Hassell, M. J.

Sims, Bromley & Martin, Huckaba Bro. & Co., Turman Helton & Co., drug stores, G. W. Boyd & Co., A. T. Collier; hotel, Thomas Young.

Waynesboro was incorporated in 1852, with the usual powers of such corporations. The following constituted the first board: Cyrus Tyree, I. Warner, S. R. Laird, J. C. Bridges, G. W. House, J. Morris and N. C. David. Of these Tyree became mayor; David, recorder, and Bridges, treasurer. The charter was allowed to lapse in 1860, but was renewed again in 1870, with Matthew Collier, mayor, and C. C. Stribling, recorder.

The first newspaper in Waynesboro was *The Family Visitor*, edited by W. L. Morris. This was in the early part of 1850. This was followed by *Waynesboro Times*, under B. A. Murtishaw, in 1856. Then came the period of the war, and no more paper till 1872, when the *Review* was started by the Malone Bros. This was followed by the *Wayne County Citizen*, on February 19, 1874, by Stribling & Warren as proprietors, with Robert Cypert as editor till December 24, 1874. On November 24, 1875, the paper was first issued at Clifton, where it has since remained.

Waynesboro Lodge, No. 127, was organized February 13, 1851, with the following officers: Jas. Anderson, W. M.; Chas. Cox, S. W.; N. F. Biffle, J. W.; D. K. Hood, Treas.; John McDougal, Sec.; A. P. Cook, S. D.; S. R. Laird, J. D.; J. C. Bridges, S. and T. Visiting members, P. Whitehead and S. D. Whitley, both Master Masons. The first members added were W. R. Kindle and J. M. Jones. The membership now numbers thirty-seven. A chapter was instituted November 1, 1879, with J. J. Comes as High Priest; C. Buchanan, King, and J. Jackson, Scribe. A Grand Army Post was organized in 1884 by Capt. Jones, of Nashville. It is known as the Wm. P. Kendrick Post, No. 5. It enrolls from fifty to sixty members.

About two miles below where Clifton now stands, formerly stood Carrollsville, named in honor of Gov. Carroll. This place was founded in 1818 on the lands of Thomas Reeves. The sale of lots began in 1821. At that time Reeves sold his interest to Johnson & Blackburn. Henry Mahon, John Blackburn, Matthew Grimes, Henry Rayburn, Stephen Stubblefield, Jacob Spencer, Malachi Wimberly, Chas. Harrington and John Elliott were the principal property owners of the place. The business men were Hugh Simpson, Chas. Teas, Hine & Ross, and R. A. McCullough. It is claimed that Carrollsville came within one vote of being made the capital of the State. On the completion of the Central Turnpike to its terminus on the river, at Clifton, Carrollsville began rapidly to decline, so that now nothing remains to mark the site of the old town. This place witnessed one of the first tragedies in the county, the killing of Dr. Green by Edward Sanford. A quarrel arose over the sale of some liquors, and Green assaulted Sanford with a gun, and was himself killed by a stone in the hands of Sanford. Clifton, it may be said, grew from the ruins of Carrollsville; it was founded in 1840, and was named from the high cliff upon which it stands. It is situated sixteen miles west of Waynesboro, on the Tennessee River, at the terminus of the old Central Turnpike. The lands were purchased of Stephen Roach by Evan Young, Granville A. Pillow, Gideon J. Pillow, W. J. Polk, L. J. Polk and James Helton, of the Turnpike Company. The first owners of lots were R. C. Hemphill, A. T. Hassell, James Walker, John O. Roberts, Edward Spears, J. Wright, R. H. Cooper and S. S. Ricketts. The first business men of Clifton were James Walker (who managed the old "Marine Furnace"), A. T. Hassell & Co., Cooper & Hemphill. Clifton has always been an excellent business point, by far the best in the county. It now has the following dry goods and general stores: Hughes & Grimes, Thompson & Cook, J. J. Nichols, T. N. Copeland. Drug and grocery stores: T. R. Ricketts & Co., Stribling & Hassell, Hardin & Duncan. Groceries: Charles Ricketts.

The Cumberland Presbyterian Church was built in 1859, on a lot deeded to them by H. W. Hunter. The Methodist Church was built much later. Masonic lodge, No. 173, called Clifton Lodge by last report, has a membership of forty-five. Clifton also has a chapter, No. 57, R. A. M., and a council, No. 37, R. & S. M. Clifton was incorporated by an act of Legislature in 1854, but allowed its charter to lapse during the war; however, it has since been revived. The first number of the *Wayne County Citizen* was issued on November 25, 1875, by C. C. Stribling and T. F. Warren. The paper, however, had been published at Waynesboro by the same firm since 1874. On December 21, 1876, Mr. T. F. Warren severed his connection with the paper. Since that time it has been owned by Mr. C. C. Stribling. It is no more than justice to say that the *Wayne County Citizen* is a paper of uncommon merit. Politically it is Independent.

Ashland is situated eleven miles northeast of Waynesboro, and was established in 1830 by Ephraim Dixon and Samuel Mitchell. The postoffice at that place is called Forty-Eight; formerly it was called Pleasant Hill. Malachi Wimberly and Anderson Stoneball sold goods near where Ashland now is in 1819. The first settlers around Ashland were Lovick Rasberry, Nathan Biffle, James Russell, Wm. Walker and Wm. Burns. Following Dixon & Mitchell, above mentioned, Buckner & Dickson were the next business firm. Ashland has usually had from one to two general stores. The principal business of the place is now done by A. H. Cunningham.

The Cumberland Presbyterian Church and Masonic lodge room, on Buffalo, was built in 1878. The trustees of the church were G. T. Walker, A. B. Wisdom, R. A. Shaw, W. F. Edwards and James Durham, and of the Buffalo Lodge, No. 329, were T. S. Evans, W. M.; Theodore Clendenen, S. W.; P. H. Craig, J. W., and others.

Flatwood is a small neighborhood village, about fourteen miles northwest of Waynesboro, founded about 1850. It is the seat of two stores, a postoffice and a school. The business firms are Harris & Hurt and Burns & Graves.

Old Town was the former seat of justice for the county. It was situated on Old Town Branch, a small tributary of Green River, about five miles from Waynesboro. The only residents of the place were Wm. Barnett and John Hill. Nothing now remains to mark the former site of Old Town, so called in distinction from Waynesboro, or the new town.

Though hardly a part of military history, it may be stated that Wayne County was, like all other counties, divided into districts embracing all subject to militia duty. The first divisions for the county were Beech Creek, Eagle Creek, Hardin Creek, Indian Creek, Cypress Creek, Buffalo River, Forty-eight Creek and Rich Creek. In these were the companies of Capts. William Gambrell, G. H. Tucker, Isaac Robertson, H. J. Ray, A. Morris, Thomas Reeves, John Rayburn, Frank Mayberry, Sherrell, Thompson and Aydlotte. These increased in number as the population grew. No regular organized body of men went from this county to either the Seminole or Mexican war. The only representatives of either of those wars is the Rev. George E. Huckaba, who commanded Company H, of the Second Tennessee (Federal) Mounted Infantry in the late war. The county was almost unanimous for the Union till hostilities began, when there was a division. The southern part of the county remained firm for the Union during the whole struggle, while the northern portion was almost unanimous in favor of the Confederacy. The first troops raised for the Confederate Government were for the Ninth Tennessee Cavalry. These troops were mainly recruited about Waynesboro and in the vicinity of Ashland and Flatwood. The first company was A. The officers of this company were J. T. Biffle, captain; J. M. Benham, first lieutenant; P. H. Craig, second lieutenant; G. P. Wells, third lieutenant. The second company had for its officers James M. Reynolds, captain; Reiley Littleton, first lieutenant; John Littleton, second lieutenant. The third company of this regiment was commanded by Capt. John A. Johnson, with B. S. Hardin, first lieutenant, and A. H. Ross, second lieutenant.

The Ninth was mustered into the service in August, 1862, at Waynesboro. The operations of the regiment were confined to the surrounding counties, in guarding railroads, bridges, rivers, etc. Later the regiment was ordered to Murfreesboro with Forrest, where it joined in an attack and capture of the same, also in the raid through West Tennessee in December, and upon Franklin and Spring Hill. In 1863, the regiment was in the pursuit and capture of Col. Streight, of the Fifty-first Indiana, in his raid through Georgia. The regiment was engaged at Chickamauga, Chattanooga, and at Knoxville in the siege of Burnside's army. In December, 1863, P. H. Craig raised Company B, consisting of about seventy-five men, and was attached to the Twentieth Regiment. Their operations were confined mainly to Alabama and Mississippi till the fall and winter of 1864, when the entire army invaded Tennessee in the advance upon Nashville. A very brilliant dash was made upon Johnsonville and the Federal supplies at that place captured and burned, amounting to more than a million of dollars. The troops then advanced upon Nashville, by way of Florence, Wayland Springs, Lawrenceville, Columbia, Spring Hill and Franklin. In that engagement the Twentieth was on the right, under Forrest. After the retreat of the Federals from Franklin the Twentieth joined in the pursuit, and struck the Federals at Hollow Tree Gap and drove in the pickets at Nashville. Forrest, with a large portion of his cavalry, was sent to assist in the operations against Murfreesboro. After the defeat of Hood at Nashville these forces were hastened to Franklin to cover the retreat from Tennessee. Those that escaped the disaster were collected at Tupelo, Miss., and soon afterward sent East to engage in the final struggle in that section. For the Ninth Battalion there recruited Company F from Wayne County. This was commanded by T. D Whitehead as captain; William M. Biffle, first lieutenant; Dr. R. W. Couch, second lieutenant; S. W. Burns, third lieutenant. These men were mustered into the service in 1861, at Camp Anderson, near Nashville. After the defeat and capture at Fort Donelson, the men captured were held till the last of August, 1862, when they were exchanged and were soon after reorganized. At the reorganization, W. L. Bromley was chosen captain; Joseph Clendenen, first lieutenant; James E. Grimes, second lieutenant; J. T. Cotton, third-lieutenant. J. H. Akin was in command of the battalion, the history of which is found elsewhere. Several companies went out in Deering's Fifty-fourth, but after the stampede and disorganization of that regiment the men were assigned to Dixon's Forty-eighth. The companies were three in number. The officers of the first were T. R. Hughes, captain; William L. Montague, first lieutenant; Jasper Benham, second lieutenant; A. K. Hardin, third lieutenant. Of the second, D. S. Skillern, was captain; D. H. Jones, first lieutenant; J. H. Shields, second lieutenant; J. B. Huckaba, third lieutenant. Of the third company, James M. Reynolds, was captain; J. N. Hollis, first lieutenant. (See history of Dixon's Forty-eighth for a history of this regiment.)

The first company for the Federal service was Company A, of the Tenth Tennessee (three years). Officers: Captain, Ed B. Bladen; Henry N. Lee, first lieutenant; John J. Brewer, second lieutenant. Mustered into service April 26, at Nashville. Henry N. Lee was afterward chosen captain. The men were mainly from south part of the county. Number of men, 92. Services were mainly garrison and guard duty. Second Mounted Infantry (one year), regimental officers: John Murphy, colonel; Owen Haney, lieutenant-colonel; J. M. Dickerson, major; Nat Brown, adjutant. Organized at Nashville in 1864. Services were mainly at Clifton and other parts of Wayne and other counties. Company A —T. J. Cypert, captain; Jas. Moore, first lieutenant; C. C. Stribling, second lieutenant. Company B—W. A. Harrison, captain (afterward Sam H. Martin); E. D. McGlamery first lieutenant; Elias Thrasher, second lieutenant. Company C—A. J. Roberts, captain; Wm. Barnett, first lieutenant; Alfred Cottham, second lieutenant. Company D—C. W. Shipman, captain; Phillip Howard, first lieutenant; Asberry Thompson, second lieutenant. Company E—Henry D. Hamm, captain; J. J. Bromley, first lieutenant; G. H. Brewer, second lieutenant. Company H—Geo. E. Huckaba, captain; John Judd, first lieutenant; Wm. A. Skillern, second lieutenant. Company I or K—A. Garner, captain; Mr. Barnett, first lieutenant; Mr. Glasgow, second lieutenant. These were all in the Second Tennessee Mounted Infantry.

Sixth Tennessee Cavalry was composed of the companies of Capt. G. Berry and Capt. D. I. Dickerson. The Eighth Mounted Infantry consisted of the company of Capt. C. W. Shipman, formerly of the Second Tennessee, as above, with E. V. Turman as first lieutenant. Eldridge's artillery consisted of Lieut. Wright and a few men from different parts of the county.

The schools of Wayne County were entirely isolated in their character till 1843, when Ashland Academy was built. This was built under the old seminary law. This building stood a short distance southwest of the Public Square of Waynesboro. The first trustees were John McDougal, Nathan Biffle, J. L. Ross, Abraham Montague, D. L. Jones, R. W. Kendel, S. D. Mack and T. M. East. In 1849 the funds had so accumulated that an additional academy was erected. This was called the Female Academy, and stood on Lot 31, where the college building now stands. The building was under the same board of management as the other. These served the public until the reorganization of the schools since the war. In 1885 was erected in Waynesboro the new school building known as the Waynesboro College. This was built by a joint stock company of the leading citizens of the place and vicinity. This is an excellent building and is managed as a consolidated school. The schools of the county were organized under the present system in 1873, by James Anderson, county superintendent. A comparison of superintendent's reports for 1880 and 1885, the only ones available, will show the increase in attendance and number of the public schools. In 1880 the number of scholastic population was white, 3,733; colored, 334; total, 4,076. Number of teachers in the county: White, 56; colored, 5; total, 61. The enrollment during the year was 2,577 white and 127 colored. The average attendance was 2,003 white and 98 colored. The county then had 1 brick, 12 frame and 20 log schoolhouses, and expended for schools $2,109.95. The scholastic population for 1885 was 4,180 white and 392 colored; total, 4,572. The pupils enrolled were 3,042 white and 297 colored; total, 3,339. The average daily attendance was 1,861 white and 200 colored, or 2,061 in all. The number of schoolhouses was 19 frame and 26 log houses, the whole number being 45. The whole number of schools in the county, however, including females' schools, was 75, 67 of which were white and 8 colored. The total amount expended for that year was $6,546.62.

The first Methodist Church erected in the county was built just east of Waynesboro, at the grave-yard, about 1820. This was a small log building, and served as a place of worship till 1840. In that year the lot opposite Capt. P. H. Cray's residence was deeded by Thomas Boshers to D. J. Jones, John McDougal, Thomas Boshers and Thomas East, as trustees of the church. This was a frame building and stood till the war. In 1878 one wall of the Cumberland Church fell, and was repaired by the Methodists and Masons. The Methodists were then allowed an interest in that building. The Methodists also have churches at Indian Creek and a camp-ground was also established there in 1859; the trustees having been A. G. McDougal, J. B. Biffle, W. T. Childress, A. P. Denning, J. J. Denning and W. Roachwell; one at Culp's Chapel, built in 1877, Eagle Tannery, Clifton, Ashland, Flatwood, Furnace Branch, El Bethel and Beech Creek.

The first Primitive Baptist Church was built near the mouth of Forty-Eight about 1820. To this belonged the Russells, Biffles, Walkers and Thompsons. This church is still sustained with a good membership. The church on Hardin Creek is half a century old; also the one at Goshen, in the Sixth District, is nearly as old. There is also a church of this denomination on Upper Indian Creek. Churches of more recent date stand in the First and Ninth Districts. The founders of these older churches have long since been "gathered to their fathers."

By far the most numerous branch of the Baptist family is the branch known as the Missionary Baptists. The oldest organizations of this church are at Indian Creek and Philadelphia, each of which dates back more than half a century. Besides the two mentioned, there are churches at Green River, Zion, Friendship, Bethlehem, Union, or Beech Creek, Holly Creek, Chestnut Grove, Oak Grove, Macedonia, Rayburn Creek, Pleasant Valley and Leatherwood. The aggregate in membership amounting to about 700. Besides these, there are a number of Free-Will Baptists in the county, there being a church of this denomination at the head of Factor Fork and at Oak Grove; also a number of others.

The first Cumberland Presbyterian Church erected in this county was, perhaps, the church at Waynesboro. This was erected about 1850 by the Presbyterians and Masons. The church at Clifton was built in 1859; they are both substantial brick buildings. This denomination has churches at Shady Grove, Ashland, New Providence and Mount Olive.

PERRY COUNTY.

THE eastern and central portions of Perry County lie on the western slope of the Highland Rim, and the western portion in the valley of the Tennessee River. It is bounded north by Humphreys, east by Hickman and Lewis, south by Wayne, and west by the Tennessee River, which separates it from the county of Decatur. Its area is about 400 square miles, or 256,000 acres, with a very small portion under cultivation. The length of the county north and south is about double its width east and west. The Buffalo River flows through the county from south to north, and so divides it as to leave about one-third of the area to the east and two-thirds to the west. The Buffalo Ridge runs through the county west of and parallel with the Buffalo River, and averages about three-fourths of a mile distant therefrom. This ridge is about 700 feet above sea level, and 300 feet above the adjacent valleys. It has a rapid descent toward the Buffalo River, and a more gradual descent toward the Tennessee. This ridge has numerous arms, or branch ridges, extending westward, between which the creeks rise and flow into the Tennessee River. The sources of these creeks are only about one and a half miles west of Buffalo River, and their names, beginning at the north are Crooked, Roan, Tom, Deer, Lick, Spring, Cypress, Marsh, Cedar, Bee and White Oak. A few spring branches flow from the eastern escarpment of this ridge into Buffalo River. The eastern part of the county is a series of ridges extending east and west, between which the creeks rise and flow westward into Buffalo River. The names of these creeks, beginning at the north, are Lost, Russell, Lagoon, Cane, Brush, Coon, Short, Hurricane, Rockhouse and Sinking. All the ridges are covered with a dense growth of the oak in its varieties, and chestnut, gum, dogwood, etc. The valleys and hillsides contain oak, poplar, walnut, beech, ash, etc. The soil of the ridges is thin, flinty and sterile, while that of the valleys is alluvial and sufficiently charged with flinty gravel and coarse sand to make it easy of cultivation. The latter soil is very productive, and well adapted to the growing of Indian corn, oats, peanuts, rye and the grasses.

The geology of the county, as given by the State Board of Agriculture, is as follows: "Blue and gray limestones outcrop in all the valleys excepting a few in the northern part of the county. These limestones belong to the formations known among the geologists as Niagara and Lower Helderberg. Many of the bluffs along the Tennessee River are made up of their strata. There are a number of glady places in the county, formed by the outcrops of the Niagara limestones, which have supplied geologists at home and abroad with fine specimens of fossils. Many of these fossils have been taken to Europe. Above the Lower Helderberg limestones, which are generally thin bedded, blue and full of fossils, lies the black shale, a formation which everywhere attracts attention, mainly because it is mistaken as an indication of stone-coal. This bed ranges in thickness from a few feet to thirty or more. Above the black shale, and constituting the mass of tops of the ridges, is the siliceous division of the Lower Carboniferous. The lower strata of this division are often silico-calcareous shales, mixed, more or less, with limestones. The upper portion contains more limestone, which often shows cherty masses; the latter, being liberated, cover, more or less, the tops of the ridges.

More than one-half of all the land in the county is charged with iron ore. There seems to be an almost inexhaustible supply of this mineral. It is found, however, in the greatest quantities along Marsh, Cedar and Sinking Creeks. "Along the creeks and on the west side of Buffalo Ridge blossoms outcrop in dark, bluish boulders, whose great weight shows iron to be the predominant ingredient." The Cedar Grove Iron Furnace was erected on Cedar Creek, near its mouth, by Wallace Dixon, about the year 1834. It was rebuilt about twelve years later by Ewing,

McNickle & Co. It was afterward run by different persons, and suspended operations in 1862, and has not been run since. It used to make 1,500 tons of pig metal annually. A rough species of reddish, varigated marble, useful and beautiful for building purposes, is found in great quantities, in different parts of the county. There is a mine of wealth in the "bowels of the earth," in Perry County, remaining undeveloped. The cheap means of transportation for heavy articles, which the Tennessee River furnishes, will undoubtedly lead capital to this mine, and cause it to be developed in some future day.

It can not be said who was the first settler of Perry County. The settlements were made in the valleys along the water-courses, and have ever since been confined to those localities. There is no account of settlements prior to 1818, but it is evident that a number of individuals settled in the territory of the county before that date. Robert Patterson, whose son William was born on Tom Creek in 1818; Ferney Stanley, who taught the first school in the county, on the same creek, in 1820; Rev. Wm. Hodge, Rev. Samuel Atkins, John Stanley, Wm. O. Britt, Enoch Hooper and John Young, all settled on Tom Creek about the year 1818. William Patterson, now deceased, if not the first, was among the first born in the county. The family of Whitwells, Thomas, John, Samuel and James Lomax, Horner Cude, James Salmon, John Anderson, Rev. Joseph Kelley and Jesse Depriest were among the first settlers on Cane Creek. Jacob Huffstedler, born on board of a sailship *en route* from Germany to America in 1775, settled with his family on Cane Creek in 1821. John Horner, Elbert Matthews, Jerry Holligan and James Wilkins and their families settled on Buffalo River, near Beardstown about the year 1824. Joseph Tucker, from North Carolina, settled on the farm now owned by E. Dodson, near Linden. Isaac W. Stanly settled on Buffalo River, and was surveyor of Perry County for many years. James Dixon (at whose house the county of Perry was organized), James Yates, Wiley Tanner, John and Jesse Newton and others settled on Lick Creek as early at least as 1818. Joseph Brown, William and Nathan Ward and Nat. Dabbs were among the first settlers on Marsh Creek. Samuel Denton, John Tracy and Jesse Childress settled on Cedar Creek about 1818. Joshua Briley, Thomas Evans, Nicholas Welch and James Scott were the first settlers on White Oak Creek. Jacob Fraley, George Hollabough and John Webb settled on Sinking Creek about 1818 or 1820, and about the same time David Hogan, Hodge Adams and Nancy Randal settled on Rockhouse Creek. Allen Barber and the Jarmons settled on Hurricane Creek, and John Siser, John Turner, Elijah Duncan and the Cobles on Brush Creek, and Thomas Dowdy, Joshua

Cotes and Abraham Barber on Coon Creek. Other early settlers of the county were Wm. Holmes, John L. Houston, Oswald Griffin, John Wims, Green B. Newsom, West Wood, John A. Rains, Aaron Lewis, Jacob Harmon, Mark Murphy and Joseph Dixon. The first steam-boat that passed up the Tennessee River, was the "General Green," in 1819. Many of the pioneer settlers visited the river to see the great curiosity.

James Dixon built the first horse-mill in the county, on Lick Creek, about the year 1820, and the first water-mill in the county was erected on Cedar Creek in 1821, by John Tracy. The first merchant in the county was James Yates, who began business about the year 1819, on Tom Creek. The first cotton-gin was erected on Cedar Creek in 1821, by Samuel Denton. The raising of cotton was not a prominent industry in the county until after the close of the civil war, when the farmers engaged in it extensively for a few years; but, finding it unprofitable, they have now almost entirely abandoned it. For some years past the leading industry among the farmers has been, and is now, the cultivation of peanuts, of which there are from 500,000 to 800,000 bushels produced annually in the county, this being one of the leading counties in the State for that product. The number of bushels of cereals raised in Perry County, in 1885, was as follows: Indian corn, 423,461; rye, 565; barley, 125; oats, 23,874; wheat, 16,051. The number of animals reported in the county were: Horses and mules, 2,462; cattle, 4,806; sheep, 4,799; hogs, 16,764. The number of dogs is not reported, but it is declared, on good authority, that there are more dogs than sheep in the county. Two or three curs and five or six hounds constitute the ordinary pack of dogs owned by many individuals. Owing to the fact that only a small portion of the land is cleared, thus leaving extensive forests, wild animals, such as deer, wildcats, foxes, coons, etc., and wild turkeys, still abound in considerable numbers. The people enjoy the sport of hunting, hence the great number of dogs. When the county was first settled the above-enumerated animals, and also bears, wolves and panthers were numerous. There are none of the latter now remaining.

Perry County is somewhat noted for its tanneries. The first yard established in the county was at a place on the Tennessee River known as Rat Tail, by Charles Gotthardt, a native of Germany. This yard was started about 1843, receiving its peculiar name from the circumstance of its having been infested with rats disembarked from a St. Louis barge loaded with hides. During the ten years succeeding the foregoing date, ten tan-yards were established at different points in the county, and the annual product of all then within the county, according to the best estimates that can now be made, was $50,000. The war and its consequences have compelled all these tanneries, excepting two, to suspend operations. Of the two remaining, the one owned by Robert Houssels was established at its present site in 1868, and now yields an annual product amounting in value to $75,000. The other one, owned by James B. Sutton, yields an annual product amounting in value to $5,000. Mouse Tail, on the Tennessee River, named in contra-distinction of the old landing, Rat Tail, now in disuse, is the principal place of shipment for the tanning products. The number of green hides required to supply these tanneries is about 7,000, nearly all of which are shipped from the North.

A number of grist-mills, sufficient to supply the demands of the county, have been erected at different points. Saw-mills have been constructed on the creeks, principally for getting out black-walnut and poplar lumber for shipment. The supply of walnut timber has been exhausted, but there is a large quantity of good poplar timber still remaining. Immense quanties of lumber, shingles and tan-bark have been shipped on the Tennessee River from this county to St. Louis and other points in the North. Between 1866 and 1880 Thomas Whitwell operated a wool-carding-mill on Rockhouse Creek. It was then removed to Hurricane Creek, where Messrs. Henderson & Williams have recently rebuilt it and supplied it with new machinery throughout. During the seventies Josiah Bastian operated a woolen-mill on Cane Creek.

The county of Perry was created by an act of the General Assembly of the State, passed in November, 1819. The act provided "that a new county be established north of Wayne, west of Hickman, and south of Humphreys, by the name of Perry County, beginning at the southeast corner of Humphreys, running west, thence south, thence east, thence north to place of beginning, and to include all the territory lying between Humphreys, Hardin, Wayne and Hickman Counties." The act also provided that, until otherwise directed, the quarter sessions and circuit court should be held at the house of James Yates, on Tom Creek, or at such other place in said county as the justices thereof might select. The territory originally included in the county embraced, in addition to what it now contains, nearly all of Decatur County.

The first magistrates (justices) of the county were James Dixon, Joseph Brown, Wm. O. Britt, Wm. Holmes, John L. Houston, Oswald Griffin, Enoch Hooper, Mr. Nunn and Green B. Newsom. The house of James Dixon, on Lick Creek, was the place selected by the magistrates for holding their first session, and there, on the first Monday of January, 1820, they met and organized the county of Perry. Joseph Brown was elected chairman of the court of quarter sessions (county court), and the first county officers were elected as follows: Wm. Jarmon, clerk; West

Wood, sheriff; John A. Rains, register; Aaron Lewis, trustee; Jacob Harmon, ranger; Mark Murphy, coroner; Joseph Dixon and four others were elected constables. The first courts were held, as stated, at the house of James Dixon, and the next at the house of Mr. Barry, on Tom Creek. In 1821, the year following the organization, the county seat was established at Perryville, on the west bank of the Tennessee River. An act of the General Assembly, passed in November, 1845, provided that all the territory of Perry County lying west of the Tennessee River be formed into a new county, to be known as the county of Decatur. Accordingly, in 1846, the county of Perry was divided and the county of Decatur established, with the Tennessee River as the boundary line between the two counties. The courts of Perry County were then adjourned to Harrisburg, a point three miles south of Linden. Here they were held two years. Meanwhile the location of the new county seat was the absorbing question of the citizens. Harrisburg and Linden were the competing points. An election was held, and it was decided in favor of Linden by a majority of six votes; and in 1848 the county seat was permanently established at Linden, where it still remains. The site of Linden, consisting of forty acres, was donated to the county by David R. Harris. He reserved a few lots, and named the place Linden at the suggestion of Maj. Thomas M. Brashear. The town was surveyed into lots, including a public square for county buildings. The lots were sold, and the proceeds of the sales thereof were appropriated to defray the expense of erecting public buildings. The county has been divided into eleven civil districts.

The first court house at Perryville was built of logs and the second one of brick. The latter was used until the division of the county in 1846. The first court house at Linden was also made of logs. This was replaced in 1849-50 with a frame building. The latter was consumed by fire during the late civil war, together with all records therein contained. Some of the public records, being in offices outside of the courthouse, were preserved. The present court house is a very substantial and quite ornamental brick structure of two stories, with the county offices on the first floor and the court rooms on the second. It was erected in 1868 at a cost of $9,500. The present jail is a small two-story brick building, with two cells for prisoners. It was erected in 1872 at a cost of about $3,500. It has recently been condemned on account of its insufficiency, and the county court is now negotiating for its reconstruction, or the building of a new one.

In December, 1880, the county purchased a farm consisting of 277 acres, with buildings thereon, of W. C. and J. L. Webb, for $5,000.

Some expenses have since been incurred in the construction and repair of sufficient buildings. On this farm, which lies on the east side of Buffalo River, about a mile above Linden, a home for the paupers of the county is provided. The average number of persons thus annually provided for is about eight. The county is without a railroad, but has for the transportation of its products the advantages afforded by the Tennessee River.

The tax duplicate for the county for the year 1886 shows 253,858 acres of land and fifty-seven town lots, assessed at $699,043, and personal property assessed at $80,913, making a total assessment of $779,956. The total tax levied and charged thereupon is $8,984.64. By reference to the last amount, allowing a small percentage to be uncollectable, the reader can approximate the receipts and expenditures for the year. The number of taxable polls in the county is 1,098.

County Court Clerks since the war—Jesse Taylor, 1865-67; John Taylor, 1867-68; R. A. Guthrie, 1868-70; T. J. Lewis, 1870-74; P. P. Pickard, 1874-82; C. L. Pearson, 1882-86. Registers since 1840 (the records of that office prior to that date having been destroyed)—J. A. Rains, 1841-46; Thomas Lomax, 1846-82; R. A. Kimbel, 1882-86. As Mr. Rains was the first register it is probable that he served from 1820 to 1846. Sheriffs—West Wood, 1820-28; John Easley, 1828-32; Larkin Baker, 1832-34; Madison Harris, 1834-36; Wm. Welch, 1836-42; Abner Coleman, 1842-43; Hugh B. Hand, 1843-46; Thomas Simmons, 1846-47; John L. Webb, 1847-48; James Kelley, 1848-52; Moses Bates, 1852-56; James H. Brown, 1856-58; Moses Bates, 1858-62; * * * James M. Dodson, 1866-68; Henry H. Long, 1868-70; John L. Webb, 1870-74; Wm. J. Flowers, 1874-76; Edward W. Easley, 1876-78; A. D. Craig, 1878-82; J. M. Hunt, 1882-86. Chancery court clerks and masters—James H. Kinzer, 1854-58; I. N. Hulme, 1858-60; R. M. Thomas, 1860; T. M. Brashear, 1865-68; H. J. Young, 1868-71; T. W. Edwards, 1871-77; W. A. Edwards, 1877-83; W. C. Webb, 1883-86. Circuit court clerks since 1846—F. H. Kimble, 1846-50; T. W. Edwards, 1850-58; B. G. Rickman, 1858 to war period; J. P. Ledbetter, 1865-70; Lewis C. Waggoner, 1870-74; T. J. Evans, 1874-78; James E. Dodson, 1878-82; J. W. Lewis, 1882-86. The county has been represented in the Legislature by Messrs. H. M. Brown, Robt. Crudup, Charles Graham, Thomas M. Brashear, Hartwell Barham, F. H. Kimble, William S. Maxwell, William N. Baker, Jesse Taylor, C. B. Dodson and J. B. Daniel, and in the State Senate by H. H. Brown, Thomas M. Brashear and Warren Smith. The population of the county is 7,200. The county tax levied for 1886 is 15 cents on each $100 of taxable property, and 50 cents on each poll.

Sufficient mention of the action of the county court has been made above. It resumed its authority at the close of the war, when martial law was succeeded by the civil, and held its first session in April, 1865. It now consists of Judge Thomas Whitwell and the following magistrates: H. A. Culp, C. Lineberry, C. T. Wiley, William Briley, W. T. Weems, J. B. Dickson, S. M. Barnett, H. H. Long, J. G. Edwin, P. Whitwell, J. B. Gregory, W. A. Hix, J. R. Bates, W. H. Lancaster, S. V. Alberson, Edmond Harder, N. J. Hinson, M. M. Little, J. P. Ledbetter and H. J. Bumpass. The first term of the circuit court was held at the house of James Dixon, on Lick Creek, in the spring of 1820, Judge Humphreys presiding. The early records of this court have been destroyed, so that no connected sketch of its actions can now be compiled. Prior to the formation of the chancery court, the circuit court had jurisdiction over the chancery practice. The first term of the chancery court of Perry County was begun and held in Linden on the first Thursday after the third Monday of June, 1854, with Hon. Stephen C. Pavatt, chancellor, presiding. This court, as well as the other courts, did not convene during the war period. The records of this court have been well kept, and were not destroyed during the war. The Perry County bar consists of James L. Sloan, T. W. Sims, L. W. Morrison and George Pearson. Other lawyers, who have resided in the county and practiced for a few years, are H. E. Rice, H. C. Carter and J. W. Doharty.

Linden, the county seat of justice, is located on the west bank of Buffalo River, about three miles southeast of the geographical center of the county, and about ten miles east of Perryville, the former county seat. The first dwelling-houses in the town were erected in 1847 by Jesse Taylor and Miles Prince. John L. Webb kept the first hotel, commencing in 1849, and Dr. Wm. C. Moore opened the first store in 1847. He was the first physician and also the first postmaster. Linden was incorporated in 1848, and the charter repealed in 1883. For some years prior to the latter date, Linden was infested with saloons and intemperance prevailed to an alarming extent. To overcome this evil, the better class of citizens petitioned the Legislature to abolish the charter. This being done, the saloons had to close up in obedience to the "four-mile law," and there is now not a saloon in Perry County where liquors are sold. The town of Linden now consists of the county buildings, two hotels, two schoolhouses (the Linden High School and the colored free school), one Union Church, three stores, one restaurant, some mechanics' shops and about twenty-five dwelling-houses and 200 inhabitants, three doctors and four lawyers. The Linden *Times*, a weekly newspaper, was published in 1881–82 by S. L. Neely, and in 1882–83 by C. L. Pearson, and in 1883-84 by W. N. Sloan, since which time it has been suspended. This was the only paper ever published in the county.

Farmers' Valley, on Buffalo River, ten miles above Linden, has a postoffice, two stores and a warehouse. Theodore is a post-hamlet on Hurricane Creek, with a wool-carding-mill, grist-mill and saw-mill. Beardstown, established in 1830, and named after George Beard, its first merchant, is a post-village pleasantly located on a high bluff on the west side of Buffalo River, about eight miles below Linden, and contains two stores and a postoffice. Lobelsville is also a post-village on the west side of Buffalo River, about five miles below Beardstown. It was established in 1854 and named after Henry De Lobel, a French immigrant, who remained here seventeen years and then returned to France. The village contains three stores and a schoolhouse and church combined. Britt's Landing, on the east bank of the Tennessee River, in the lower end of the county, was established in 1839. As early as 1844 it became a point of considerable commercial importance, and still continues as such. The imports of goods for Beardstown, Lobelsville and several other points, are received at this landing. The postoffice at Britt's was established about 1850. Cotton, in considerable quantities, was once shipped from this point, but peanuts have usurped its place, and now no cotton is exported, but from 100,000 to 120,000 bushels of peanuts are shipped annually. Wm. O. Britt & Son are the proprietors of the landing, and also of a large general store and warehouse. Mouse Tail Landing, on the east bank of the Tennessee River, was established in 1840-45, after which Homer & Blackburn conducted a grocery store for a number of years. A warehouse was finally built, and since the era of peanut culture began the place has become an important shipping point. Immense quantities of tan-bark have been shipped from this landing. The postoffice was established here at the close of the late war. The place contains a store and warehouse. Other landings in Perry County on the Tennessee River, are Denson's, Webb's, Cedar Creek, Peters' and New Era. At each of these landings, excepting Webb's, there is a postoffice, store and warehouse; at Webb's there is only a postoffice and warehouse.

Perry County has no military history, prior to the late civil war, worthy of mention. Some of her early settlers were survivors of the war of 1812, and some of her later citizens participated in the war with Mexico. At the outbreak of the Rebellion, a strong Union sentiment prevailed, which was maintained by its adherents throughout the entire struggle. The people were greatly divided, the majority, however, being in favor of a Southern Confederacy. With the citizens of the county the war became intestine. Those favoring the Southern cause were the first to enter the struggle. Early in the spring of 1861 Capt. Lewis Shy enlisted the Perry Guards, and joined the Confederate Army with his company, which became Company G, Twentieth Tennessee Infantry, Zollicoffer's brigade. The Captain had his leg broken early in the war, and then resigned. He was succeeded by Capt. Robert Anderson, and he by Capt. George Pettigrew. This company lost more men in the battle of Fishing Creek, Ky., than any other company in the regiment. Capt. N. N. Cox (afterward colonel of the Tenth Tennessee) raised a company in Perry County in July, 1861, and with it joined Wheeler's battalion of cavalry. Capt. Wm. H. Harder enlisted the third company in the county, in 1861, mostly from Cedar Creek Valley. This company joined the Twenty-third Tennessee Confederate Infantry. Capt. I. N. Hulme raised the fourth company, the Perry Blues, in November, 1861. This became Company G, Forty-second Tennessee Infantry. The next and fifth company was raised by Capt. W. H. Whitwell early in 1862. This became Company C, Tenth Tennessee Confederate Cavalry. The sixth company was raised by Capt. Bass, and became Company A of the last named regiment. Capt. Elisha Stephens, of Perryville, raised a company (B) for the same regiment. About half of this company enlisted from Perry County. Capt. B. G. Rickman's Company H, of the Tenth Tennessee, was also from Perry County. Enough men to make half of a company went out of the county and joined the Twelfth and Twenty-seventh Tennessee Regiments. There were about 600 men of the county who joined the Confederate Army.

The union men of the county tried to avoid the war by remaining at home. But finding it dangerous to remain where they were constantly harrassed by their enemies, concluded to take up arms and fight for their principles. Accordingly Capt. W. C. Webb took the initiatory step, and with about forty men joined the Sixth Tennessee Federal Cavalry and became a part of Company G of that regiment. Afterward Capt. R. A. Guthrie raised a company for the Second Tennessee Mounted Federal Infantry, and Capt. J. W. Taylor raised another company for the same regiment. A number of citizens of the county who were pressed into the Confederate Army early in the war escaped therefrom, and joined different commands in the Federal Army, so that it is fair and safe to estimate the number of Union soldiers furnished by the county at something over 200. In the spring of 1863 Col. Frierson, with about 120 Confederate soldiers, had possession of and commanded the post of Linden; and early one morning Col. Breckenridge and Capt. Webb, with a portion of the Sixth Tennessee Federal Cavalry, took the place by surprise, and captured Col. Frierson and over 50 of his men, and about 100 horses, a number of mules, a wagon load of arms, and burned the court house in which the Confederates were partially quartered. Only two or three men were killed in this engagement. Near the close of the war a dash was made through Linden by a troop of Confederate Cavalry, when the Federal soldiers were not holding it in force. A few Federal soldiers, however, were there, and all made their escape except one who was captured and killed. The war became desperate here before it closed, as it was conducted mostly by mounted men who ceased to take prisoners. Happily, however, since it has closed, those who were bitter enemies then have become friends, and all bitterness engendered by the war has been forgotten, or at least forgiven.

The first school in the county of Perry was taught by Ferry Stanley on Tom Creek in 1820; and the first school in Linden was taught by Edwin H. Eldridge about 1848. There were scarcely any educational advantages in Perry County prior to the adoption of the present school system. And for some years after its adoption, the county failed to levy any school tax, thus leaving the schools dependent for support upon the tax derived from the State levy, which was entirely insufficient. Of late years the county has made an annual levy of school tax, and for the year 1886 the county levy is 10 cents on each $100 of taxable property and $1 on each poll. The scholastic population of the county for the year 1885 was as follows: White males, 1,418; white females, 1,313; colored males, 117; colored females, 121—total 2,969. The number of pupils enrolled in the schools during the year were: White males, 1,290; white females, 1,210; colored males, 60; colored females, 50—total 2,610. This shows that 91 per cent of the white children attend the free schools, while only 46 per cent of the colored children attend. The number of schools taught in the county in 1885 were 41 white and 4 colored, and the number of teachers employed were 36 white males, 5 white females, and 4 colored males. The average number of days taught during the year were 70, and the average compensation of teachers per month was $27.50. The total amount expended in the county for school purposes for the year ending June 30, 1886, including teachers' salaries, buildings, superintendent's salary, etc., was $5,641.33.

The Methodists and Primitive Baptists seem to have been the pioneer Christians of Perry County. Rev. John Craig, of the Methodist Church, was the first minister that preached in the county, beginning his labors in 1818–19. The first church edifice was a log structure, erected on Lick Creek by the Primitive Baptists in 1825. Revs. William Hodge and Samuel Akin (or Atkin) were the first ministers to preach in it. The Baptists also erected the first church edifice—a log building—in

Linden in 1849, and Rev. Greenberry Mitchell was the first pastor. The first camp-meeting in the county was established on Lick Creek in 1826. Afterward another was established on White Oak Creek, and another near Linden. Services continued to be held at the White Oak camp-ground up to the late war, and since that period no camp-meetings have been held in the county. The leading religious denominations now in the county are the Methodists, Christians and Primitive Baptists. The Cumberland Presbyterians have a church at Lobelsville, and the Free-Will Baptists one on Cedar Creek.

Minnie Duncan, of Perry County, one year old, daughter of Wm. R. and Lizzie Duncan, has more living ancestors than any other person in the State. In the paternal line she has E. T. and Catharine Duncan, grandfather and mother; Elijah and Nancy Duncan, great-grandfather and mother, and in the maternal line of her father a great-grandmother, Mrs. Mary McDonald. In the maternal line B. F. Campbell, grandfather, and W. H. and Martha C. Campbell, great-grandfather and mother. In the maternal line of her mother, Sally Bryson, great-grandmother, and "Granny" Quarles, great-great-grandmother. All of these twelve ancestors live in District No. 10, except the Campbells, who live in District No. 6, both in Perry County. All are Republicans in politics, and useful citizens.

HICKMAN COUNTY.

HICKMAN COUNTY is situated on the western side of the Highland Rim of Middle Tennessee, and is the leading county in what is called the Western Iron Region. The surface of the county is much broken, being composed of high, rolling ridges and deep ravines, pointing generally toward the numerous streams. In the northern part of the county are plateau lands, they being a continuation of what is known as the Tennessee Ridge, which extends through the adjoining county of Dickson, forming the watershed between the Cumberland and Tennessee Rivers. As they approach Duck River these plateau lands sink, but appear again on the south side of that stream. The soil of the ridges is sterile and unproductive, being thin and rocky, while in the valley or bottoms the soil is rich and alluvial, notably in the valleys of the Duck and Piney Rivers and of several of the other larger streams. The streams of the county are Duck River and its numerous tributaries: Piney River, Sugar, Beaver Dam, Swan, Lick, Leatherwood, Cane, Taylor and Mill Creeks, Wade and Bird Branches. At a point about nine miles west from the county seat the waters of Piney River disappear under a bluff, and after passing underground to considerable extent, reappears upon the face of another bluff, about 150 feet high, and make an abrupt fall of about 10 feet. Duck River is navigable for small steamboats at certain seasons, and boats have, at different times, ascended the river as far as Centreville, and attempted to establish a carrying business, but never met with success.

Several mineral springs of note are situated in the county, the waters of which consist of white sulphur and freestone, said to equal the celebrated white sulphur water of Virginia. The springs of note are Bon Aqua Springs, situated in the northeastern part of the county; Beaver Dam Springs, in the southern part, and Prim Springs, in the eastern part. The iron ore found in Hickman County excels that found in any other county in the State. The ore crops out at points all over the county, and lies in beds or banks, more or less mixed with cherty masses, and will yield from the furnace 54 per cent of metal. The ore banks of consequence lie on both sides of the Duck, and are as follows: 6 on the waters of Beaver Dam, 7 on the waters of Swan Creek, 2 on the waters of Garner's Creek, and 1 each on the waters of Jerry Branch, Haley Creek, Defeated Creek and Piney River. The development of these iron deposits was inaugurated in 1858, by the erection of the Ætna Furnace, on Beaver Dam, and in 1859 Oakland Furnace was established. These furnaces continued until the late war, and since that time the Etna was put in blast again and continues in operation at the present. Two other furnaces are in operation at present in the county, they being Warner's Furnace, in the northern part of the county, in the Fifth Civil District, and Goodrich's Furnace, also in the northern part of the county, in the Seventh District.

Surface lead has been picked up in many parts of the county, but no effort has been made to develop this mineral. The crops of the county consist of corn, wheat, tobacco, oats, peanuts, and all the grasses, and the timber of white and red oak, gum, hickory, poplar, maple, beech, walnut, dogwood and mulberry. Years ago a fine article of potter's clay was found on Beaver Dam Creek, and a pottery was established, which continued in operation for several years, and was abandoned as uprofitable.

The first white men to set foot in what is now Hickman County, or at least the first of whom there is any record, were the surveyors under Edmund Hickman, who came in 1785 to survey a tract of land on Piney River.

On this trip Hickman lost his life at the hands of the Indians, who attacked the surveying party near the mouth of Defeated Creek, on Duck River, where the body of Hickman was buried by his companions. During the years 1801–02 the Natchez Road, which touches this county on the east, was opened by United States soldiers, under command of Capt. Robert Butler and Lieut. Edward P. Gains. In the latter part of the first year the soldiers reached what is now known as Gordon Ferry, on Duck River, where they went into winter quarters and established a trading house. In 1805, upon the extinguishment of the Chickasaw Indians' title to the lands, Capt. Gordon, then living in Nashville, made a settlement on Duck River, north of the ferry by his name, though he did not himself settle there until in 1812. Thomas H. Benton, the distinguished Missouri senator, who served in the United States Senate for thirty-six years, was in the employ of Capt. Gordon as clerk in his store at Gordon Ferry, in 1807–08, where, it is said, he prosecuted his law studies at odd times and at nights. Among the first settlers in the Gordon Ferry neighborhood were Samuel Oliphant and Rosin L. Bishop, who located there in 1806–07.

Adam Wilson, from East Tennessee, was the first settler on Piney River, he clearing away the cane and undergrowth in 1806, and raised the first crop in the county. During the winter of 1806 other settlers located in the Wilson neighborhood, among whom were William Curl, Reuben Copeland, Samuel Walker, John Lowe, John Ward and Eli Hornbeck, the two former coming from East Tennessee and the latter from South Carolina. A year afterward Ship Landing, on Duck River, was settled by Josiah Ship, John Huddleston and Joseph McConnell.

Between 1807 and 1810 settlements were made as follows: James Peery (and sons, George, Levi and Buchanan), James Anderson, William Duncan, Samuel Aydelott, Henry Jones, Hugh Wallace, Henry Young, William and Jerry Horder, James Campbell, Joseph Morris, John and Boswell Clayton, John Buchanan and Jonathan Toll, on Swan Creek; James Inman and Henry Mayberry, on Lick Creek; Robert Dean, John Nicks, David Dunn and Gabriel Fowlkes, on Mill Creek; David Herrin, on Taylor Creek; John Ward, on Bird Creek; Samuel Walker, on Sugar Creek; William Richardson, on Piney River; Obediah Finn and Samuel Lomax, on Duck River, below the mouth of Piney River. Other early settlers were Robert Wade, Bartley Milam, Joseph Jones, John Bates, Joseph Kimmins, Mark Black, Henry Breece, Levi Garrett, Elias Morris, Mervin Hinson, Charles Warren, Robert Beery, William, Elijah and Gilbert Hicks, Elias Deaton, Willis Dodson, Daniel Davidson, Spencer Tinsley, Clayborn Berryman, Jerry Booth, Hooton and

William Harris, William Morrison, John and Clere McCann, John Angel, Thomas Green and George Hinson. The first mill erected in the county was built in 1808, on Mill Creek, by William Hale, an East Tennessean. Previous to this mill the settlers crushed the corn in old-fashioned mortars, or traveled to mill in Dickson County. Hale's mill was of water-power, and ground nothing but corn. In 1809 the first horse-power corn-mill was erected by Andrew Carrothers, on Sugar Creek. These mills did the grinding for the county for several years, and then numerous other similar mills were erected. In 1828 Edward Corender erected a mill on Lick Creek, water-power, which has been in operation from that time to this, and at present is owned by John Tatum. William Briggs erected a water-power corn-mill on Swan Creek in 1830, long since abandoned. William McCutchen erected a mill and carding machine in Mill Hollow, near Centreville, in 1833, which is in operation at present, being the property of Dr. Montgomery; the Montgomery Mills, on Piney River, about eight miles from Centreville, were established by John Montgomery in 1835. The power for this mill is furnished by an over-shot wheel, and flour and corn are ground, and also lumber sawed. The mills are in operation at the present, and are owned by Josiah Bastin. In 1840 Joshua Downing erected a water-power corn-mill on Cane Creek, which is still operated by him; William Foster erected a water-power corn-mill on Marvin Creek, which is owned and operated by Rufus Gardner; John G. Tarkington erected a water-mill on Lick Creek in 1846, since abandoned; S. G. Williams established a water-mill on Defeated Creek in 1850, now owned by J. T. Warren; Jackson Stamfield erected a water-mill on Swan Creek, now gone; Erastus Anderson has a water-power, grist and saw-mill on a branch of Lick Creek; a tobacco factory, owned by William Dean, on Dogwood Creek, where plug and twist chewing tobacco is manufactured, and the Standard Charcoal Company's works, on the railroad, make up the manufacturing establishments of the county, outside of the iron works, before mentioned, and the manufactories of Pinewood, an account of which may be found in the sketch of that village. The above-mentioned works of the Standard Charcoal Company were established in 1883 by a syndicate of capitalists, and are under the management of Dr. H. M. Pierce, the superintendent. The capital stock is $250,000, the same selling at a premium when in the market, which is seldom. The works consist of twenty large charcoal ovens, with a monthly capacity of 50,000 bushels of charcoal, and other necessary buildings. From the wood is also obtained pyroligneous acid and incondensible gasses, and from the former alcohol is distilled, and the latter is used in running the machinery. It is the second establishment of its kind in the United States, if not of any continent. Joseph Ship erected a cotton-gin on Duck River in 1811, which was the first one in the county. Subsequently other gins were erected, but as the production of cotton was small, they were not long continued in operation. In 1811 Jesse Rodgers built a small powder-mill on Mill Creek, which was the first, and so far as known, the only one in the county.

Hickman County is bounded on the north by Dickson County, east by Williams and Maury, south by Lewis, and west by Perry and Humphreys, and has an area of 559 square miles. The act creating the county out of Dickson County was passed by the General Assembly in 1807, and was named in honor of Edmund Hickman, the surveyor, who was killed on Duck River by the Indians in 1785, an account of which is given above. The act authorizing the establishment of Hickman County appointed David Love, Joel Walker, John S. Prim and Joseph Lynn as commissioners to run the boundary lines, establish the county and select a county seat site. The same act appointed the following magistrates for the new county: Robert Anderson, William Curl, William Wilson, Alex Gray, Joshua McConnell, John Huddleston, Robert Dean and Gabriel Foulkes.

The total area of Hickman County is 390,400 acres, of which 76,215 acres are improved. The population is 12,100, of which 3,000 are voters, four-fifths being members of the Democratic party. The total valuation of property assessed for taxation in 1885 was $1,142,336, an average of $3.10 per acre. In 1885 there were in the county 4,688 head of horses and mules, 7,779 head of cattle, 8,568 head of sheep and 25,464 head of hogs. During the same year the cereal products of the county amounted to 192 bushels of barley, 165 bushels of buckwheat, 828,117 bushels of corn, 42,448 bushels of oats, 1,221 bushels of rye, 37,491 bushels of wheat. The Nashville & Tuscaloosa Narrow-guage Railroad passes entirely across the county from north to south. This road was begun in 1877, by private subscription, but has since passed entirely into the hands and control of the Nashville & Chattanooga system. There are no turnpikes and but two county bridges of consequence in the county, and the roads and highways are fit subjects for improvement.

The magistrates met at the house of William Joslin, on Piney River, two miles north of Vernon, on the first Monday in April, 1808, and organized the county court by electing William Wilson, chairman; Millington Easley, clerk; William Phillips, sheriff; John Easley, Sr., trustee; Bart G. Stewart, register; James Lynn, ranger, and Alex Gray, coroner.

The commissioners appointed by the General Assembly for that purpose met in 1809, and selected a county site on the lands of James Wilson and Joseph Lynn, on a high bluff on the east bank of Piney River, eight miles west from the present site of Centreville, and, laying off a town, named the same Vernon, in honor of Washington's home, in Virginia. A log court house was erected during the following year, when the courts adjourned thereto, and the records were also removed from the temporary court house at Wilson's dwelling.

After the purchase of the Chickasaw claim, on the south side of Duck River, in 1818, that part of the county was rapidly settled up, and the question was sprung of removing the county seat to a more central location. After much excitement and confusion the question was carried by election, and the present site of Centreville was selected, it being on a tract of sixty-one acres of land owned by John C. McLemore and Charles Stewart, both of whom generously donated the same to the county. In 1823 the courts and records were removed to Centreville, and the log court house at Vernon was torn down, and with the same logs another court house erected at the new county seat. In 1825 a brick court house was erected, and was enlarged in 1849. This building was burned by Federal soldiers during the late war, and in 1867 the present court house was erected. It is a two-story brick building, with a court room above and county offices below, and cost about $10,000. There have been three county jails erected in the county. The first one was a little log hut at Vernon, which served until the removal of the county seat, when a brick jail was erected, which was in use until 1848, when it was set fire to by a prisoner and destroyed. The third and present jail was built in 1850. It is a brick building and is provided with suitable apartments for a jailor and his family. There are four strong cells and necessary corridors to the jail.

The county officers have been as follows since the organization of the county: County Court Clerks—Millington Easley, William Stone, Samuel Stebastian, J. D. Easley, J. W. Hornbeak, M. H. Puckett, J. D. Murphy, A. M. Reeves and W. P. Coleman. Sheriffs—William Phillips, Gabriel Fowlkes, Pleasant Walker, William H. Coruthers, Reeves A. Huddleston, William Phillips, John W. Huddleston, Solomon J. George, Levi McCollum, Daniel D. Smith, Joseph Beasley, John Baker, Ephraim A. Dean, Horatio C. Hunter, J. H. Harvill and William Phillips. Registers—B. G. Stewart, W. T. Murrill, E. B. Hornbeak, P. M. Hornbeak, N. F. Fowlkes, E. W. Easley, John Hines, E. W. Lawson, T. J. Walker and W.' D. Thompson. Circuit Court Clerks—Robert Estes, Steven Lacy, Millington Easley, D. B. Warren, Samuel Whitson, A. C. Deshozer, John L. Griffin, W. G. Clagett, E. G. Thompson, J. D. Flowers and W. T. Atkinson. Trustees—Samuel Whitson, John McGill, Benj. Grimmitt, Jesse Briggs, Daniel Dean, S. McE. Wilson and A. W. Warren.

The first session of the Hickman Circuit Court was held at the house of Wm. Joslin in 1808, with the Hon. Parry W. Humphreys presiding as judge, and Joseph B. Reynolds solicitor-general. Robert Estes was appointed clerk. Upon the completion of the court house at Vernon the court and records were removed thereto, and removed to Centreville in 1823. During the years 1830-32-33 the supreme court of Tennessee met at Centreville, but of this court there is now no record, save that it met here.

The judges who have presided over the circuit court of Hickman County together with the attorney-generals, are as follows: Judges—Parry W. Humphreys, West W. Humphreys, M. A. Martin, Edmund Dillahunty, Elijah Walker, ——— Hurst, A. M. Hughes, Elijah Walker, T. P. Bateman and Edward Patterson. Attorney-Generals—Wm. K. Turner, Alex. Hardin, James H. Thomas, Nathan Baxter, ——— Bentley, Noble Smithson, John M. Taylor, M. H. Meaks and John L. Jones. The chancery court held its first session in Centreville on the 6th of September, 1852, with Chancellor John S. Brien presiding, and John W. Whitfield as clerk and master. Chancellors—John S. Brien, Samuel D. Frierson, Stephen C. Pavatt, Robert Rose, Hillary Ward, J. C. Walker, G. H. Nixon and Andrew J. Abernathy. Clerks and Masters—John W. Whitfield, S. H. Williams, O. A. Nixon, P. M. Hornbeak, William M. Johnson, J. C. Walker, Wm. M. Johnson and O. A. Nixon. The members of the local bar have been many, and in many cases distinguished. The early lawyers were James R. McMinn, Henry Nixon, Elijah Walker, W. K. Stebastian, James M. Howney, R. H. Smith, J. J. Williams, A. C. Deshozer and J. R. Hubbard. Those of the present are Col. J. H. Moore, W. C. Clark, O. A. Nixon, Henry Nixon, J. A. Bates and John H. Clagett.

Hickman County was represented in the war of 1812 by only individual volunteers, there being no regularly organized company sent out from the county. Such was also the case in the war of 1836—the Florida war. For the war with Mexico, in 1846, however, Hickman County furnished her full quota. Under the call of the State for volunteers a company was organized in the county and sent out under command of Capt. J. W. Whitfield, in May, 1846. These were enlisted for twelve months, and at the expiration of that time the survivors, or most of them, returned home, with them their captain. At the second call for volunteers Capt. Whitfield organized a second company, and went into service in 1847. Of the regiment to which they were assigned Capt. Whitfield was elected colonel, when Edward Fowlkes was elected to succeed him in command of the company. Of the members of these companies the following names have been secured: J. D. Easley, Ransom Dean, Joseph Weams, Robert Whitson, Henry Darden, Alfred Darden, Lewis P. Trotty, Barnett Trotty, Zachariah Trotty, John C. Lewis, Thomas Dansbee, Dr. Ward, D. Montgomery, W. E. Burchard, William Vinyard and Joshua Burnum.

Hickman County responded promptly to the call of Gov. Harris for State troops in 1861, the people being enthusiastic for the Confederacy. The first company organized in the county was commanded by Capt. T. P. Bateman, and went out in May, 1861, joining the Eleventh Regiment of Tennessee Infantry at Nashville. Then followed companies as follows: Capt. Levi McCollum's company, which joined the Forty-second Regiment of Infantry; Capt. Josiah H. Hubbard's company joined the Forty-second Regiment of Infantry; Capt. J. J. Williams' company joined the Twenty-fourth Regiment of Infantry; Capt. William Beal's company joined the Twenty-fourth Regiment of Infantry; Capt. S. J. George's company joined the Forty-eighth Regiment of Infantry; Capt. J. P. Morrison's company joined the Forty-eighth Regiment of Infantry. Later on, R. M. Whitson and George Mayberry each raised companies of cavalry, of which they were elected captains, and joined the Ninth Battalion of Cavalry, and Capt. F. S. Easley organized another company of cavalry and joined the Tenth Tennessee Cavalry.

Throughout all the engagements of their respective regiments the Hickman County companies participated, losing many men, but acquitting themselves nobly each time they went into battle. This county was overrun by raiding parties sent out by the Federals, and while many Federal troops passed through the county, destroying much valuable property and confiscating arms, stock, and such, no regular encampments were made in the county, nor did any engagements occur in the county between the Federals and Confederates. The guerrillas were also present in the county during the war, and preyed unmercifully upon the farmers, stealing horses, cattle and provisions of all kinds, and committing many depredations.

Centreville, the county seat and principal town of Hickman County, lies in a horse-shoe shaped bend of Duck River, fifty-five miles southwest from Nashville, on the Nashville & Tuscaloosa Railroad, and has a population of 700. The town was founded in 1823, by the commissioners appointed to select a county seat, and was located within two miles of the center of the county—hence its name—on the lands of John C. McLemore and Charles Stewart. The first citizen was Eli B. Hornbeak, and he and his partner, Robert Shegog, were the first merchants of the town, they opening a general store in 1823. Peter Morgan opened the first boarding-house in the town, in 1823, and at that time Dr. Joel Walker was the postmaster, and Dr. Samuel Stebastian the physician. The business men since then have been as follows: From 1825 to 1830—Irwin & Whitson, Irwin & Fry, Robert Charter and Dale & Philips. From 1830 to 1840—Bullock, Irwin & Co., Shegog & Whitson, E. B. Hornbeak, Robert Charter, Dale & Phillips, Bullock & White, Clagett & Fowlkes, W. G. & H. Clagett and S. H. & A. M. Williams. From 1840 to 1850—W. G. & H. Clagett, Russell & Williams, Bird & Peerey, Bird & Fowlkes, B. C. White, Whitfield & Bliss, T. J. Whitfield, S. H. & A. M. Williams and Bird & Williams. From 1850 to 1860—W. G. & H. Clagett, Russell & Williams, Bird & Williams, P. M. Hornbeak, Hornbeak & Nunnelly, John F. Stanfield and Huddleston & Mayberry. From 1860 to 1870—Clagett & Bro., S. H. Williams, Wilson & Williams, Prim & Cunningham, Bates & Cunningham, Bates & Prim and Cunningham & Thompson. From 1870 to 1880—Clagett & Bro., Cunningham & Thompson, Thompson, Jones & Co., E. G. Thompson, S. A. Craig, M. Stewart, S. McE. Wilson and John F. Walker. From 1880 to 1886—Clagett & Bro., general store; Walker & Barnwell, same; S. McE. Wilson, dry goods and drugs; S. A. Craig, general store; S. L. Dodd, same; A. T. Thompson, same; J. T. Prim, family grocery; John P. Brown, same; J. H. Russell, drugs; E. A. Dean, hotel; Huddleston & Bro., livery stable; McFarlan & Co. have a saw-mill on the edge of town, and Charles Whitsides and Robert Hornbeak are the blacksmiths.

The First National Bank of Centreville, with a capital of $50,000, was established in February, 1885, and of which H. Clagett is president, John T. Walker, cashier, and Allen Thompson, teller. The bank has its own building, a handsome two-story brick, and is fitted up with improved vaults, safes, etc. It enjoys a good patronage, being the only bank west of Nashville, between that city and Paris, W. Tenn. The Centreville Peanut Recleaning & Storage Company, a stock concern, was organized in June, 1886, with $10,000 capital, of which H. Clagett is president and J. A. Bates, secretary and treasurer. The company have almost completed a large frame factory or warehouse, which, when ready for operation, will have cost between $7,000 and $8,000.

Centreville was incorporated in 1825, when James D. Easley was elected mayor; since then the town has been incorporated at various times, and at present is a taxing district, having been working under the four-mile law since 1880, and is consequently not annoyed by the sale of whisky within its boundary. The secret societies of the town are Polk

Lodge, No. 83, F. & A. M.; Good Templar Lodge, No. 59; Lodge, No. 311, K. of H., and Hickman Commandery, No. 227, N. O. G. The churches are two in number, being of Methodist and Christian denominations. The schools are the Centreville High School and Fenelon Hall, a private school. The following is a list of the physicians who have practiced medicine in Centreville and vicinity, their names being given in the order in which they have practiced down to the present: Drs. Thompson, Wm. E. McConnell, Samuel Stebastian, S. B. Moore, Wm. E. Douglas, J. M. Douglas, S. P. Stebastian, J. C. Ward, K. I. Sutton, Andrew Norris and S. McE. Wilson, the latter four being the present practitioners. The *Hickman Pioneer*, the first and only newspaper of the county, is published at Centreville by J. F. Martin. The *Pioneer* is a neat and substantial paper, Democratic in politics, and though a doubtful venture and experiment at the time of its establishment by Mr. J. F. Martin, in 1878, has secured a good foundation, and is one of the fixtures of the town and county. The office is fitted up with first-class material, and being one of the best county papers in the State, reflecting credit upon its editor, the town and county, should be liberally patronized by the citizens, and from its present prosperity surely receives the deserved patronage and support.

Pine Wood is exclusively a manufacturing village, situated on Piney River, in the Sixth District, twelve miles north from Centreville, and three miles from Graham's Station on the Nashville & Florence Railroad, and has a population of between 350 and 400, composed entirely of the mill operators and their families. Pine Wood was founded in 1851 upon the lands of and by Samuel Graham, and derived its name from the fact that its original buildings were constructed entirely of pine wood. Mr. Graham upon founding the town established a cotton factory upon a small scale, which was run by water. In 1855 the factory was enlarged and steam power added. In 1871, the mill was accidentally destroyed by fire, and was immediately rebuilt. The machinery consists of 44 looms, 2,330 spindles, 2 sets of wool carders, and 2 rope machines, with a flour and corn-mill attached. Mr. Graham has a large store in connection with his mill, and a good blacksmith shop. The school is the Pine Wood Academy, a splendid one, and the church Methodist. There is a Masonic Lodge and Good Templar organization. Shady Grove was founded in 1848 upon the south side of Duck River, in the Third Civil District, fourteen miles southeast from the county seat, has a population of about 100, and took its name from the shady grove in which its first storehouse was located. Henry Michels was the first citizen and first merchant. The present business men are Michael Hoover, S. W. Cotton and

Q. A. Dean, all general merchants, and M. S. Jones, undertaker. W. J. Thompson is the blacksmith. The churches of Shady Grove are the Methodist, Christian and Mormon, all of which are frame buildings. Shady Grove High School is the one educational institute of the village. The Masons have a lodge, with hall above the Methodist Church. Vernon, the first county seat, was founded in 1809 by the commissioners, two miles northwest from the present county seat, and named in honor of Gen. Washington's home. Robert Shegog was the first merchant of the town. Between 1815 and 1820 the town flourished, but upon the removal of the county seat in 1823, the place rapidly declined, and at the present there remains nothing of the once prosperous village. Walter S. Nunnelly has a general store near where the town once stood, and Philip Claud has a blacksmith shop. Little Lot, on Duck River, in the Second District, has a population of between forty and fifty. John A. Jones has a general store and a cotton-gin and saw-mill; J. H. Martin, Sr., has a grist-mill, and Wash. Martin a blacksmith shop. The Methodists and Christians have churches and the Masonic fraternity a lodge. Green Wood Academy, a chartered institute of learning is located at Little Lot. At Etna, Warner and Goodrich Furnaces there are from 250 to 300 inhabitants each, they being the operatives and their families.

Probably the first school taught in Hickman County was located on the site of Vernon, the first county seat, on Piney River, in 1808, by George J. Peyton. The school was a subscription one, only the rudiments of an education being taught, and the school term lasted from three to five months each year. The schoolhouse was a small log hut, with room for the accommodation of not more than 20 or 25 pupils. George Gantt and Wylie V. Harper taught schools on Lick Creek, and Wm. F. Tulley, John T. Prim and Wm. R. Dickey, near the present site of Shady Grove, at an early date. In 1824-25, a school was taught in a log schoolhouse at Centreville by Canty Nixon, and in 1842 Hickman Academy for males was established in Centreville, under a charter obtained from the Legislature under the provisions of the act passed in 1806 by Congress, appropriating lands in Tennessee for the purpose of establishing State universities and county academies in that State. A substantial brick building was erected for this school at a cost of about $3,000, which was destroyed by fire in 1868. In 1847 a female academy was established in Centreville, and in 1851-52 a two-story brick building was erected, which cost upward of $5,000. Upon the burning of the male academy building the two schools were consolidated and taught in one building. The building has since been enlarged, and is now the Centreville High School building. The one other school in Centreville is Fenelon Hall, a classic school for both male and female, which was established in 1885, by Miss Amanda Phillips. The other schools of the county, other than the common schools, are Greenwood Academy, at Little Lot, on Duck River; Mrs. Shouse's private school, on Duck River, for young ladies; Shady Grove Academy, at the village by that name; Pine wood Academy, at Pinewood; Lick Creek Academy, on that creek, in the Fourth Civil District; Whitfield Academy, in the Ninth District; Cane Creek Academy, in the Tenth District, and Leatherwood Academy, in the Thirteenth District—all of which are excellent schools with large patronage. On June 30, 1885, the scholastic population of Hickman County, between the ages of six and twenty-one years, was as follows: White—male, 2,002; female, 2, 193; total, 4,195; colored—male, 596; female, 543; total, 1,049. Total white and colored, 5, 244. During the above years teachers were employed in the county as follows: White—male, 58; female, 13; total 71; colored—male, 14; female, 5; total, 19. Total white and colored teachers, 90. The schools in the county were as follows: white, 68; colored, 19; total 87. There were five graded schools and one consolidated school in the county. During the year there were six institutes held in the county, which continued for a total of twelve days, and teachers, licenses were issued as follows: White—male, 60; female, 14; total, 74; colored—male, 14; female, 5; total, 19. Total white and colored, 93. The following gentleman here served as superintendents of the county schools since the establishment of that office in 1873: A. J. Stanfield, O. A. Nixon, J. A. Cunningham, W. P. Clark and Isaac Hunter.

The first religious denomination to effect an organization in Hickman County were the Primitive Baptists, who, in 1808, erected a church —the first in the county—on what was afterward the site of Vernon, the first county seat. Revs. Andrew Caruthers, Willis Dodson and Elias Deaton were the pioneer preachers of this church. In 1810 the Methodists organized and erected a church near the mouth of Piney River, which they called Jacob's Pillow. A camp-ground was also established at that point. In 1825 a Methodist Church was built on Dog Creek, eighteen miles northeast from Centreville, which was one of the first in the county of that denomination. At a very early date camp-grounds were established by the Methodists in Gray Bend of Duck River and at Centreville In 1828 the Methodists erected a log church in Centreville—the first in the town—which stood until 1848, when the present brick meeting-house was erected by the Masonic lodge and church together, at a cost of about $5,000. Among the early Methodist ministers were Rev. Mr. Nixon, Rev. James Forsence, Rev. Jordan Moore, Rev. Wm. Mullen, Robert L. Andrews and Wm. E. Doety. Probably the first Cumberland Presbyterian Church in the county stood on Swan Creek, which was erected in about 1816. A camp-ground, called Peery's camp-ground, was also established in connection with the church. During the fifties the Cumberland Presbyterians had a small organization in Centreville, and would hold occasional services in the Methodist church building at that place, but they did not erect a house of their own, and at the present have no organization at all in the town. The Christians made their first organization and built their first church near Shady Grove in about 1840, which they christened Dunlap. In 1848 Little Rock Church was erected on Mill Creek, and in about 1852–53 the church at Pinewood. In 1873 the Christians erected their present substantial frame church in Centreville at a cost of $1,000. Among the early preachers of this denomination were Rev. J. M. Trimble, Rev. Barton W. Stone and Rev. Gooch. At an early date, probably as early as 1839–40, this county was visited by a number of Mormon elders, who gathered around them a few followers and sought to establish a church. They were principally successful and strong in the neighborhood of Shady Grove. The Christian Church was the chief antagonist of the Mormons in that section, and a joint debate or discussion was arranged in 1840 between Rev. Gooch for the Christian Church and Elder Litts for the Mormons. A great crowd was present and much interest manifested. The Mormon disciple was badly worsted in the discussion, which gave his church quite a backset. However, an organization was established, but no church erected, which organization was in a flourishing condition until the memorable " Mormon massacre " in Lewis County in 1884, since when it has been on the decline, yet is still in existence. The members of the organization in this county are upright, law-abiding citizens, and are respected by their neighbors, as they do not embrace the " plurality of wives " doctrine, nor do they make any attempt to practice polygamy.

The present churches of the county, outside of the towns and villages, heretofore mentioned, are as follows: First District, Jacob's Chapel, Union (in which meet the Methodist Episcopal Church South, Christian and Primitive Baptists), Mt. Carmel Methodist Episcopal Church South and Gray Bend Methodist Episcopal Church South. Second District, Primitive Baptists, near Little Lot. Fourth District, Walnut Grove Methodist Episcopal Church South, and Missionary Baptist. Fifth District, Bon Aqua Springs Methodist Episcopal Church South, Cedar Hill Methodist Episcopal Church South, Little Rock, Christian and Warner Furnace Union. Sixth District, Eno Methodist Episcopal Church South, Garner Creek Methodist Episcopal Church South, and Cumberland Presbyterian, Methodist Episcopal Church South, and Christian

Union Church. Seventh District, Nunnelly's Ore Bank Union Church, and Brigg's Chapel Methodist Episcopal Church South. Eighth District, one each of Methodist Episcopal Church South and Baptist. Ninth District, one Union Church, Methodist Episcopal Church South and Cumberland Presbyterian. Tenth District, Pleasant Grove Methodist Episcopal Church South. Eleventh District, one Cumberland Presbyterian and Methodist Episcopal Church South Union Church. Twelfth District, one Union Church and camp-ground, Methodist Episcopal and Cumberland Presbyterian. Thirteenth District, Leatherwood Methodist Episcopal Church South. Fourteenth District, Rawley's Chapel Methodist Episcopal Church South. Fifteenth District, Poplar Church Methodist Episcopal.

LEWIS COUNTY.

LEWIS COUNTY, situated on the Highland Rim, is bounded north by Hickman, east by Maury, south by Lawrence and Wayne, and west by Perry. It contains about 325 square miles, or 208,000 acres of land, only a small portion of which is under cultivation. The county is located on a plateau, higher than the adjoining counties, and is drained from the center outward toward nearly all points of the compass, by Buffalo and Big Swan Creeks and their tributaries. Bordering the valleys, the lands lie in ridges, and the soil is flinty and sterile, and in many places underlaid with slate.

These ridges are covered with a dense growth of red and white oak, chestnut, poplar, etc. The soil of the valleys is alluvial, and equally productive with other bottom lands, being well adapted to the growing of corn, wheat, oats, peanuts and grass. This class of lands compose a very small portion of the area of the county, and are about the only lands under cultivation. Passing from the valleys over the ridges, we come to the "barrens," which are flat and open and lightly covered with scrubby oaks. The soil of the barrens is thin and naturally sterile, but large portions of it have a good foundation, and could be made productive by proper fertilization. Other portions of the barrens, and also of the ridges, are so leachy that they will not hold fertilizing matter, and consequently can not be made productive. However, all portions of the high lands, so far as they have been tested, are especially well adapted to the raising of all kinds of fruit. There is a strip of barrens about three miles wide, extending through the county from the southeast to the northwest. Iron ore abounds in great quantities in the ridges, especially in the southern part of the county. About two-thirds of all the lands in the county are charged with iron ore, the greater portion, however, being confined to the hilly and rolling lands. There are many excellent springs of freestone water, and some of mineral. The elevation of the county is so great, and the fall of the streams so rapid, that it is a remarkably healthy location.

The first settlement in the county was made on Big Swan Creek about 1806–10, by John Sharp and his sons (William, Edward, Nehemiah, Samuel and Joshua), Elijah, Samuel and James Mayfield, all from Kentucky; James Rhoads and Bryson B. Venable, from South Carolina; Ambrose Blackburn, from Georgia; Daniel Garrett, Larkin Hensley and his brothers (William, Samuel and James), Edward Dycus, John Johnson, John Clayton, the Kirkseys, the Condors and Benjamin Lankford, all from North Carolina. Mr. Dobbins was proprietor of "Dobbins' Stand," on Big Swan Creek, where the "Natchez Trace" crosses said creek. Robert Grinder was proprietor of "Grinders' Stand," on the "Natchez Trace," near where it crosses Little Swan Creek, and about two and a half miles west of Newburg. William Johnson, Daniel Sims and Young Simmons were among the first settlers on Pond Creek. John McClish, a half-breed Indian, lived on a reservation in 1812–15, and kept a "stand" on the Natchez Trace, where it crosses the Big Buffalo Creek. The Natchez Trace was opened by Gen. Jackson and his army, on their way from Nashville to New Orleans, during the war of 1812. The stands above referred to were places where travelers were entertained.

The early settlements were made along the streams, and to the present day have been mostly confined thereto. But very little of the upland has been brought into cultivation. By keeping away from the streams and valleys, one may now travel for hours without seeing a human habitation. Deer, wild turkeys, wild cats and venomous snakes still abound in the extensive forests.

The first water-mills built in the territory composing Lewis County was Tom's mill, on Cathey Creek, and the Widow Cavitt's mill, on Swan Creek, both being built about the year 1812, but which was completed first we are unable to say positively. An iron forge was built on Buffalo Creek, at the crossing of the Natchez Trace, and operated in an early day. It was afterward moved to the site of the Napier Furnace, which stands on Chief Creek, about nine miles south of Newburg. The Napier Furnace was erected in 1834, by Napier & Catron. Mr. Catron died over forty years ago, and the Napiers have owned the property ever since. The furnace has been operated part of the time by the proprietors and part of the time by lessees. Since 1880 its operation has been suspended. When operated it required about twenty-five hands, and produced about ten tons of pig iron per day.

The Rockdale Cotton Factory was erected on Big Bigby Creek by Skipwith & Nightengale about the year 1825. It manufactured cotton yarn only, and about twenty-five persons, mostly women, were employed to run it. It suspended operations during the late civil war, and has not been run since. There are now no manufacturing establishments in the county, except a few saw and grist-mills, and a barrel factory at Carpenter's Station.

Lewis County was created by an act of the General Assembly of the State, passed December 23, 1843, providing that a new county should be formed out of fractions from Maury, Lawrence, Wayne and Hickman Counties, and that it be named Lewis County, in honor of Merriwether Lewis,* who accompanied Gen. Clarke in his famous overland route to Oregon Territory in 1803–06.

The act defined the boundary line of the county, and appointed John Akin and Albert G. Cooper, of Maury County; Shadrack Morris and James Voss, of Lawrence; James Gullet and David Voorhees, of Wayne; Hugh B. Venable and John Clayton, of Hickman; to employ a competent surveyor to make the necessary surveys, to hold elections in each fraction, to select and purchase a site for the country seat, to lay out a town with a public square, to sell the lots on a credit of twelve months, and to appropriate the funds arising from the sale of said lots to the erection of county buildings. Elections were accordingly held in the fractions of the old counties, and a majority of the electors thereof voted in favor of the new county. The commissioners then proceeded and organized the county as further provided in the act of creation. The county was divided into eight civil districts, and the first county election held in 1844, when the following officers were elected, to wit: David C. Mitchell, chairman county court; Josiah K. Strayhom, clerk of county court; Hugh B. Venable, trustee; and Alexander King, register. The magistrates elected were John Clayton, Redding Reeves, Drury D. Goodman, William Hines, James F. Hensley, David C. Mitchell, John Akin, Gideon G. Carter, Kincheon Carter, John S. Layton, George Nixon, John W. Killpatrick, C. Y. Hudson, Griffith Cathey, John M. Sharp and James G. Shaw.

---

*" In the very center of the county, on the line of the Natchez Trace, while on a journey from the territory of Louisiana, of which he was governor, Merriwether Lewis, on the 11th day of October, 1809, committed suicide, being at the time a little over thirty-five years of age. On this very spot he was buried, and the Legislature of Tennessee, in 1848, had a suitable monument erected to his memory. This monument, with a pedestal of the hard, siliceous rock of the region, and a shaft of limestone, in imitation of a giant of the forest, untimely broken, is typical of the hard, rough life and premature death of the man. The monument is twenty-five feet high."—*Resources of Tennessee*. The inscription on the west front reads as follows: " Merriwether Lewis—Born near Charlottville, Va., Aug. 18, 1774. Died Oct. 11, 1809. Aged 35 years." Appropriate inscriptions are cut on each of the other three fronts. It is claimed by old citizens of Lewis County that it is not certain whether Lewis committed suicide or was murdered.

The first courts were held, as provided in the act, at the house of John Blackburn, on Swan Creek, which is about four miles east of the present site of Newburg. Here, on the lands of said Blackburn, the first county seat was located in 1846, and named Gordon for Powhattan Gordon, of Columbia. The place never grew much, having only a log court house, one store, and the dwelling of Mr. Blackburn. Nothing of the place now remains except the aforesaid dwelling in which the courts were first held. A resurvey of the boundary of Lewis County was made, and the line moved farther from the county seats of the old counties. In 1848 the county seat was changed from Gordon to its present site, and located in the woods, on the dividing ridge between Big and Little Swan Creeks. It was located on a fifty-acre tract donated by Hugh B. Venable and Robert O. Smith, and took its name from the fact that it was then the last named burg in the State, and consequently a "New-burg." It is about two and one-half miles east of the Lewis monument, in a broken and healthy section, and where the water is excellent.

The first court house was a log building erected at Gordon, and afterward moved to Newburg. It was torn down in 1857, and the present one was erected at a cost of $1,500. It is a two-story frame building, 40x40 feet, with the court-room on the first floor and county offices on the second. A log jail, 18x20 feet, was erected at Newburg, but there has not been a prisoner incarcerated therein since the late war, and for several years last past the authorities, in their annual report, have said "no jail." The paupers are supported by appropriations made by the county court, there being no "poor asylum" in the county.

The annual receipts from taxation, and otherwise, are about $1,500, and the expenses of the county about the same. The indebtedness of the county is about $500. The tax-duplicate for 1886 shows 161,387 acres of land assessed at $217,188, and personal property at $4,500, making the total assessment of taxable property in the county $221,688, and the total tax charged thereon $2,689.61.

The Nashville & Florence Railroad passes through the eastern part of the county, and has one station within the county at Carpenter. The survey of the Nashville & Tuscaloosa Narrow-guage Railroad passes from north to south through the center of the county, and about two and one-half miles west of Newburg.

The county court clerks have been Joseph Strayhorn, 1844–48; C. Y. Hudson, 1848–52; William H. Flanigan, 1852–56; John S. Hunter, six months in 1856; William H. Flanigan, 1856 to civil war; John Hale, 1865–66; Samuel V. Perkins, 1866–70; W. C. Dabbs, 1870–82; J. W. Stockard, 1882–86.

The county trustees have been Hugh B. Venable, 1844-48. William Sharp, 1848-54; Richard Downey, 1854-58; James Lindsley, 1858-60; Milton D. Brown, 1860-62; Rev. John Hensley and others, 1865-70; George W. Hunt, 1870-74; Redden Reeves, 1874-76; Paris Cooper, 1876-82; R. W. Grimes, 1882-86.

The county registers have been Alexander King, 1844-48; John W. Ricketts, 1848-52; J. H. S. Anderson, 1852-56; A. G. Cooper, 1856-60; John Holmes, 1865-72; J. W. Stockard, 1872-78; J. W. Haley, 1878-82; S. L. Massey, 1882-86.

The circuit court clerks have been R. M. Cooper, 1844-56; Richard Downey, 1856-60; Wm. H. Napier and W. T. Brown, 1860-70; Richard Downey, 1870-74; James Craig, 1874-77; Richard Downey, 1877-82; S. Q. Weatherly, 1882-86.

The county sheriffs have been A. P. Buckner, 1844-47; N. B. Akin, 1847-52; Alex. King, two months in 1852; Andrew Johnston, 1852-56; Thos. S. Easley, 1856-58; Samuel A. Whitesides, 1858-60; Green B. Dean, 1860-61; Thos. T. Christian, 1861-65; Milton D. Brown, 1865-70; A. F. Goodman, 1870-72; Allen J. Noles, 1872-78; John Carroll, 1878-84; J. W. Christian, 1884-86. William H. Flanigan served as chancery court clerk, 1871-86.

The attorneys-at-law of the county are John H. Vandiveer, at Hohenweld; J. W. M. Frain, in the western part, and F. A. Plummer, near Palestine.

The first term of county court was held early in 1844, at the house of John Blackburn, at Gordon. And the court continued to hold its regular sessions, at the places provided for holding the courts, until December, 1861, when it suspended its sessions through the war period, and until June, 1865, since which time it has held its regular sessions. The first term of circuit court was begun and held at the house of the said Blackburn on Monday, March 25, 1844; Edmund Dillahunty, judge presiding, and Robert M. Cooper, clerk, and Nathaniel Baxter, attorney-general. The business of this court was also suspended during the war period. The first term of chancery court was begun and held on Monday, April 24, 1871, at Newburg, with Hon. George H. Nixon, as chancellor, and William H. Flanigan, clerk and master. By an act of the General Assembly, passed January 31, 1844, Lewis County was attached to the chancery district of Maury County. But the citizens of Lewis were allowed to file their bills, either at Columbia or in the chancery court at Lawrenceburg. Consequently, all business in chancery for Lewis County, was conducted in those counties until the Lewis County chancery court was organized.

The first dwelling house in the town of Newburg was erected by William H. Flanigan, who kept the first hotel. The postoffice was established in 1848, and Mr. Flanigan was the first postmaster. James Patton, the first merchant, opened his store in 1849, and John H. Cooper taught the first school the same year. Dr. John Bowman was the first physician, and located in 1853; John L. Miller, the first attorney, located in 1850. Newburg was incorporated in 1852. The charter of incorporation has since been abolished. The town had its greatest prosperity in 1854–55, when it contained four stores, two saloons, two hotels, and several mechanics' shops. It began to decline before the war, during which, at one time, it was wholly deserted. It now contains the court house, one store, the postoffice, one schoolhouse, one hotel, five dwellings, and a population of about thirty souls. It has neither lawyer, doctor nor preacher. Hohenweld has two stores and a postoffice. Napier Furnace, one store and postoffice. Voorhies, one store and postoffice. Nutt, two stores and postoffice. Carpenter's Station, one store, saw-mill and barrel factory. Palestine, on Swan Creek, six miles northeast of Newburg, was established in 1835, and had its prosperity about 1860, when it contained a postoffice, store, grocery, school, church and about a dozen dwellings, and fifty inhabitants. It now contains only one store, a church and a few dwellings.

"About a mile north of the Lewis monument, on the old Natchez Trace, and on the east bank of Little Swan Creek, is where Gen. William Carroll disbanded his troops on his return from New Orleans in 1815. An eye witness states that he made them a farewell address, and bid them adieu, crying like a child." The following veterans of the Mexican war are now residing in the county: Abel T. Hensley, Samuel L. Tarrant, A. W. Weatherly and William C. Story. In the late civil war the county furnished three companies for the Confederate Army, as follows: Company H, Third Tennessee Infantry, Capts. Samuel L. Tarrant and R. T. Cooper (the latter was killed at Raymond, Miss.); Company C, Forty-eighth Tennessee Infantry, commanded by Capt. Samuel Whiteside, and Company H, Ninth Tennessee Cavalry, commanded by Capt. Thomas H. Beatty. It is claimed that with these companies, and the individuals who joined organizations outside (the county furnished in the aggregate for the Confederate Army, about 400 men), a number nearly equal to its voting population. The farmers of this county suffered considerably during the war, by the loss of property seized by foragers.

Education in Lewis County has been very much neglected. To show the condition of the schools is given a synopsis of the report of the Superintendent of Public Instruction for the year ending June 30, 1885.

Scholastic population—White, male, 353; white, female, 364; colored, male, 71; colored, female, 72; total, 860. Number of pupils enrolled—white, male, 160; white, female, 200; colored, male, 30; colored, female, 16; total, 406. This shows that less than one-half of the scholastic population of the county attend the schools. The number of schools taught and the number of teachers employed, 14; teachers average monthly wages, $22; average number of days taught in the year, 80; amount of school funds received during the year, $1,760.75; amount expended, $1,031.98; balance on hand, $728.77.

The first church established in the county was the Ebenezer, at Palistine, established about the year 1824, with Rev. James Tarrant as pastor. The Cumberland Presbyterians erected the first church at Newburg, in 1849, Rev. William Walker being the first pastor thereof. The Methodists, Cumberland Presbyterians and Christians are the leading religious denominations in the county, and have their churches at different points throughout the same.

[NOTE.—Acknowledgments are due to the Tennessee Historical Society for a portion of the foregoing facts pertaining to Lewis County.]

LAWRENCE COUNTY.

James M. Alford was born in Tennessee in 1832, son of Isaac W. and Mary P. (Edmiston) Alford. The father was a North Carolinian by birth, and was an early immigrant to Tennessee. He was a farmer and merchant, and held the office of trustee for ten years. He was a follower of the Democratic party and died in Lawrence County in 1859. His wife died in 1876. James M. clerked in his father's store until twenty-five years of age, and closed out the stock at the latter's death, and also settled up the estate. In 1858 he wedded Martha F. Childress of Tennessee, born in 1838, daughter of Adian D. and Nancy (McGuire) Childress. The following are the children born to the union of Mr. and Mrs. Alford: Emma C., William R. (deceased), James B., Charles A., Edward C. (deceased), George T. (deceased), Joseph H. and Maggie S. Mrs. Alford died May 25, 1886. In 1862 Mr. Alford enlisted in Company D, Ninth Tennessee Cavalry Confederate States Army, as a private, and was elected orderly sergeant and served faithfully until the close of the conflict. Since his return in 1865 he has farmed and worked at the carpenter trade. In 1868 he was elected circuit court clerk, holding the office until 1870, when he resigned and opened a general merchandise establishment at the noted watering-place, Wayland Springs. He also carries on farming and is a stanch Democrat in politics, and a member of the Masonic fraternity. He is a member of the Cumberland Presbyterian Church, as was his wife previous to her death.

Demosthenes Buchanan is a native of Giles County, Tenn., born February 23, 1840, son of Samuel G. and Sarah E. (Bodenhammer) Buchanan, both of whom were born in Tennessee. The father was one of the family of John Buchanan, who was one of the early settlers of Lawrence County, and a member of the State Legislature a number of terms. The father was a prosperous farmer and secured a comfortable competency. His death occurred in May, 1853. The mother yet resides in Giles County. Our subject secured a good common school education, and at the age of twenty-one enlisted in Company D, Third Tennessee Regiment, and served as high private. He was wounded at Fort Donelson, and after residing at home until his wound healed, he, in 1862, joined Company G, Forty-eighth Tennessee Regiment, and served until October of that year, when he was again wounded, for which he was discharged the following August. He farmed in Giles County until 1871, at which time he purchased his present place and has been engaged in farming and stock raising up to the present time. Mr. Buchanan is a Democrat and has been magistrate of the Tenth District a number of years. Alonzo L., Solon, Walter, Franklin, Samuel, John and a little girl deceased are the children born to his marriage with Mary J. Quarles, which took place June 17, 1864. Mrs. Buchanan is a member of the Missionary Baptist Church.

William M. Busby may be mentioned as a prominent and successful planter of Lawrence County, Tenn. He was born near Lawrenceburg October 15, 1827, the youngest of five children. His father was born and reared in North Carolina, and after his marriage to a Miss Hale moved to Tennessee. After her death he wedded Verlinda Thomas, daughter of Samuel Thomas, who was born near London, England, about 1758, and came to the United States prior to the Revolutionary war. He served in that conflict and participated in the battle of Bunker Hill. Our subject's mother, Miss (Thomas) Busby, was born in the Bluegrass State March 30, 1797, and is still living at the advanced age of ninety years. William M. was married in Lawrence County July 27, 1854, to N. C. Springer, daughter of Jacob and granddaughter of Aaron Springer. Mr. and Mrs. Busby's children are as follows: Sallie J. (Mrs. W. C. Smith), James F., Stephen J., Samuel T., William A., Paul Jones, John S. and George H. Their mother was born in Lawrence County May 25,

1833, and died at her home July 28, 1882. Mr. Busby is a tiller of the soil, and is the owner of 319 acres of land. He gives considerable attention to stock raising, and is an extensive raiser of the cereals. He is a Democrat in politics, and, although not a member of any church, is prominently identified with all enterprises for the public good.

Hugh A. Campbell was born in Maury County, Tenn., in 1850, and is a son of Richard and Adelia (McMackin) Campbell, who were Tennesseeans by birth. The father was a fairly successful tiller of the soil, and he and wife are members of the Methodist Episcopal Church South, and at present are residing in the village of Chinnabee. Our subject was united in marriage, in 1870, to Miss Lou Voss, who was born in this State in 1849, and is a daughter of Levi and Sarah Voss. Hugh A.'s early days were spent on his father's farm, and there he resided until he attained his majority, when he farmed three years for himself, and then worked alternately at the carpenter's trade, blacksmithing and wagon-making in Chinnabee. His residence is located on a seven-acre lot near the village. He and Mrs. Campbell are worthy members of the Cumberland Presbyterian Church, and in politics he has always given his support to the Democratic party, and is also a strong supporter of prohibition.

Francis M. Cannon was born near Wayland Springs, Lawrence Co., Tenn., September 24, 1837, son of James M. and Temperance (Thomas) Cannon. His early educational advantages were very limited, but by close observation and contact with business life he has acquired a good education. He began farming for himself at the age of fifteen and continued that calling up to the age of twenty-three years. He then married Carrie E. True, daughter of Shiloh and Sarah A. (Slayden) True, and eight children blessed their union: William E., born February 17, 1865; James E., born December 9, 1866; Thomas F., born December 8, 1868; Geneva H., born November 12, 1870; Shiloh T., born December 19, 1872; Emma C., born September 30, 1876; John C., born November 25, 1878, and Mary E., born November 18, 1882. Mr. Cannon was elected circuit court clerk in 1870, which office he faithfully filled the greater part of the time up to 1882. He continued to reside in the town of Lawrenceburg until April 9, 1885, when he removed to his farm of 120 acres near Lawrenceburg. Besides this he owns several thousand acres in another part of the county. In politics he is a Democrat. His parents, James and Temperance Cannon, were born in Virginia August 16, 1816, and Alabama in 1818, respectively. The father came to Tennessee when quite young, and there resided until 1857, when he took up his abode near Florence, Ala., where he died in 1877. The mother is at present residing in Lawrence County, Tenn.

Matthew F. Carrell is the sixth of twelve children born to the marriage of Stephen A. and Mary Frances (Stribling) Carrell, and is of Irish descent. He was born at Lawrenceburg October 3, 1853, and there acquired his education in Jackson Academy. In early life he was a school-teacher, but has followed farming as his chief occupation. He was married, March 4, 1879, to Julia A. Simms, daughter of Paris L. and Mary E. (McGlamry) Simms. The father was a farmer of the Tenth District and the father of twelve children. Mrs. Carrell was born May 22, 1863, in Lawrence County, and is the mother of two children: Mary L., born in 1880, and Paris A., born in 1882. Mr. Carrell is a Democrat and a man of intelligence and liberality. His farm of 160 acres is devoted to the production of the cereals principally, but stock and cotton are also raised. His father was born in Lawrence County and is one of its wealthy farmers, being the owner of six farms, which amount to about 3,000 acres. He has served in official capacities nearly all his life, and has been clerk of the county court for thirteen years, and judge of the same. He was a representative in the State Legislature in 1853, and is one of the highly respected and honored citizens of the county. The mother was born in Lawrence County, and, although in her sixty-third year, enjoys remarkably good health.

T. J. Choate was born on the 27th of February, 1831, in Maury County, Tenn., son of Richard and Martha (McMackin) Choate, who came from East Tennessee to Maury County at an early day. Both parents are deceased. Our subject was reared in Lawrence County and received limited early education in his boyhood days. Since that he has gained a fair education by careful observation and study. After attaining his majority he began doing for himself, working as a mechanic, and now owns what is known as the Fall River Wool Factory, which he successfully operates. In connection with this he owns and farms 242 acres of land. He was elected magistrate in 1882, and still serves in that capacity. He is a Democrat, and a member in good standing in the Methodist Episcopal Church. In 1856 he took for his companion through life Eliza J. Morgan, daughter of Daniel and Mary (Bird) Morgan, and their union was blessed in the birth of eight children: Mary Ellen, Charles A., John Rufus, Nancy, Daniel R., Ella T., James T. and Andrew Lee. Mary Ellen is deceased.

William C. Cocke is a son of Peter P. and Alice (Hooe) Cocke. The father was born in Westmoreland County, Va., and died in Ohio in 1850. Mrs. Cocke was born in Prince William County, Va., and also died in the Buckeye State, in 1872. William C., our subject, was born June 18, 1814, and was reared in his native State, Virginia. When eighteen years of age he began farming for himself, and in 1836 immigrated to Ohio, where he remained until 1881 and then came to Lawrence County, Tenn., where he still resides. His farm consists of 478 acres of choice land. March 22, 1838, he was united in marriage to Lucy Ann Hines, daughter of John and Hester Hines. These children were born to their union: Dade W., Albert H., Peter P., Taylor F., Walker A., Jackson M., George W., John C., Thornton H., Adaline F., Frances, Maria L. and Mary D. Mr. Cocke is a Jacksonian Democrat, and, so far as his means will allow, has always been a liberal contributor to all laudable enterprises. He was on the first passenger train ever run in the United States, extending from Harper's Ferry to Baltimore, Md., in 1832.

Fred W. Cornell was born in Michigan on the 27th of September, 1858, son of Robert B. and Margaret (DeLaney) Cornell, who were born in York State. The father removed to Michigan about 1840, and there farmed until 1851, when he went to California via Chicago, Mississippi River and the Isthmus of Darien, and engaged in mining and gardening for two years at Placerville. He then returned home, and in 1856 purchased a farm in Kent County, Mich., where he resided until 1878, then came to Lawrence County, Tenn., and purchased 1,000 acres of land, on which he lived for three years. In 1882 he returned to Michigan and there now resides on a farm. His wife died September 6, 1866. Their son, Fred W. Cornell, resided with his parents on a farm until twenty-one years of age, when he engaged in the mercantile business in Michigan, but came to Tennessee in 1881, and here has since made his home. In April, 1885, he established his present hotel and controls the leading trade in this line in the town. June 18, 1884, he and Alice Ribble were united in marriage. She was born in Indiana. Mr. Cornell and wife are members of the Methodist Episcopal Church, and he is a Republican in politics. He is a prominent business man of Lawrence County and is recognized as a moral, upright citizen.

John A. Couch, son of Thomas and Charity Couch, was born in Lauderdale County, Ala., December 19, 1848. The father came to Tennessee in 1865, and settled on a farm. He died in 1875, and his wife in 1883. John A. resided with his father on the farm until twenty years of age, when he became the architect of his own fortunes and chose the free and independent life of a farmer as his calling through life. He settled on and tilled a portion of his father's farm, consisting of 160 acres of very good land. His farms contains considerable ore and is well adapted to raising the different cereals and cotton. He joined the Methodist Episcopal Church South in 1879, and has always voted the Democratic ticket. In 1868 he and Mary J. Cobb were united in marriage.

She was born in Alabama, in 1850, and is the daughter of James and Mary J. Cobb. To their union were born five children: Manda E., Emily C., Mary E., William A. and Charles E.

James Craig, a native of Maury County, was born October 25, 1822, son of Johnson and Martha (Blackwood) Craig, both natives of Orange County, N. C. His father came to Maury County in 1808, and was a mechanic by trade. He farmed and raised stock also, and was an intelligent man and a useful citizen. His death occurred in October, 1848, his age being seventy-six years. His wife died in 1856. James was reared on the farm with a limited education, and when twenty-two years old began farming for himself, and has continued thus until the present. For a short time he lived in Lewis County. In July, 1844, he wedded Miss Melissa Voorhies, who bore him ten children: Johnson, Sidney, Emily, Elizabeth, Anna, Millard, Mattie, Joseph, Willie and Walter. Mr. Craig is a Democrat and was clerk of the Lewis County Circuit Court in the seventies, and also served several years as magistrate. He is a Mason, and himself and family are members of the Methodist Episcopal Church. He is one of the most substantial citizens of the county. His son, Millard, is the proprietor of a general store at Summertown, having established his business in 1884. He keeps a fine stock and has a good and growing trade. He is one of the most enterprising and promising young business men of the county.

Jonas Crews, who was born on the 22d of September, 1821, in Person County, N. C., is a son of Arthur and Louvisa (Hicks) Crews, both of whom were born in the same State and county as our subject, in 1799 and 1801, respectively. The father immigrated to Lawrence County, Tenn., on Christmas Eve, 1831, and died in that county in 1862, his wife dying in March of 1882. Our subject was reared in Lawrence County, and had few opportunities for gaining an education, but in later years has gained a good business education. He began the battle of life for himself after attaining his majority, and engaged in farming and stock raising, being very successful in the latter occupation. He owns about 1,800 acres of land, about 700 of which is under fence. On the 25th of September, 1844, he was married to Mary Virginia Hensley, daughter of Simeon and Charity (Bryant) Hensley. The father died when Mrs. Crews was quite young, and his widow married a Mr. Taylor and moved from Lawrence County, since which time nothing has been heard as to her whereabouts. To our subject and his wife were born the following family: William James, born August 4, 1845, and died July 18, 1867; Martha Ann, born May 18, 1847, and died in July, 1865; Arter Simeon, born May 1, 1849. Mrs. Crews died June 3, 1849, and June 3, 1859,

Mr. Crews married Eliza Emeline Helton, and their children are Melvina Catherine, born July 20, 1861; George Washington, born May 29, 1863; Zachariah F., born June 20, 1866; Jeremiah Benjamin, born August 11, 1869; Louvisa Amanda, born July 11, 1871, and died in September, 1882; Jonas, born September 27, 1873; Jonathan McClane, born August 11, 1876; Henry Clay, born May 29, 1879, and Daniel Webster, born October 15, 1881. Mr. Crews was not in the late war. In 1852 he was elected justice of the peace, and served six years. In 1882 he was re-elected to the same office. He was formerly a member of the Methodist Church, and still retains his religious views.

Capt. Thomas D. Deavenport was born in Lawrence County September 18, 1837, son of Thomas D. and Maria P. (Lucas) Deavenport. The father, when a boy, came from Virginia to Tennessee about 1810, his father being Matthew Deavenport. They settled in Giles County, where Matthew Deavenport was a prominent Baptist divine. About 1821 our subject's father moved to Lawrence County, where he farmed, sold goods, manufactured cotton and worked at the brick mason's trade. He was a Jeffersonian Democrat and an influential citizen. He represented his county in the State Legislature during the forties. His death occurred in 1854, and his widow's in 1862. Capt. Thomas D. Deavenport was reared on his father's farm, and completed his education at Jackson College, Columbia, but left school one session before graduation, owing to his father's death. He soon went to Kansas, where he remained during the difficulties in that State over the question of squatter sovereignty. He assisted in the Government surveys there. In 1857 he returned to Tennessee, locating in Hardin County, where he began clerking in a mercantile establishment. Later in the same year he began studying law under John S. Kennedy, at Florence, Ala. In 1858 he taught school in Lawrenceburg, continuing his legal studies, and was that year admitted to the bar, and soon began practicing. In 1861 he assisted in organizing Capt. W. P. Moore's company of the Thirty-second Regiment, and was made lieutenant, and upon the reorganization of the regiment was promoted to the captaincy. More than once on the field he was in command of his regiment, notably at Jonesboro, Ga., where he was shot through the lungs by a minie-ball. This incapacitated him for further service. After the war he resumed his practice, and has thus continued since. Capt. Deavenport is an uncompromising Democrat. In 1870 he was a member of the Constitutional Convention, and in 1877 served with distinction in the State Senate. In 1858 he married Miss Amanda Finch, who died in 1863. By this marriage he has three daughters: Martha M., Jennie D. and Mannie F. In 1875 Mr. Deavenport married Mrs. Zuba

(Dustin) Fillmore, who has presented her husband with two sons: Thomas E. and William H. Capt. Deavenport is a Mason and an adherent of the Cumberland Presbyterian Church. His wife is an Episcopalian.

Alexander T. Dobbins (deceased) was born in Limestone County, Ala., September 15, 1815, and was a prominent and successful planter. He was one of three children of David and Martha Dobbins, who were born in North Carolina, and after their marriage moved to Alabama, where they resided a few years. They then came to Tennessee, and here our subject acquired such education as could be obtained at that early period. He at one time owned and managed three mercantile houses, one in Center Star, Ala., one in Lexington, Ala., and one at his home at Appleton, Tenn., and his business career was marked with wonderful success. He dealt extensively in stock, besides superintending his extensive plantation. He was a man of generous and benevolent disposition and contributed liberally to all enterprises for the public weal. He was never under the influence of intoxicating liquor, nor indulged in the use of tobacco or profane language. He died of cancer, July 30, 1884. He was three times married. His first wife, Zilpha McMasters, bore him five children, four of whom are living: James P., John J., Favor A., and Elizabeth Calladonia. Their mother was born April 19, 1824, and died December 15, 1856. In 1859 Mr. Dobbins married Nancy C. Cox and five children were born to them. Zilpha M. (widow of William Couch), George W., William P., Martha Camilla and Robert T. Mrs. Dobbins was born July 14, 1828, and died October 28, 1870. November 7, 1871, Mrs. Mary J. (Hammond) Powell became his wife. She was born in Lawrence County April 22, 1833 [for biography of her family see sketch of G. W. Hammond], and resides on a fine farm of 525 acres, and is assisted by her step-sons in raising the cereals and live stock.

Thomas Dunn, a well known and prosperous business man of Lawrenceburg, Tenn., was born in Louisville, Ky., January, 1841, and is a son of James and Maria (Scully) Dunn, both natives of Ireland. Our subject was reared and educated in the city of Louisville. When but nineteen years of age he began the mercantile life as a clerk, and so continued until the war broke out. He enlisted as a private in Company A, Louisville Legion, at the beginning of the war, and served three years in the Federal Army as a soldier, when he was mustered out and accepted the post of sutlership in the Federal forces at Pulaski, Tenn. May, 1865, he came to Lawrenceburg and engaged in the general merchandising business with Mr. W. H. Dustin, with whom he has remained ever since. The firm, having met with more than ordinary success, carries the largest stock of general merchandise goods in the county, and controls the leading trade in this line in the town and county. The firm extended the scope of their business and engaged rather extensively in the cotton trade, conducting the Eagle and also Crescent cotton factories in the county. In 1873 Mr. Dunn married Sarah T. Sykes, a native of Lawrence County, Tenn., and the fruits of this union were four children. Our subject is strictly independent in politics, and a member of the Roman Catholic Church.

William H. Dustin, a native of Louisville, Ky., was born July 1, 1848, and is the son of Eli and Ellen Dustin, natives of Kentucky. Our subject received a liberal education in Louisville, and in early life was engaged as clerk by James Ridgeford & Co., of that city, where he remained until 1862, after which he entered the army as clerk for a sutler, and was thus engaged until the close of the war. At that time he moved to Lawrenceburg, Tenn., and engaged in the dry goods, general merchandise and cotton manufacturing business, at which he is still engaged. The firm is known as W. H. Dustin & Co., and Dustin & Dunn. They are the proprietors of both the Eagle and Crescent cottonmills. Mr. Dustin is also president of the Shoal Mills Manufacturing Company, in Lawrence County. He has been a very successful man in all his undertakings. He is considered a prosperous and accurate business man, and a good citizen. In 1867 he married Maggie J. Sykes, daughter of James and Eliza Sykes, natives of England and Connecticut, respectively. To our subject and wife were born two children: Gertrude E. and Willie S. Our subject is a Democrat in politics, a member of the F. & A. M., and also a member of the Methodist Episcopal Church South. Mrs. Dustin is a member of the Cumberland Presbyterian Church.

J. W. Fleeman is a Giles County Tennessean, born in 1836, son of William and Nancy (Leath) Fleeman, who were Tennesseans by birth and among the early settlers of Giles County. Our subject was reared in his native county and received quite a limited early education. This, however, he greatly improved in later years. When about twenty-one he began farming for himself, and has followed that occupation very successfully to the present time. He owns 100 acres of good farming land near Lawrenceburg. He joined the Federal Army September 21, 1864, and was in Company I, Fourth Tennessee Mounted Infantry, being elected first sergeant of the company, and was on guard duty most of the time. He was honorably discharged August 25, 1865. In 1870 he was elected magistrate and has since held the office, his present term expiring in 1888. He is a Republican politically, and a member in good standing in the Methodist Episcopal Church. In 1857 he was married to Elizabeth J. Bishop, daughter of Reden and Elizabeth (Price) Bishop. To Mr. and Mrs. Fleeman were born the following family: James William (deceased), James R., Mary Lure, Wiley Perry, Sarah E., Etta E., John T., Ernest T., Katie W. and Mattie Liou.

Daniel M. Foster, merchant and native of Wayne Station, Lawrence Co., Tenn., was born May 12, 1840, son of George W. and Celia (McGrew) Foster, born respectively in Kentucky and Tennessee. The father was one of the pioneer settlers of Lawrence County, coming here in 1830. He was a successful farmer, and is yet living at the advanced age of seventy-six years. The mother died in 1843. After attaining man's estate our subject began farming and carpentering, at which trade he served an apprenticeship under his father. In 1876 he began merchandising, establishing a store at Blake's Mill on Buffalo Creek, which he managed three years, also carrying on farming. He then engaged in farming and stock raising exclusively, at which he was very successful. In 1883 he began keeping a general merchandise store at Wayne Station, and carried a complete and full line of family groceries and country produce, controlling a large trade. October 9, 1860, he and Martha N. Wooten were united in marriage. Of twelve children born to them two are dead. Those living are John H., Julia A. (Mrs. J. A. Keeton), James W., Maggie B. (Mrs. T. H. Colley), Alice (Mrs. J. W. Escua), Dora, Daniel W., Albert W., Willie and Cora. Mr. Foster is a Republican in politics, and has been magistrate of the Tenth District for six years. He and family are leading members of the Methodist Episcopal Church, and he has been a Master Mason since 1870.

James W. Garrett, register of Lawrence County, is a native of Washington County, Ark., and was born January 20, 1859, the son of Joseph and Millie E. (Rice) Garrett, natives of Tennessee. The parents moved from Hickman County, Tenn., to Arkansas, in 1858. When the late war broke out the father enlisted in the Confederate service as a lieutenant, and afterward became a wagon master. He contracted sickness in the service and died. His wife returned to Hickman County in 1866, where she still resides. James W. was reared on a farm, and when seventeen years old began farming for himself. He taught school and soon went to Lawrenceburg, and attended school there ten months, and then engaged as clerk in the mercantile business. In 1879 he engaged for himself in the mercantile business, and continued until the autumn of 1884. Politically Mr. Garrett is a strong Democrat. At the age of twenty-one years he was elected magistrate, and in 1882 was elected register of the county. June 8, 1882, he married Miss Alice L. Chaffin, who has borne her husband one son—Joseph C., deceased. Mr. Garrett and wife are members of the Cumberland Presbyterian Church.

James M. Gilmore, clerk of the Lawrence County Court, was born in Giles County, Tenn., February 17, 1843, son of John S. and Elizabeth (Simms) Gilmore, both natives of Tennessee. The parents died when James M. was a small lad, consequently he knows but little of his ancestral history. He worked as a farm hand, after his father's death, in Giles County, and in 1861 enlisted in Capt. Cooper's Company, Third Regiment, Tennessee Confederate Infantry. He served as private and non-commissioned officer in the late war until its close, and was slightly wounded three times, but never seriously enough to leave his company. At the close of the war he resumed his agricultural pursuits in Lewis County, and later in Hickman County, until 1876, when he came to Lawrenceburg and engaged as clerk in the mercantile business. He was also deputy county court clerk, which latter position he filled until he was elected to the office of county court clerk in 1882. He also engaged in the general mercantile business for himself four years before and up to the time of his election to the office. Mr. Gilmore has served one term of four years in the office in an able and efficient manner, and was re-elected in August, 1886, by a handsome majority. In 1867 Permelia E. Flowers, of Hickman County, became his wife, and the fruits of this union were five children: Anna (wife of W. P. McClanahan, of Lawrenceburg), Narcissa, Mattie (who died August 28, 1886, aged fourteen years and nine months), Willie D. (who died in his fifth year), and Lillie. In politics Mr. Gilmore is an unswerving Democrat. He is a Mason and a member of the K. of H. Himself and family are members of the Methodist Episcopal Church South. He is recognized as one of the enterprising and public-spirited citizens of Lawrence County, and is a popular official.

John A. Hagan (deceased) was born in Kentucky December 1, 1811, son of John and Rebecca (Wilson) Hagan, and of Irish descent. He was a prominent citizen and business man of his county and succeeded in accumulating a comfortable competency for himself and family. He owned large iron works and cotton-mills, and also owned and controlled a large and paying plantation, besides being in the mercantile business, the latter consisting of three different houses—one located at Lawrenceburg, one at West Point, and the other at his home, near the cotton-mills He afterward owned and managed a store and grist-mill, on Fall River, which he continued to manage up to the time of his death, which occurred while on a visit to his son, at Mt. Pleasant, Maury Co., Tenn., July 22, 1868. Mr. Hagan was a stanch Union man during the war, and used all his influence to keep his State from seceding. He suffered great losses in slaves and other property. February 18, 1835, he wedded Mary A. Bumpass, daughter of Hartwell J. Bumpass, of Giles County, Tenn., and James W., William H., John H., Francis M. A., Mary T., Etha J., Susan R., Burgeous B., Lewis N., Marcella R., George W., Andrew A. and Charles M. are their children. Their mother was born in Lawrence County February 6, 1816. Her father, Hartwell J. Bumpass, came from South Carolina to Tennessee at an early day. He was a soldier in the war of 1812. He died about 1878. James W., John A. Hagan's eldest son, wedded Mollie E. Potts, and James A., Robert H., John W. and Alonzo A. are their children. William H., the second son, wedded Mollie E. Sykes. Their children are William J., Edward W., Minnie B. and Burgeous M. Their mother died in 1873, and he then married Mattie B. Smith, and Mattie E., Hartwell B. and Ethel May were born to them. John H. served in the late war and died at his home February 8, 1864. Francis M. A. was killed during the late war at Jackson, Miss. Mary T. died November 13, 1868. Etha J. (Mrs. Alonzo Lindsey) is the mother of the following children: Edward A., Dannie, Eugene S., Maizy, Willie and Bessie. Susan R. died October 27, 1851. Burgeous B. married Bettie A. Powell, and to this alliance were born two children: Mary E. and Cecil. Lewis N. married Calladonia E. Dobbins, and of their four children, John E., Willie and Bessie are living. George W. and Malenia A. Hammond were married and have no children. Andrew A. took for his wife Mary F. Appleton, who died in 1884. To Charles M.'s marriage with Lurilla A. McMasters two children were born: Marcella T. and Henry. The majority of the Hagan family are members of the Methodist Episcopal Church South. Mrs. Hagan, wife of John A. Hagan, owns 832 acres of land, which she manages, with the aid of her youngest sons. The Hagan family are highly respected citizens, and are Democrats of the old-line type.

William F. Hail is a native of the county in which he now resides, his birth taking place in 1828. His father was a Virginian and came to Tennessee with his parents when quite young. He was a farmer, and served under Jackson in the Indian wars. During one of the battles he obtained possession of an Indian boy, whom he afterward reared and educated. He gave him a medical education and he practiced that profession in Maury County until his death. The father married Tolitha Badgett, who bore him nineteen children, fourteen of whom lived to be grown, and six are living at the present time. The mother died in 1838, and the father wedded Martha Sullivan, who bore him five children, three yet living. The father died in 1852. William F. Hail was married in

1851 to Mary A. Vaughn, who is a Tennessean, born in 1826, and a daughter of Thomas and Mary A. (Westmore) Vaughn. To Mr. and Mrs. Hail were born the following family of children: John T., Laura N. (deceased), Tolitha E., Mary A., Margaret E., Margie A. and William F. Their mother died in 1867, and Mr. Hail took for his second wife Margaret McLaren, who was born in Tennessee in 1833, and died in 1880. In 1882 Mr. Hail wedded Ella Joyce, daughter of Henry and Nancy (Kimbrew) Joyce, who were born in South Carolina and Tennessee, respectively. Mrs. Hail was born in 1845. Our subject has always resided on a farm, and began doing for himself at the age of twenty-three years. He served in the late war, enlisting in 1862. He was a brave and faithful soldier, and returned home in April, 1865. In 1866 he purchased his present farm of 160 acres and is doing well financially. He is a member of the Cumberland Presbyterian Church, and a Democrat in politics.

George W. Hammonds is a son of Willis and Ursley (Newton) Hammonds, born in North Carolina and Tennessee in 1800 and 1805, respectively. He was an early pioneer of Tennessee and owned 250 acres of land. His wife died in Giles County July 14, 1869. George W. was educated in the common schools of his native county and at Lexington, Ala. He became salesman in a country store near his home and held that position about one year before the war. At this juncture he joined the Confederate Army, holding the position of first lieutenant in Company H, Thirty-second Tennessee Regiment. At the fall of Fort Donelson he was captured and held a prisoner at Camp Morton, Indianapolis, Ind., for seven months. He was exchanged at Vicksburg, and was in the memorable battle of Chickamauga, where he was seriously wounded and disabled from further duty. He was married, in Lauderdale County, Ala., February 7, 1883, to Maria C. Landman, daughter of Samuel Landman. They have one child, Jesse Wade, born February 22, 1884. Mrs. Hammonds was born in Ala., June 7, 1852. Mr. Hammonds is a notary public, and has been magistrate for seven years. He owns 644 acres of good land, which he devotes in a small way to the cultivation of cotton, but gives his chief attention to raising the cereals.

Eli F. Hannah was born in Lincoln County, N. C., June 30, 1829, the son of John and Mary (Wells) Hannah, both natives of the same State. In 1830 the father came to Rutherford County, Tenn., but soon moved to Giles County. His occupation was blacksmithing. He died in 1879, and his wife in 1882. Eli F. was reared on his father's farm, securing in youth a fair education. Soon after attaining his majority he engaged in mercantile pursuits, but after one year returned to the farm on Craw Fish Creek. Here he farmed and worked at blacksmithing until 1882, when he removed to his present place. He is successful in farming and stock raising. In 1857 he married Miss Mary O., daughter of Hardy and Nancy (Compton) Willeford, who has borne him five children, four still living, viz.: Sallie R. (wife of E. C. Locke), John W., James H. and Clinton C. The other child, Mary A., died in 1874, aged four years. Politically Mr. Hannah is a Republican, and himself and family are members of the Christian Church. He is recognized as one of the county's most respected and substantial citizens.

Charles J. Herrin is a North Carolinian by birth, born in 1804, and immigrated to Tennessee when a young man. He has been a farmer and merchant all his life, and has held the office of magistrate for many years. He has also served as constable, county surveyor, notary public and registrar. He first married a Miss Allen, who bore him one child, named Mary, who died when about twenty years of age. His wife lived but a short time. Mr. Herrin then wedded Martha Abernathy, and the following children are the result of their union: James L., Charles F., Emma E., Amanda F., Benjamin F., Martha J., Napoleon B., Theodore and Joseph. The last three are dead. Their mother was born June 26, 1817, and died June 14, 1859. Mr. Herrin married his first wife May 25, 1862. She was Eliza S. Hale, who was born in Tennessee May 16, 1845, and is the mother of three children: Jennie L., Dora J. and Joel M. The eldest son, James L., resided with his father until attaining his majority; since that time he has farmed, and is engaged in merchandising, but closed out the latter business in 1882, and has since given the most of his attention to farming, and owns 160 acres of very good land near West Point, besides two other farms of 150 and 175 acres each. He was born December 2, 1837, and has been a member of the Methodist Church since 1883. In May, 1861, he enlisted in the Confederate service, and was in some of the hardest fought battles of the war. He was captured at Fort Donelson, and was a prisoner for six months at Fort Warren. He was quartermaster in the Third Tennessee Regiment, and in 1872 was married to Mary J. Welch, who was born in 1859, and is the mother of five children: Horace, born in 1874; Emma H., in 1876; May J., in 1878; Blanche, in 1880, and died in 1882, and Frank, born in 1885. Mr. Herrin is a Democrat.

Daniel G. Harrison was born near Winchester, Franklin Co., Tenn., January 19, 1840, the second of ten children of David and Eliza (McCoy) Harrison. He is of English descent, and after remaining with his parents and attending the common schools until nineteen years of age he joined the Sixteenth Alabama Infantry and served in the late war four years. He was wounded at Chickamauga and was disabled from duty one year. He was captured at Murfreesboro, but was soon exchanged at Richmond, Va. He was finally released from duty, owing to the wound he had received just prior to the close of the war. August 27, 1865, he was married, in Lauderdale County, Ala., to Sarah A. Dickson, daughter of Thomas Dickson, a prominent planter of that county. Mrs. Harrison was born in Lawrence County, Tenn., September 17, 1839, and is the mother of the following children: William T., Daniel M., David L., Lulu E., Eliza E., Charles O'Connor, James K. Polk and Sarah A. Mr. Harrison is an old line Democrat and has been magistrate of his district for sixteen years. He has a fine farm of 240 acres, and is succeeding well financially. He is a member of the Masonic fraternity. Subject's father was born in Virginia in 1813, and was reared by an uncle, his parents having died when he was a small lad. He came to Franklin County, Tenn., at an early period, and after sixteen years' residence in that county moved to Alabama, where he resided until his death in the autumn of 1879. The mother is yet residing in Lamar County, Ala. She was born about 1821 and is a native of Winchester County, Tenn.

Dr. Robert H. Harvey, an influential citizen of Lawrence County, Tenn., was born in Williamson County, of the same State, August 31, 1841, and is a son of John W. and Mildred (Bailey) Harvey, both native Virginians. The subject's grandfather, Isom Harvey, came to Williamson County, Tenn., about 1830, and resided there until his death. John W. was born February 15, 1811, and came to Williamson County, after his marriage in 1836, where he has since resided, following farming and stock raising successfully. He has been magistrate in the county for a number of years. Our subject was reared on a farm and secured but a limited education in his youthful days. He was attending school when the war broke out, and in 1861 he enlisted in Company H, Twentieth Regiment Tennessee Confederate Infantry, and served until the close of the war, being early promoted to the staff of Gen. Zollicoffer, where he remained until the death of the General. He then served on the staff of John C. Breckinridge, Gen. (now Gov.) Bates, and finally with Thomas Benton Smith as staff officer, ranking at close as first lieutenant of artillery. In November, 1865, he came to Lawrenceburg, and engaged in the drug business, and also began the study of medicine, graduating from the medical department of the University of Nashville (now Vanderbilt) with the degree of M. D. in 1868. He then practiced in Wayne County eighteen months, after which he returned to Lawrenceburg, where he has since resided, and engaged actively in the practice of his profession until

1880, since which time he has given his entire time to selling lands in the county, controlling about 10,000 acres in this county. He has also given some attention to cotton manufacturing, having an interest in the Crescent Cotton Mills of this county. August 5, 1869, the Doctor married Matty J. Bentley, a native of this county. Two children, Robert B. and Mildred M., were born to this union. The Doctor is a Democrat in politics, a Mason, and a member of the Baptist Church; Mrs. Harvey is a member of the Methodist Episcopal Church. Dr. Harvey is one of the few successful business men of our county. He has always taken an active interest in all laudable public enterprises, and has contributed largely to the interest and welfare of the county.

Harvey Bros. are dealers in furniture and general merchandise and also undertakers of Lawrenceburg, Tenn. The firm is composed of Isham O. and John H. Harvey, and was established by the present firm February, 1885. Isham O. was born in Williamson County, Tenn., June 10, 1850, son of Holcomb and Mary (Wilson) Harvey, natives respectively of Virginia and Georgia; was reared on the farm in Williamson and Maury Counties, Tenn., and removed to Lawrence County in 1867. He then went to Texas and engaged in the cattle business for nine years, after which he returned to Williamson County, in 1879, and engaged in agricultural pursuits until March, 1884, when he returned to this county and in 1885 engaged in their present business. Mr. Harvey is a strong advocate of the principles of democracy and is one among the popular and successful young busniess men in the County.

Snowden B. Herbert, M. D., of Wayland Springs, Tenn., is a native of Madison County, Ala., born in 1828. He resided with his mother until seventeen years of age, and then came to Wayland Springs and read medicine under his brother, Dr. C. L. Herbert, for two years. Owing to ill health he was compelled to abandon the study of medicine, and for two years was engaged in government surveying, after which he clerked two years in a general merchandise establishment in Florence, Ala. About this time he and his brother, F. C. Herbert, purchased an interest in the establishment, and the firm became Dean & Herbert. The same year they opened a similar establishment at Wayland Springs, the firm being F. C. Herbert & Co. They carried on a successful business four years, when there was a decline in cotton and they were compelled to make an assignment, closing out the entire business in the spring of 1855. Soon after our subject entered the University of Louisville, Ky., attending the sessions of 1855 and 1856. He then practiced medicine in Hardin County, Tenn., until 1861, when he made an extended tour of Texas and Arkansas, looking out a suitable location. On his return home in 1861 there was so much excitement owing to the war that he was compelled to remain here, and located at Wayland Springs. The property was first purchased by F. C. Herbert, and after being in the possession of several different owners was purchased in 1867 by our subject's wife. The springs are four in number, and contain chalybeate, lime and freestone water and one contains carbonate of magnesia, carbonate of soda, chloride of sodium, protoxide of iron, potash, iodine and bromides. Dr. Herbert is a Democrat and a member of the Methodist Episcopal Church South. He is a Mason and I. O. O. F., and was married to Martha A. Koger, April 14, 1853. She was born May 5, 1833, and is the daughter of William and Martha A. (Westmoreland) Koger. Our subject's parents were Peter and Rebecca (McComb) Herbert, of South Carolina, who moved to Alabama in 1816. The father was a tanner and farmer, and was a soldier in the war of 1812. He died in Alabama in 1835, and his wife in 1864, being in Georgia at the time of her death.

Young M. Hudson was born in Maury County, Tenn., September 11, 1811, son of Adam B. and Priscilla (Thomas) Hudson, who were born in Maryland and were early emigrants to Davidson County, Tenn. They soon after removed to Maury County, Tenn., where they resided until 1836, and then moved to Mississippi, where he died the following year. The mother died in 1822. Young M. attended the common schools, and after attaining his twenty-first year farmed in Maury County until 1860, and then purchased his present farm, where he has since resided and tilled the soil. In 1836 he married Eliza B. Pickens, who died in 1853 leaving five children: William D., Mary C., James S., Eliza J. (Mrs. Robert Brothers), and Jesse J. In 1854 Mr. Hudson married Amanda J. Williams, of Giles County, and their union has resulted in the birth of five children: Isaac D., James S., Andrew N., Robert M. and Nora E., all of whom are living. Mr. Hudson's political views are democratic, and he has been a member of the Masonic fraternity for upward of thirty years. He and Mrs. Hudson are members of the Cumberland Presbyterian Church.

Simon Isaacs, merchant, was born in Poland in the year 1857. He came to the United States in 1873, and for three years followed the mercantile business in Nashville. He then returned to the old country, and in 1878 again came to the United States and began business in Pulaski. In February, 1883, he engaged in the dry goods and clothing business at Lawrenceburg, and has thus continued until the present. He carries a large, select stock of goods and has a constantly growing trade. He carries the only line of ready-made clothing in the town or county. He also carries hats, boots, shoes and notions, and controls much of the trade in these articles. In November, 1882, he married Annie Solinsky at Pulaski, who has borne him one son, Seymour. Mr. Isaacs is independent in politics. Himself and wife are members of the Jewish faith. He is one of the most enterprising business men of the town or county, and possesses all the shrewdness and sagacity of his race.

William W. Johnson, a pioneer citizen of Tennessee, is a native of Lawrence County, Tenn., born in 1820. His father, Robert Johnson, was born in North Carolina and came to Tennessee when quite young. He was a farmer, and married Mary McLaren, of South Carolina, who bore him eight sons, seven of whom lived to be grown, and four are yet living. The father was a major and colonel in the State militia, and died in 1836. His widow then married a Mr. Thornton. She died in 1857. William W.'s early days were spent on his father's farm, where he resided until 1844, and then emigrated to Mississippi, and was first employed in keel-boating on Chickasaw River. He farmed for some time, and also acted as overseer for several men. After traveling several months in Arkansas he was united in marriage to Mary A. Shoffner, who was born in Tennessee in 1830, daughter of Martin and Jane (Johnson) Shoffner. Soon after their marriage they purchased a farm, but sold out in 1856, and after being employed as overseer for two years he purchased and moved on to his father's farm, and there now lives. This farm is near the noted Wayland Springs, and contains about 900 acres. He and wife are members of the Cumberland Presbyterian Church; he is a Democrat and his first presidential vote was cast for Martin Van Buren. His family consisted of seven children, six of whom are living: Mary J. (deceased), Robert A., Andrew, Laura L., Emma, Wiley B. and Albert S. Andrew is a practicing physician on the home place, being a graduate of the Vanderbilt University.

Josephus S. Johnson, a native of Lawrence County, Tenn., was born in 1832, and was reared to manhood on a farm. When about twenty-five years of age he removed to Arkansas and was engaged in teaching school, farming and clerking in a general merchandise establishment, remaining in the State two years. At that time he entered the Confederate service and remained until 1863, being a participant in the battle of Shiloh and others of less note. At the last named date he returned home and began pedagoging, meeting with good success for five years. He then united his fortunes with those of Amanda Herrin, who was born in 1844, and the daughter of C. J. and Martha (Abernathy) Herrin. Their union was blessed in the birth of ten children: Richard F., Martha O., Joseph L., Robert C., Ann Eliza V., Edna E., Eldridge H., Loulie H., Emma M. (deceased), and Mary E. Mr. Johnson taught school every year until 1873, when he purchased his present farm of 238 acres of well cultivated land. In 1876 he was elected magistrate of District No. 1, and has faithfully discharged the duties of that office up to the present time. He was elected county surveyor in 1881 and holds that office also. He has always been a stanch Democrat in politics.

Columbus M. Joiner was born in Lauderdale County, Ala., March 12, 1860, the son of James and Lucy (Rust) Joiner, natives of Alabama. The father died at Jackson, Miss., in 1863, of sickness contracted in the Confederate service. Columbus M. was reared by his mother, and in 1868 was taken by her to Shawneetown, Ill. Here she died, in December, 1870. In 1871 Columbus went to Mississippi, remaining there until 1873, when he returned to his native county. In 1877 he went to Texas and herded cattle in that State for two years. He returned in 1879, and engaged in the liquor and mercantile business, continuing until 1883, when he came to Lawrenceburg and engaged in the retail liquor business, and is thus engaged at present. In 1886 he opened a general hardware and agricultural implement store, and now has a good and growing business. January 16, 1881, he married Lydia Ann Beavers, and by her has two sons. He is a Democrat and an enterprising citizen.

John B. Kennedy, clerk of the circuit and criminal courts of Lawrence County, Tenn., and a native of Giles County, of the same State, was born November 6, 1843, son of John and Patsy Kennedy, both natives of Kentucky. The father came to Tennessee in the twenties and located on a farm in Giles County, where he followed agricultural pursuits and stock raising successfully, being the first man to introduce the celebrated Kentucky blue grass in that region. He died there when our subject was but seven or eight years of age. John B. was reared on a farm in his native county, and secured a fair literary education, having just completed his sophomore year in Centre College, Danville, Ky., when the war broke out. He enlisted in the Southern Army as private in Company A, Third Tennessee Infantry (Gov. John C. Brown's regiment), and served gallantly and faithfully in that sanguinary struggle until, at its close, he was seriously wounded at Chickamauga, and also at Jonesboro, Ga., having his musket shot from his hand at the latter place and losing a finger. At the close of the war he returned home and engaged in mercantile pursuits until 1868, when he repaired to his farm, in Giles County, where he remained until 1871, after which he removed to Lawrence County and soon after engaged in the mercantile business. At the end of four or five years he returned to Pulaski, and engaged in the same business at that place. In 1884 he returned to this county, and the same year was elected to fill the unexpired term of T. L. Bentley (deceased) in the circuit clerk's office, and has discharged the duties of this important office in a highly satisfactory manner, to the present time. November 17, 1869, he wedded Alice L. McClain, a native of Lawrence County, Tenn. They have one son, named Joseph McClain. Mr. Kennedy is, and always has been, an unswerving Democrat. On the 5th day of August, 1886, Mr. Kennedy was re-elected circuit court clerk by a handsome majority.

Allen H. Kidd is a son of George and Nancy N. Kidd, who were born, respectively, in North Carolina and Tennessee. George Kidd was one of the early immigrants to Tennessee, and followed the vocation of farming in Giles and Lawrence Counties. He died in 1843, and the mother in 1876. Allen H. was born in Lawrence County March 18, 1843, and his early days were spent on the farm with his mother. He received a practical education, and, at the age of fourteen, began clerking in Henryville, Tenn., where he remained one year and a half. In 1861 he joined Capt. Armstrong's company, Twenty-third Tennessee Regiment, and served as high private of that company until 1863, when he joined the cavalry, under the command of Gen. Forrest, and was elected to the office of second lieutenant, but was soon after wounded near Lawrenceburg and disabled for further service. He returned home after the close of the conflict, and for two years tilled the soil, and the following two years was a merchant of Columbia. He established a mercantile store at Henryville, and some time later built a large saw and grist-mill on Water Fork of Buffalo River, which he operated in connection with a store. In September, 1883, he established a store at Carpenter Station, but in January, 1886, opened up his present general merchandise store. He is doing well financially and controls a large trade. Mr. Kidd has seen fit to remain a bachelor. He is a Democrat in politics, and is one of the successful and enterprising business men of the county.

William K. Lackey, an influential citizen of Lawrence County, Tenn., is a native of Giles County, born in 1844. His father was a native Tennessean and was reared on a farm, but followed teaching the greater portion of his life. The mother, whose maiden name was Flora McCollum, was born in North Carolina, and came to Tennessee with her parents when quite young. Mr. and Mrs. Lackey became the parents of four children, two of whom are yet living. The father died in 1863, and the mother six years later. Our subject resided at home until twenty-six years of age. After his mother's death, at her request, he attended school about ten months and acquired a good education. He then taught school in Tennessee and Missouri for some time, and in 1875 was united in marriage to Nannie M. Spencer, daughter of A. J. and M. E. (Wayland) Spencer. Mrs. Lackey was born in Tennessee, in 1859. Her grandfather, S. H. Wayland, was the founder, and at one time the owner, of the noted Wayland Springs. Our subject and his wife are the parents of three children: Minnie L., William P. and Ida. In 1880 Mr. Lackey purchased his present farm, consisting of seventy-five acres of fairly improved land. In 1883 he was elected county superintendent of Lawrence County, and is holding the position at the present time. He is a Democrat in politics and cast his first presidential vote for S. J. Tilden.

David C. Legg was born in East Tennessee January 4, 1814, and is a son of William Legg, who was also born in East Tennessee in 1798. After attaining his majority he married Nancy Coffman, and soon moved to Jackson County, Ala., where he remained about five years. He then moved to Limestone County, and there resided until his death in 1880. The mother was born in Jefferson County, Tenn., in 1800, and died in Limestone County, Ala., in 1880. David C. Legg was educated in the common schools and chose the free and independent life of a farmer as his calling through life. At the age of twenty-three he began working on his own responsibility, and in 1837 moved to the Lone Star State. The Indians were very troublesome, at this time, to white settlers, and he assisted the Texans in their war against them, and for his services received 320 acres of land. Besides this, he took land to the amount of 1,280 acres, and if these claims can be established, they will result in a handsome fortune to Mr. Legg. To his marriage with Mary Halbert, in 1835, two children were born: James A. and Susan S. Mrs. Legg died in Texas in 1840. In 1843 he wedded Mary J. Carlisle; and William W., Eliza J., Joel E., Rufus E., Theodocia, Emily E., Celestia and Emma Clarinda are their children. Their mother died October 14, 1882. Mr. Legg married Mrs Keziah Basshan, daughter of James Roper, September 24, 1884. Our subject is a Democrat and Mason, and he and wife are members of the Baptist and Methodist Episcopal Churches, respectively.

James W. Locke, farmer, of Lawrence County, Tenn., is a son of Walter Locke, of North Carolina, who was one of the pioneer settlers of Giles County, Tenn. He was a farmer and married Rachel Ross, of Kentucky. He died about 1852, and the mother six years later. James W. Locke was born in Giles County September 13, 1813, and attended the primitive log schoolhouse of his boyhood days. At the age of twenty-one he began farming in Giles County, and at the death of his father purchased his farm. In 1861 he bought and located on his present place, where he has been a prosperous farmer and stock raiser. In 1835 he wedded Asenath C. McCreary, who died in 1843, leaving four children, three now living: Nancy C. (deceased), Eliza M. (Mrs. James Carter),

John S. and Martha A. (Mrs. James Brownlow). In 1846 Mr. Locke married Elizabeth A. Braly, and nine children are the result of their union: Nathaniel H., William M., Sarah F. (who died in 1881), Ephraim C., Robert N., Mary A. (Mrs. J. W. Cross), Asenath C. (Mrs. James Spreegle), Walter S. and Cora E. Mr. Locke is neutral in politics, and himself and family are leading members of the Christian Church.

James M. Lumpkin is the eldest of eight children, and was born on Knob Creek April 26, 1837, son of William H. Lumpkin, who was born in North Carolina in 1811, and came to Tennessee when a young man. Here he married Eliza Smith and reared his family. He breathed his last at the old homestead when about sixty-six years of age. The mother was born September 24, 1816, and is still living. James M. received his early education in the common schools and has made farming his chief calling through life. He served in the Ninth Tennessee Cavalry under Col. Biffle, Confederate States Army, in the late war, and was in many skirmishes. He took the oath of allegiance at Columbia just before the close of the war. He has been married three times, and had three children by his first wife, Sarah M. Springer. Their names are Sarah C., James F. and William S. Mrs. Lumpkin died in 1865. His second wife, Eliza C. Belew, who died March 16, 1873, bore the following four children: Telie A., Mollie L., Anna E. and Robert Lee. Margaret L., Katie Jane, Louis N., John C. (deceased), Charles and Richard Earl are the children of his third wife, Malinda C. Kelley, who was born in Georgia January 24, 1853. Mr. Lumpkin is rather independent in politics, but leans toward the Democratic party. He owns 100 acres of good land and is a member of the Masonic fraternity. He and wife are worthy members of the Methodist Episcopal Church South.

William G. Lumpkin, farmer, is the fourth of eight children, and was born in Lawrence County, Tenn., March 1, 1844. [See James M. Lumpkin's for parents' sketch]. He received the education and rearing of the average farmer boy, and at the breaking out of the late war enlisted in the Confederate service in the Ninth Tennessee Cavalry, and served about two years, taking an active part in the battles of Franklin and Nashville. March 30, 1865, was the date of his marriage with Caladonia Springer. To them were born the following children: William J., Gustavus H., Andrew J., Barney P., John B., Lucius T. and Jane Gertrude. Mrs. Lumpkin was born in Lawrence County October 19, 1846. Her father was born in South Carolina, and came to Tennessee when a young man, where he married and reared his family. Mrs. Lumpkin can trace her ancestry back eight centuries. Our subject is a liberal Democrat and is a wealthy farmer, owning, at the present time, over 700 acres of land, 500 acres being in the home place. His chief attention is given to fine stock raising and the production of the cereals.

Ephraim McClain, M. D., was born July 29, 1827, in Maury County, Tenn., one of twelve children born to John and Elizabeth (McMillen) McClain, who were born in South Carolina and Kentucky, respectively. The father was born the year following the Declaration of Independence, and when a young man moved to Kentucky, where he was married and came to Tennessee about the beginning of the present century. He was a soldier in the war of 1812, and was with Jackson at New Orleans. He soon after returned to Maury County, and followed a long and useful life as a farmer. He died at the remarkable age of one hundred and four years, respected by all who knew him. Our subject was reared and educated in his native county, and taught school a number of years. In 1853 he began the study of medicine, and the same year came to Lawrence County and studied with Dr. J. M. Hamilton, and in 1855 began practicing. He has met with more than ordinary success, and has a large practice in this and adjoining counties. August 2, 1849, he wedded Annie Clendennin, a native of North Carolina, who died May 4, 1885, leaving one child—Alice (Mrs. J. B. Kennedy), who was engrossing clerk in the House of Representatives in 1883-85. She is a lady of culture and intelligence, and filled the position in a very satisfactory manner. The Doctor is a Democrat, and belongs to the Masonic and Odd Fellow fraternities. He belongs to the Cumberland Presbyterian Church. He served three months in his professional capacity in the Ninth Tennessee Cavalry, under Col. Biffle.

H. D. McClure, M. D., a prominent physician and citizen of Wayland Springs, Tenn., was born in Alabama in 1853, son of Harvey B. and Rebecca (Herbert) McClure, who were born in Tennessee and Alabama, respectively. The father was a farmer by occupation, a member of the Methodist Episcopal Church South and a Democrat in politics. He died in Alabama in 1869. Our subject's early days were spent on a farm, and in attending the country schools. He was salesman in a family grocery store for two years, after which he resided on a farm until 1873. He then began studying medicine under Dr. S. B. Herbert and remained with him three years. He then practiced with the Doctor for three years, when they dissolved partnership, and Dr. McClure has since practiced his profession alone, meeting with merited success. In 1878 he wedded Emma Alford, who was born in Tennessee in 1861, and is the mother of three children: Maudie R., Fannie S. and Claudie A. Mrs. McClure's parents were James M. and Fannie (Childress) Alford. Dr. McClure is a member of the Masonic fraternity and a Democrat, casting his first presidential vote for S. J. Tilden.

James H. McKey was born in Alabama, in 1838, son of Charles and Eveline (Fisher) McKey. Charles McKey was born in the Palmetto State, and moved to Alabama with his parents about 1810, where he first married Eliza Cauthen. She died about seven months later, and he then married Miss Fisher, who bore him two children. The father was a farmer and served in the late war under Col. Murphy, being a Federal soldier. During his service he contracted a disease which resulted in his death, in September, 1877. Our subject received a good education in the country schools and resided with his father on a farm until 1857, when he wedded Martha A. Fondren, born in 1839. Dovey E., Charles A. (deceased), Elizabeth S. (deceased), and Edward T. are their children. Mrs. McKey died in 1870, and in September, 1871, Sarah F. Earnest became his second wife and the mother of the following family: Alice C., Taylor H., Luther A., Pink L. and Rufus B. Mrs. McKey was born in 1854, and is the daughter of Moses and Mary Earnest, of Alabama. She died in 1882, and a year later he took for his third wife Sarah A. Jones, daughter of John and Mary A. Jones. They have one child, Rob Roy. Mr. McKey served as sheriff two years and was United States deputy collector one year, and has held various minor offices. He fell heir to 265 acres of his father's estate, and has added to it until he now owns 500 acres. His farm contains rich ore beds, and he also has a bluff of fine variegated marble, and a good deposit of fine sandstone that will rank with the best known. In 1880 Mr. McKey was admitted to the Lawrenceburg bar, and has given the most of his attention to his profession since that time. He is a member of the Methodist Episcopal Church South, and is a Democrat. In 1862 he enlisted in Company H, Sixth Tennessee Cavalry, and served until the surrender, participating in many of the principal battles. He served in the Federal Army and was a true and tried soldier.

John C. McLaren is a Bedford County Tennessean, born in 1819. He resided on his parents' farm until the father's death, when he took charge of the home place, and afterward fell heir to a portion of it and purchased the remainder. It consists of 270 acres, and is in a good state of cultivation. The dwelling in which he lives was erected in 1833, and was used for several years, at intervals, for public worship and school. John C. wedded Chanie A. Blythe in 1854, and Theodore D., Mary J., Susan C., Charles T. and William F. are their children. Mrs. McLaren was born in 1838, and is a daughter of Jacob and Jane (Holland) Blythe. She and her husband are members of the Cumberland Presbyterian Church, and he is a Democrat and cast his first presidential vote for James K. Polk. Subject's parents, Daniel and Susan (Rutledge)

McLaren, were born in North Carolina, and came to Tennessee when quite young. The father was an agriculturist, and served in the war of 1812, and also in the Creek and Seminole wars. He died in Lawrence County in 1838, and his widow married Samuel McClain, who lived but a short time. She lived a widow the remainder of her life, and died in 1882. Daniel McLaren, grandfather of our subject, was a soldier in the Revolutionary war, and died in Lawrence County, Tenn., in 1840. His father, Daniel McLaren, served five years in the Revolutionary war, and held the rank of major. He died in Hickman County in 1844.

R. L. McLaren was born in Lawrence County, Tenn., May 1, 1825. John McLaren, his father, was born in South Carolina, and when about twenty-three years of age married Mary McDougal, of Alabama, who bore him nine children, all residents of Texas, except our subject. The father was a farmer and an early resident of Tennessee; he died in 1863. R. L. McLaren began doing for himself when about twenty-two years of age, and in 1848 was united in marriage to Sarah E. Hale, daughter of John A. and Tolitha (Badgett) Hale. She was born in Tennessee in 1830, and is one of nineteen children, three of whom are living. Her mother died in 1835, and her father then married Martha Sullivan, who bore him six children. The father was a private in the Creek and Seminole wars, and died in 1853. Shortly after our subject's marriage he purchased a farm of 195 acres near Factory Creek, where he resided until 1868. He then purchased the farm on which he now lives, consisting of 333 acres. He was chosen magistrate in 1856, and faithfully performed the duties of the office for twelve years. He was enrolling officer of his district during the late civil war, and since 1863 has been a member of the Methodist Episcopal Church South; his wife belongs to the same church. He is a stanch Democrat in politics, and cast his first presidential vote for James K. Polk.

John L. McLean, county trustee, was born in this county December 4, 1840, the son of Samuel D. and Elizabeth C. (Wasson) McLean, natives, respectively, of Kentucky and Indiana. Samuel D. when a boy came to this county, in 1817, locating at McLean's Spring, three miles east of Lawrenceburg. Here the grandfather, Samuel, raised a family of five sons and four daughters, and followed the occupation of farming until his death, in 1850. The father of John L. was reared in this county, married here and reared his family on the old homestead. He was a useful citizen, his death occurring in 1880, and his wife's in 1884. John L. was reared a farmer, securing a limited education. At the age of twenty-four years he began farming for himself on his father's farm. In 1872 he bought land in the Eighteenth District, where he resided until 1880, when he moved to near Lawrenceburg. Mr. McLean is a Democrat, though his ancestors were Whigs. In 1861 he enlisted in Company K, Third Tennessee Confederate Regiment, and served until the cessation of hostilities. Twice he was seriously wounded. At Raymond, Miss., his leg was broken by a bullet, and at Jonesboro, Ga., he was wounded in the face and head by a minie-ball. He was also slightly wounded at Fort Donelson and at Powder Spring Road, Ga. In 1871 he was made deputy sheriff, and in 1884 was elected county trustee. In 1870 he married Miss Rachel C. Norman, who died in 1874, leaving two children: Coda and Thomas. In 1881 he married Mrs. Dora I. Carter, who has borne two children: Walter and Burgie.

Thomas H. Meredith, livery man of Lawrenceburg, Tenn., was born in Giles County, Tenn., May 23, 1846, and is a son of Thomas H. and Jane J. (Hodge) Meredith, both natives of Giles County, Tenn., where the father followed farming successfully until his death, in 1860, and the mother died in November, 1882. Our subject was reared in Pulaski and educated in Giles College. In 1861 he enlisted in Company K, First Regiment Tennessee Infantry, Confederate Army, and served until the close of the war. He then returned home and engaged in agricultural pursuits until 1875, after which he traveled, selling nursery stock until 1880. He then engaged in the livery business in Pulaski until March, 1883, when he came to Lawrenceburg and erected his present large and commodious stable and engaged in the livery business, which he has continued to the present time. He has met with good and well deserved success, having a monopoly of the trade in the town and county. He is a Democrat in politics, and is recognized as one of the enterprising and reliable business men of Lawrence County. Mr. Meredith received a slight wound in the head at Cheat Mountain, and a serious wound in the body at Missionary Ridge; he also was slightly wounded in the foot at Perryville, Ky.

George H. Mester, proprietor of the Lawrenceburg Hotel, is a son of Kasper and Mary (Nieman) Mester, natives of Prussia, where they lived and died. George was born in Munster, Westphalia, Prussia, September 19, 1837, and was reared and educated in his native country, learning the baker's occupation of his father. At the age of seventeen years he came to the United States, locating at Cincinnati, where he learned the cabinet-maker's trade. He worked at this for twelve years and then engaged in the grocery business three years. In 1868 he prospected through the Southern States for a suitable place to locate, and finally, in 1870, came to Lawrenceburg and engaged in the cabinet-maker's trade and carpentering at that place. At the end of four years he built his present hotel and engaged in this business in connection with the other; but during the last five years he has given almost his entire attention to the first-class accommodation of the traveling public. January 21, 1858, he married Anna M. Riesenbeck, a native of that city, and the result of this union is an interesting family of six children: Anna M., George H., Frances, Katie, John W. and Louis H. Mr. Mester and family are members of the Catholic Church. He is a good citizen and one of the best business men of the county.

James M. Metcalf, a native of Lincoln County, was born June 1, 1845, being a son of William H. and Jane (Kennon) Metcalf, natives, respectively, of Kentucky and Tennessee. The father moved to Tennessee in 1840 and followed merchandising until his death, in 1873. The mother died in 1863. Upon reaching his majority James M. (after securing a good classical education, finishing in Bethany College, in Giles County), began life for himself. In 1862 he enlisted in Freeman's (Confederate) battery, with which he continued to serve until the close of the war. At Parker's Cross Roads, Tenn., he was seriously wounded, from which he has never completely recovered. After the war he traveled three years and then engaged in the mercantile business at Petersburg, as a clerk. After two or three years he continued the same business at Fayetteville, and about four years later started in the mercantile business for himself at Columbia. In 1878 he removed to this county. In 1882 he established his present business. In 1876 he married Miss Felicia, daughter of Gen. F. K. Zollicoffer, who has borne her husband four children, two living—Mary L. and Felicia L. Mr. Metcalf is a Democrat and was appointed postmaster by President Cleveland. He is a Mason, and his wife is a member of the Episcopal Church.

Wiley W. Neal, M. D., of Lawrenceburg, Tenn., was born in Giles County, of that State, June 4, 1833, and is a son of Wiley and Nancy (Goggins) Neal, both natives of Newberry District, S. C., where they were married. They came to Tennessee in 1818, locating in Giles County, where they both spent the remainder of their days. Our subject was reared on a farm in Giles County, and secured a fair literary education in his youthful days, attending the Cumberland University at Lebanon, Tenn. At the age of eighteen he engaged in the mercantile business with his brother, in Giles County, where he remained three years. He then taught school and read medicine under Dr. Fields, of Pulaski, after which he taught again in order to secure means to enable him to pursue his medical studies to completion. He attended medical lectures in 1857–58, at the University of Nashville, and then practiced one summer, after which, the following session, he returned and graduated in the spring of 1859. He then returned to Lawrenceburg and entered regularly on the practice of medicine until the breaking out of the civil war. He then enlisted as a private in Capt. B. F. Matthews' company, Third Regiment Confederate Tennessee Infantry, and, after serving a few months, was honorably discharged on account of disability. Returning home he resumed his practice at West Point, where he acquired a large and successful practice. January, 1886, he removed to Lawrenceburg, and has continued practicing here, having also bought the only drug store in Lawrenceburg or the county, which he conducts in a successful manner, assisted by his son, Paul A., a practicing physician also. November 18, 1859, our subject married Sarah M. Tidwell, of Giles County, who died January 2, 1880, leaving a family of five children. July 7, 1880, the Doctor married Amanda H. Sowell, of Lawrence County, and one child blessed this union. The Doctor is a Democrat in his political views, but of the more conservative class. He is a Mason, and he and wife are members of the Methodist Episcopal Church.

Hon. William T. Nixon, clerk and master of the chancery court of Lawrence County, Tenn., and a native of that county, was born November 19, 1846, eldest son of Chancellor George H. Nixon. He received a preparatory education at Jackson Academy, of Lawrenceburg, and later attended the literary department of the Cumberland University at Lebanon, Tenn., from which institution he graduated in 1875. He had in the meantime been studying law, and was admitted to the Lawrence County bar in 1870. After graduating he entered regularly into the practice of his profession, until 1869, when he was elected to the State Legislature, and served in the session of 1869 and 1870. In 1871 he was appointed to his present position by his father, upon the universal recommendation of the Lawrence County bar, and has continued in the discharge of the duties of that office up to the present time. November 19, 1868, Mr. Nixon married Elizabeth G. Parkes, a native of Staffordshire, England. To this union were born three children. He is a Democrat in politics, a Mason, and himself and wife are members of the Cumberland Presbyterian Church, of which he has been ordained a minister. His brother, Henry Nixon, a prominent lawyer of Lawrenceburg and a native of Lawrence County, was born August 18, 1852. He grew to manhood on the farm, and finished his education at Vanderbilt University, at Nashville, where he also studied law, graduating from that department in 1875. He then returned to Lawrenceburg, and was admitted to the Lawrence County bar, and has since practiced in its courts. In 1877 he married Laura Parkes. of this county, and four children blessed this union. Mr. Nixon is a Democrat in politics, and a Master Mason. He was chief engineer in the first survey of the Nashville & Florence Railroad, and was secretary, treasurer and superintendent of the road the first three years.

Ira North, Jr., a prominent farmer of Lawrence County, Tenn., was born in Ohio February 3, 1844, son of Ira and Harriett (Egleston) North, natives, respectively, of New York and Ohio. The father farmed in Ohio and immigrated to Tennessee in 1849, where he followed farming and stock raising. In 1850 he removed to the edge of Wayne County, where he kept an inn. About 1863 he returned to Lawrence County and the next year moved to Davidson County, twelve miles from Nashville, but returned to Lawrence County in 1865, and there now resides, engaged in farming and stock raising. His wife died in 1850. Ira North, Jr., received a limited education and was reared on a farm. In 1862 he enlisted in Company A, Tenth Tennessee Regiment Federal Army, the company being known as the Governor's Guards. He served first as corporal and afterward as sergeant, until the close of the war, when he returned home and engaged in farming. In 1871 he purchased his present farm of 135 acres of fine land. August 6, 1866, he married Sarah F. Locke, who died December 24, 1879, leaving two children: Mary I. (Mrs. A. L. Spiegel) and William Lee. October 6, 1880, Mr. North married Mary E. Gooch, who bore him four children, two living: H. and N. M. The family are leading members of the Christian Church, and Mr. North is classed among Lawrence County's most enterprising and successful farmers.

Joshua B. Parker, attorney at law, of Lawrenceburg, Tenn., and a native of Giles County, is a son of John A. and Nettie (Baker) Parker, both natives of Giles County, Tenn. The father removed to this county from Giles in 1882, and now follows farming in the Fourteenth District. Our subject was born December 12, 1863; received his education in his native county, and finished in Giles College, at Pulaski, in 1883. In 1878, however, he began reading law in a desultory manner, as he had to support himself and assist in supporting his family. He was a student or protege of Hon. Noble Smithson, and also received some assistance from Col. Solon E. Rose. Our subject came to this county in 1884, and in December of that year was admitted to the bar. He has continued ever since in the practice here, having met with merited success. In November, 1885, he was sworn into practice in the Federal court in Northern Mississippi, and in December of the same year was sworn into practice in the Federal and supreme courts of Tennessee, enjoying the distinction of being not only the youngest legal practitioner of the county, but one of the youngest attorneys admitted to practice in the Supreme Court of Tennessee. He is a Democrat in his political views, but of the younger and more progressive class. He is a member of the Methodist Episcopal Church, and is one of the promising young lawyers of the county.

William A. Pierce, citizen of Wayland Springs, Tenn., and native of the State, was born in 1843, son of George W. and Araminta (Mitchell) Pierce. The father was a tailor and for many years was a citizen of Lawrenceburg. After residing a short time in Alabama, he returned to Lawrenceburg, where he died in 1855. His wife died in 1845. The grandfather, Spencer Pierce, was a North Carolinian, and settled in Tennessee in 1818. His son George, our subject's father, was a very active man and was noted for being very swift of foot. He was twice married, and by his first wife was the father of two children. Lucy Welsh, his second wife, bore him six children. William A. Pierce married Mary L. Green in 1866, daughter of William and Edie Green. She was born in Tennessee in 1846, and died in 1865. A year later Mr. Pierce wedded Maggie C. Goats, daughter of Philip and Nancy (Yarbrough) Goats. Six children blessed their union: Lulu E., Minnie J., Annie L., Maggie V., William H., and Alexander A. Our subject made his home with his father until 1855, and then resided with an uncle until 1861, when he enlisted in Company B, Twenty-third Tennessee Regiment, and participated in many hard-fought battles. Owing to a wound received at Shiloh, he was unfitted for service for about one year. He then joined Roddy's cavalry, and shortly after the battle of Moulton, Ala., was captured and kept a prisoner at Rock Island, Ill., for about nine months. He was then released, owing to the cessation of hostilities, and returned home in March, 1865, and began clerking in a general merchandise store, and at the expiration of one year, opened a similar establishment at Wayland Springs, where he has prospered financially. He is also postmaster at the Springs and is a Mason and K. of H., and is also a member of the K. & L. of H. lodge. Mr. Pierce is a Democrat and cast his first presidential vote for Horace Greeley.

Aaron A. Pierce, merchant of Wayland Springs, Tenn., and native of the State, was born in 1850, son of Samuel and Jemima (Carter) Pierce. The father was a farmer and a Democrat, and a participant in the late war. He belonged to the Cumberland Presbyterian Church, and died in March, 1883. His wife died in 1880. The subject of our sketch spent his juvenile days on a farm, and lived with his father up to the time of the latter's death. In 1874 he united his fortunes with those of Miss Laura Johnson, who was born in Tennessee in 1858, and by her became the father of the following children: Emmett L., Bertie M., Ida G. and Mannie M. Mr. Pierce followed the occupation of farming up to

1881, when he purchased the mercantile stock of M. M. Fisher, at Wayland Springs, and controls a large and lucrative trade. In January, 1886, the family took up their residence at Wayland Springs. Mr. Pierce gives his support to the Democratic party, and his first presidential vote was cast in favor of Horace Greeley. Mrs. Pierce's parents were W. W. and Mary (Shoffner) Johnson.

M. M. Powell was born in Lawrence County, Tenn., December 5, 1843, son of J. M. and Sarah L. (Pullen) Powell, who were born in South Carolina and Tennessee, in 1819 and 1824, respectively. The former died May 26, 1876, but the latter is still living in Lawrence County. Our subject's grandfather was a soldier in the war of 1812, under Gen. Jackson. M. M. was reared in Lawrence County, and began doing for himself at the age of twenty-five. His principal occupation has been farming, in which he has been fairly successful, owning at the present time 687 acres of land. November 14, 1867, he married Hannah P. Comer, daughter of Jesse and Margaret (Springer) Comer, and by her is the father of two children: John D., born September 30, 1869, and Calvin T., born October 25, 1873. Mr. Powell served in the Federal Army in the late war, enlisting at Nashville, November 3, 1863, and was mustered out May 16, 1865. He was elected justice of the peace in August, 1876, and was re-elected in 1882 and is now serving in that capacity. He is a Democrat, and not a member of any church, but is in sympathy with the Methodists.

J. B. Powell, M. D., was born June 12, 1857, in Lawrence County, Tenn. His parents, Andrew and Malinda (Welch) Powell were born in Marshall and Lawrence Counties, Tenn., in 1830 and 1836, respectively. Both are living and are residents of Lawrence County. Dr. Powell was reared in his native county, and received good early educational advantages. He attended Jackson Academy at Lawrenceburg about two years, and at the age of twenty-one began studying medicine under Dr. James Kyle, of Florence, Ala., and graduated as an M. D. from the Vanderbilt University of Nashville, Tenn., in 1879. He immediately located at Wayland Springs, where he remained until April, 1886, when he came to St. Joseph and was appointed United States examining surgeon. In connection with his practice he keeps a drug and general merchandise store at St. Joseph, and is the owner of about 2,300 acres of unimproved mineral lands. Nannie E. Reynolds became his wife December 5, 1880, and the mother of his two children: Lillian E., born February 14, 1882, and George, born July 29, 1884. Mrs. Powell's parents are Hugh R. and Mary A. (Carter) Reynolds. Dr. Powell gives his support to the Democratic party and is one of the directors of the Shoal

Creek Iron Company, organized February 24, 1886. The mines are in Lawrence County, near St. Joseph, and the ore, analyzed, has been found to be brown hematite, yielding over 56 per cent of metallic iron. The mines are being operated under the management of Col. Thomas Sharp, of Nashville, who is president of the company.

William J. Price, a leading citizen of Lawrence County, Tenn., is of Scotch-Irish descent, and was born in the State in 1849, son of Ezekiel and Martha Price, who were natives of North Carolina and settlers of Tennessee in 1821. The father was a teacher and merchant in early life, but retired to the farm after marriage. He was a member of the Cumberland Presbyterian Church, and died in Lawrence County in 1883. William J. was raised on a farm and educated at West Point, Tenn. At the age of twenty-eight years he began teaching school, and at the expiration of three years began farming, which he has continued up to the present time. In 1876 he purchased the farm of fifty acres, on which he now lives, and in 1882 was chosen magistrate of his district, and has faithfully discharged the duties of that office up to the present time. He is a Democrat, and he and wife are members of the Methodist Episcopal Church South. In 1881 he wedded Mary T. Kelley, a daughter of John and Susan Kelley. She was born in Tennessee in 1845, and is the mother of one child, named Lillie S., who was born in 1883.

David T. Quarles, sheriff of Lawrence County, was born in Giles County March 24, 1853, the son of Amon T. and Elizabeth (Vaughn) Quarles, natives of Virginia. The father lived upon a farm in Lawrence County, Tenth District, from 1868 until 1880, when his death occurred. David T. was reared upon a farm, securing during youth a limited education. At the age of eighteen years he began farming and stockraising for himself, which pursuits he followed until he was elected to the office of sheriff in August, 1884. This position he has filled with honor to himself and satisfaction to his fellow citizens. His official term will expire in August, 1886. In 1872 he was united in marriage with Mary E. Meredith, a native of Georgia, by whom he has the following family: William L., Mary T. and Russell A. Mr. Quarles is a stanch Democrat and a useful citizen.

Judge Robert H. Rose, the oldest living member of the Lawrence County bar, was born in Brunswick County, Va., January 2, 1818, and is a son of William and Elizabeth (Meredith) Rose. Our subject was reared in Giles County, and secured a good academical education in his youthful days. He was a soldier in the Florida war, and at its close, in 1836, he began the study of law. He entered the office of E. J. Shield, of Pulaski, member of Congress from this district, and was admitted to the Giles County bar in 1840. He remained and practiced law in that county until 1850, when he came to Lawrenceburg, and has since taken an active and leading part in representing his profession at this bar. In 1861 he was elected judge of this circuit, which office he held in an able manner until 1865, when he was elected chancellor of the district. In 1868 he, with many others, was removed by Gov. Brownlow's orders, causing another election. Since then the Judge has been incessantly engaged in the practice of his profession, in which he has been justly successful. He is a Democrat in politics, an ancient Odd Fellow, and an Episcopalian in his religious faith. He is a lawyer of ability and high standing in the profession.

Alfred H. Rose, merchant of Lawrenceburg, Tenn., was born in Brunswick County, Va., November 23, 1808, and is a brother of Judge, R. H. Rose, of Lawrenceburg, whose sketch appears elsewhere in these pages. Our subject's parents, William and Elizabeth (Meredith) Rose, were natives of the "Old Dominion." The father emigrated westward and located in Giles County, Tenn., with his family, in 1814. Here our subject was reared and educated. After attaining his majority he located in West Tennessee, in Hardeman County, where he followed agricultural pursuits successfully for fifty-five years, although, like many others, his financial condition was sadly impaired during the late war. He was magistrate in Hardeman County for twenty-eight years, and for twelve years was chairman of the county court. He is, and always has been, an unswerving Democrat in politics, casting his first presidential vote for Jackson, in 1832. In June, 1884, he left Hardeman County, and after a short stay, both in Lawrence and Giles County, he engaged in the mercantile business in Lawrenceburg which he has continued up to the present time. January 28, 1828, he married Mildred Eastham, of Virginia, who died in October, 1858. To this union were born eight children, three now living, viz,: W. S., Medora (wife of James J. McCollum) and Mary Ann (wife of Mc. Alexander). April 11, 1871, Mr. Rose married Mrs. Victoria Maddox, who died May 3, 1883. She left one son, Alfred P. Although Mr. Rose is comparatively a new citizen of Lawrence County, he is one of the pioneers of Tennessee, and a reliable, enterprising citizen.

John Schade, Jr., editor and one of the proprietors of the *Lawrence Union*, of Lawrenceburg, Tenn., is a son of John Schade, Sr., a merchant of Lawrenceburg, Tenn., who was born in Germany, kingdom of Bavaria, October 24, 1838, and a grandson of George and Margaret (Rubbert) Schade, both natives of the same country. The father of our subject came to the United States in 1831 with his parents, and located in Baltimore,

Md., where his parents died. He learned the shoe-maker's trade in that city, which he followed until the late war. He enlisted from Dayton, Ohio, in Company E, Fifty-eighth Ohio Regiment, and served nine months. He then resided in Ohio, being unfit for work on account of disabilities contracted during service. In 1872 he came to Lawrenceburg and followed his trade until 1880, when he engaged in his present business. In 1860 he married Christina Zeigler, a native of Wurtemburg, Germany, and this union resulted in the birth of five children: John, Charles C., Joseph B., Mary C. and Theresa B. John Schade, Sr., is a Republican in politics, but of rather independent views. Himself and family are members of the Catholic Church. Our subject, John Schade, Jr., was born in Dayton, Ohio, October 10, 1862, and came to Lawrenceburg with his parents in 1872. He received a good German and English education, and in 1880 began learning the printer's trade, working on the *Lawrence Press* one year. In 1882 he worked on the *Pulaski Herald*, but returned to the Lawrenceburg *Press* during 1883 and 1884. During 1885 he was in the mercantile business, and in February, 1886, he, in company with his brother, Joseph B., bought out the Lawrenceburg *Press* office, and established the *Lawrence Union*, which they have since conducted successfully as a Republican paper. August 7, 1883, John, Jr., married Lizzie Cook, of Cincinnati, Ohio, and two children (twins), named Henry and Christina, were born to this union. In politics our subject is a stanch Republican, and he and family are members of the Catholic Church.

William R. Sexton is one of six children of John J. and and Elizabeth A. (Yeager) Sexton, and of English and German descent. He was born in Lincoln County, Tenn., November 6, 1843, and attended the common schools in boyhood. He learned the tanner's trade and followed that occupation many years. He served in the Confederate Army in the Thirty-second Regiment Tennessee Infantry, and was captured at the fall of Fort Donelson, and kept a prisoner at Camp Morton, Indianapolis, Ind., for seven months, when he was exchanged at Vicksburg, and was afterward at Lookout Mountain, Missionary Ridge, Moulton, Athens and Johnsonville, and was severely wounded on the march to Nashville, which disabled him from further service. January 1, 1865, he was united in marriage to Mary E. Sparkman, daughter of James G. and Delany M. Sparkman, and to them were born the following family: Alice J., born April 15, 1868; Edward H., born July 27, 1870, and Lewis A., born March 25, 1874. Mrs. Sexton was born in Williamson County, Tenn., June 11, 1844, and she and her husband and daughter are members of the Missionary Baptist Church. Mr. Sexton is a

Mason and a Democrat, and is the owner of 225 acres of fertile land. His father was born in Tennessee, in 1820, and was a farmer by occupation. He moved to Arkansas in 1851, but soon returned to Tennessee, thence to Alabama, and in 1861 returned to Tennessee, where he resided until his death, October 23, 1868. His wife was born in Lincoln County, in 1824, and is still living on the old homestead. She and her husband were active and useful members of the Primitive Baptist Church.

John B. Simms is a native of Lawrence County born November 22, 1859, being the son of Paris L. and Mary E. (McGlamery) Simms, natives of Tennessee. The father came to this county in 1848 and followed farming until 1877, when his death occurred on February 14 of that year. He was a Whig before, and a strong Union man during the war. He was a magistrate about sixteen years, and was chairman of the county court three or four years, and was one of the most substantial citizens of the county. John B. was given an academic education in youth. At the age of twenty-one years he began the study of law in the office of Capt. Deavenport. In 1882 he was admitted to the bar, since which time he has continued in active practice. For twelve months he was in partnership with S. A. Carroll, Jr., and is at present associated with George T. Hughes, of Columbia. July 22, 1885, he married Mannie F., daughter of Capt. Deavenport. They have one daughter. Mr. Simms is a Republican. In 1881–82 he served as sergeant-at-arms of the Tennessee House of Representatives, being elected without solicitation on his part. Since 1884 he has held the office of county entry-taker. He is the local counsel of the Nashville & Florence Railroad Company. He is a rising attorney.

William Smith was born in the Hoosier State in 1810, and is the youngest of six children of James and Martha (Gilbert) Smith, and is of English descent. His parents were born in North Carolina, where they were married, but reared their family in Tennessee. Previous to this they resided a short time in Indiana, but finally moved to Mississippi, where the mother died in 1850, and the father a few years later. Our subject received a limited early education and made his home with his parents until he attained his majority, when he began farming on his own account, and now owns 860 acres of land, which are furnished with a number of fine inexhaustible springs. Mr. Smith wedded Alice Nelson in October, 1833. She was born in Lawrence County in 1817, daughter of John Nelson, one of the prominent farmers of the county. Their union has been blessed with fourteen children, only eight now living: Louisa W., Martha J., James H., William R., Calvin T., Samuel J., Andrew J. and John N. Mr. and Mrs. Smith have resided on their present farm since 1844, and are yet quite hale and vigorous. Mr. Smith was too old to take part in the late war, but his sons, Robert W. and William R., both served. The former died soon after enlisting, and the latter served four years. Previous to the war our subject was an old line Whig and did all in his power to prevent his State from seceding, but after it was inevitable he espoused the cause of the Confederacy. Since that time he has voted the Democratic ticket.

William R. Smith, a prominent and energetic farmer of Lawrence County, Tenn., is a native of the county, born February 22, 1841, the second son of William and Allie (Nelson) Smith, both born in Tennessee. The father was one of the pioneer settlers, and has lived on his present farm, near Lawrenceburg, since he was eight years of age. Both parents are yet living and are hale and hearty. Up to the age of twenty years our subject resided on a farm, and secured a common school education. At the breaking out of the war he enlisted in Company I, Third Tennessee Regiment, and served first as private, and afterward as sergeant. He was captured at Fort Donelson, and for seven months was imprisoned at Camp Douglas, Chicago. He was exchanged at Vicksburg, and was made sergeant of Company K, Third Tennessee Regiment, and remained such until October, 1864, when he was taken prisoner at Jonesboro, and remained in captivity until the close of the war. He then returned home and farmed on his father's land until 1867, when he purchased a farm in Alabama. In 1877 he purchased his present place, on which he has been extensively engaged in farming and stock raising. In 1867 he united his fortunes with those of Miss Ruth Springer, and seven children blessed their union, two of whom are dead. Those living are A. Wildie, Robert N., Jonas C., Louisa and Mary T. Matilda J. died in August, 1885, and Sarah C. in April, 1870. Mr. Smith is a Republican of the old Whig type, and he and wife are members of the Missionary Baptist Church.

Henry B. Sowell, attorney at law, of Lawrenceburg, Tenn., was born in Hickman County, Tenn., July 24, 1854, and is a son of Hon. Joseph M. and Mary A. (Blakely) Sowell, natives respectively of North Carolina and Maury County, Tenn., the father being reared, however, after his third year, in Maury County, where he resided until his marriage. After a short residence in Hickman County, he removed to Lawrence County in 1854, where he has since resided. He has twice represented the county in the State Legislature. Our subject was reared in Lawrence County, and educated in its schools. He completed an academical course of learning, at Columbia, in 1876, and in 1877 began reading law here with Judge John T. Allen, with whom he remained as a pupil until

1878. He was then admitted to the Lawrence County bar, and entered actively into the practice of his profession, which he has continued with very flattering success to the present time. In 1885 he formed his present partnership with J. B. Parker, and has contributed largely to the established success of this well known legal firm. Mr. Sowell is, and always has been, a stanch and uncompromising Democrat in politics. He held the office of circuit court clerk of this county by appointment part of 1884. He has also held the office of magistrate for the last four years. Perhaps no man in the county is better acquainted with the books and affairs in the various county offices, as he has held irregularly the position of deputy in nearly all the offices. He is recognized in the county as an active party leader, an enterprising citizen, and an able member of the Lawrence County bar. He is a steward in the Methodist Episcopal Church South, and one of the county's best citizens.

Aaron F. Springer, a prominent planter, and native of the county in which he resides, was born near his present residence December 3, 1836, being the fourth of eleven children of Jacob and Malinda C. (Todd) Springer, who were born in South Carolina in 1808 and 1812, respectively. The father came to Lawrence County, Tenn., when about sixteen years of age, and here married, and reared his family, and died October 5, 1869. His wife's death occurred at the old homestead June 11, 1865. Aaron F. Springer has made farming his chief calling through life. Mary S. A. Carrell became his wife May 10, 1860, and their union was blessed in the birth of eleven children: James C., Mollie C., Robert C., Lillie S., Sallie E., Alix C., Emma B. and Alice Leslie and three who are dead. The mother of these children was born near Lawrenceburg in 1843, and is the daughter of Judge Stephen A. Carrell, who was born in Lawrence County in 1817, and served as clerk and judge of the county court. Our subject served in the Confederate Army in the Ninth Tennessee Cavalry, and was in the battles of Franklin and Nashville. He was captured at one time and held a prisoner at Rock Island, Ill., for about four months. He was paroled at Gainsville, Ala. He is an old line Democrat and a member of the F. & A. M. fraternity. He owns 500 acres of land, on which he raises the cereals and live stock. His wife is a member of the Methodist Episcopal Church South.

William A. Stewart, lawyer and postmaster of Lawrenceburg, Tenn., and a native of Lawrence County, of the same State, is a son of Daniel M. and Sarah F. (Evans) Stewart, natives, respectively, of Tennessee and North Carolina. The father was reared in this county, and early in life adopted the medical profession. He practiced here until 1876, when he removed to Denton County, Tex., where he now resides. His only brother, John W. Stewart, a highly enterprising and public-spirited citizen of Lawrence County, was sheriff of that county during the war, and held the office of surveyor regularly from the time he attained his majority until his death, in November, 1884. Our subject's grandfather, Alexander Stewart, came to Lawrence County about 1820, and here he resided, following farming, until shortly before his death, which occurred in Alabama October 14, 1883. Our subject was reared and educated in this county, completing an academic course at the West Point High School. At the age of twenty he began the study of law with a view of making it a profession. He read law in the office of Judge R. H. Rose, and in 1872 was admitted to practice in Lawrence County courts and entered regularly in the practice of his profession, first with W. C. Davis, but soon after with his former preceptor, until 1879, since which time Mr. Stewart has been engaged in the practice alone. He is a Democrat in politics, although his ancestors were of the old Whig stock. His father and uncle were both in the Confederate service during the late war. In August, 1885, our subject was appointed, by President Cleveland, postmaster at Lawrenceburg, which position he now fills. At the same time he became connected with the *Lawrence Democrat* in the capacity of associate editor and publisher, having contributed equally with others to the success of this official organ of democracy in Lawrence County. January 1, 1880, he married Loulie S. Parkes, a native of Giles County, Tenn. Two children, Jennie L. and Parkes Evans, were born to this union. Mr. Stewart is a member of the K. of H., and himself and wife are members of the Cumberland Presbyterian Church.

Col. James L. Stribling, a prominent and well known citizen of Lawrence County, Tenn., was born in Giles County, March 9, 1829, son of Obadiah T. and Mary (Simonton) Stribling, natives respectively of South and North Carolina. The father came to Tennessee in 1818 and practiced medicine there in Athens, Ala., until 1829, when he came to Lawrenceburg, where he resided at the time of his death in July, 1833. James L. has made his home in Lawrence County since 1843. In 1847 he and W. P. Horne purchased the *Middle Tennessean*, a weekly newspaper, in the interest of the Whig party, and the only paper printed in the judicial circuit at that time. The paper had been established in 1845, by Dr. W. P. Rowls, under the name of the *Academist*, and was afterward run by S. E. Rose, John A. Tinnon, Lee M. Bentley and Horne & Harrison. Col. Stribling purchased Mr. Harrison's interest and continued the publication of the paper until 1850, when the firm sold to Hatcher & Jerrett. After retiring from the newspaper business Col. Stribling engaged in farming, but in 1872 returned to Lawrenceburg and engaged in the hotel business, and continued successfully about six years. Since that time he has given his time and attention to farming and general trading. In August, 1885, he became connected with the grist mill of Lawrenceburg, being a partner of Daniel Guthrie. July 15, 1849, he married Mary J. Alexander, of Maury County, who bore him six children: Edward L., Mary A., Fannie K. (Mrs. A. M. Looney), James H., Rose E. and Robert Lee. The Colonel is a Democrat but previous to the war was a Whig.

William H. Sykes, of Athens, Ala., formerly a resident of Lawrence County, was born in Dayton, Ohio, August 10, 1842, son of James and Elizabeth (Mulholland) Sykes, natives respectively of England and Pennsylvania. The father came to Lawrence County in 1843 and engaged in cotton manufacture northeast of Lawrenceburg at Oak Factory. He was a useful citizen and died in 1865. William H. was reared in this county, securing an academic education. After his father's death he assumed control of the Crowson Cotton Mills, which were built by the father in 1856. Since his father's death he has managed these mills. He uses 350 to 400 bales of cotton per year, manufacturing yarns, carpet-warps and batting, finding his principal market in Cincinnati. He uses water power and employs about twenty-five hands. June 8, 1875, Mr. Sykes married Jennie P. Hayes, of Athens, Ala., who has borne her husband three children—one son and two daughters. He is a Democrat and a member of the Masonic fraternity.

John C. Tarpley was born in the "Old Dominion" November 21, 1804. His father was a soldier in the Revolutionary war, and came to Tennessee in 1808, and for three years was a resident of Nashville, which then consisted of a few scattered log houses. A few houses marked the cities of Franklin and Columbia, and the city of Pulaski was an uninterrupted cane brake. Our subject is the fourth of twelve children of Alexander and Elizabeth (Abernathy) Tarpley, and is of English descent. The mother was a daughter of William Abernathy, a prominent citizen of Giles County, who lived a long and useful life. Our subject received a common school education, and by energy and economy is now the owner of 437 acres of land. He has been twice married, the first time to Temperance M. Stone, in 1827, daughter of Thomas Stone, of Virginia. Their children are as follows: William A., Elizabeth Agnes (Mrs. Robert Johnson), Catherine D. (Mrs. James Parks), Leonidas J., Sarah P. (Mrs. M. B. Harvey) and John R. Leonidas was killed at the battle of Perryville, and Benjamin M. at the battle of Shiloh, during the late war. Mr. Tarpley's marriage to Helen M. Black, in 1857, resulted in the birth of three children: Charles C., Thomas D. and Mary

V. Mr. Tarpley is an old line Democrat, and is a man noted for his integrity and fair dealing.

Darling M. Tidwell is a son of Vincent and Phœbe (Rackley) Tidwell. The father was born in the Palmetto State, and was an early pioneer of Tennessee. Of their twelve children eight of them lived to be grown, and six served in the Confederate Army. Vincent Tidwell and his wife died in 1873 and 1883, respectively. Darling M. Tidwell was born in Tennessee in 1832, and in 1850 wedded Roxanna W. McCracken, born in Tennessee in 1835, daughter of Calvin and Amanda (English) McCracken. Mr. and Mrs. Tidwell had eighteen children: John V., Phœbe E., Mary J., James C., Calloway H., Frances L., Thomas M., Charles W. and William J. (twins), Andrew J., Robert E. L., C. D., Wiley N., Emma L., Lulu and Nancy D. Two died in infancy. Eleven of these children are living, and five are married. Our subject began doing for himself at the age of eighteen, and by perseverance and energy accumulated considerable property. When about twenty-eight years of age he was appointed deputy sheriff, and held the office about six years, after which he was elected constable of his district, holding that position about four years. He served in the late war in Company D, Biffles Cavalry, and participated in many hotly contested battles. After his return he was constable of his district about two years. In 1873 he purchased the farm on which he now lives and which contains 1,100 acres. He deals extensively in cattle and mules, and in 1880 began merchandising on his farm, but is now closing out. In June, 1878, his wife died. He is a member of the Methodist Episcopal Church, and he is a Democrat in politics. His children are all living in this State. John B. moved to Texas in 1876, and died in 1878, leaving a widow and three children to mourn his loss. They are now living in Tennessee.

T. K. True is a son of David H. and Ellen (Glasscock) True, and was born in Maury County, Tenn., June 16, 1839. The father was a Virginian and came to Tennessee when quite young with his father, who was a soldier in the Revolutionary war. David H. was a farmer and followed merchandising and stock trading for many years. He died in 1871, and his wife five years later. Our subject became the architect of his own fortunes at the age of twenty-one, and followed farming up to the breaking out of the late civil war, when he enlisted as a private in Company K, Forty-eighth Tennessee Regiment, and acted as adjutant the greater part of the war, yet held no commission. He participated in many hard-fought engagements, and returned home May 19, 1865, and associated himself with Thomas H. Payne (present State superintendent of schools) and opened a high school at West Point, Tenn. Ten months later he was licensed to preach and was an itinerant minister of the Methodist Episcopal Church South for several years. He was recently employed by the I. O. O. F. Grand Lodge as State lecturer, and visited various portions of the State in behalf of that organization, doing very effective work. Since 1872 he has resided on his farm of 110 acres on Factory Creek. Mr. True is a Democrat and Prohibitionist.

Theodore D. Vaughn, farmer and native of the county in which he resides, was born in 1840, son of Thomas and Mary A. Vaughn, who were Tennesseans by birth and died in 1863 and 1862, respectively. Our subject was reared on his parents' farm, and resided with them until 1861, when he entered the Confederate service and participated in the battle of Fort Donelson. He was there captured and taken to Camp Douglas, where he was retained six months and was then taken to Vicksburg and exchanged. Here the company reorganized and took an active part in the battle of Chickasaw Bayou and was in several other engagements, the most noted of which was Murfreesboro. On Hood's retirement from Tennessee Mr. Vaughn gave up army life and has since been a tiller of the soil. In 1876 he purchased his farm of 100 acres, on which he raises principally corn and cotton. In 1866 Araminta T. Hail became his wife; she was born in Tennessee in 1847, and is a daughter of John A. and Martha Hail. Mr. and Mrs. Vaughn are members of the Methodist Episcopal Church South, and in politics Mr. Vaughn has always favored Democratic principles.

John W. Welch, M. D., was born in Tennessee in 1829, son of John L. and Rachel (Archer) Welch, born in South Carolina and Georgia, respectively. John L. Welch came to Tennessee with his parents in 1806. He was a farmer and lived in Lawrence County until his death in 1876. His wife died in 1873. After residing on the farm for some time John W. attended the Jackson Academy at Lawrenceburg. In 1851 he began the study of medicine under Dr. H. H. Dodson and later under Dr. W. P. Hale, and began practicing at Pleasantville, Hickman County, where he remained two years. He then practiced in Linden, Perry County, four years. He then enlisted in N. N. Cox's Company of Cavalry, remaining twelve months, and at the reorganization of the battalion he was elected first lieutenant. A year later he was discharged under the conscript law and came home, remaining seven months. He then enlisted in Company B, Twenty-third Regiment Tennessee Infantry, and remained in the service until October, 1864, when he was taken sick and was in the hospital at Richmond until the surrender. After being kept a prisoner about one month he took the oath of allegiance and returned home. He was married in 1852 to Elizabeth McMackin, born in Tennessee in 1835. The following are their children: John A., Martha E., Mary J., James A., Albert S. (deceased), Ben T., Josephine R. (deceased), Georgia A., Kate E. and Elroy E. In 1870 Dr. Welch purchased his farm of 275 acres, and in 1881 he formed a partnership with his brother, George K. Welch, in the merchandise business in Chinnabee, and has met with fair success. Doctor Welch inherited about $1,600 from his father's estate, but the most of his property has been gained through his own exertions. He and wife are members of the Methodist Episcopal Church, and he is a Democrat.

George K. Welch, merchant, is a Tennessean, born in 1843 [see sketch of J. W. Welch for parents' biography], and resided with his father on a farm until eighteen years of age, at which time he enlisted in the Confederate service and was in some of the hardest fought battles of the war, Shiloh, Chickamauga and Murfreesboro being the principal ones. He served through the entire war and surrendered with Gen. Lee at Appomattox Court House. He returned home and attended school for some time, and has followed clerking, milling, farming and merchandising, having a general stock of goods in the village of Chinnabee, his brother, J. W. Welch, being in partnership with him. In 1871 he wedded Maggie E. Shannon, daughter of Gazaway and Jane Shannon. Mrs. Welch was born in 1850, and is the mother of five children: Ella J. (deceased), Maude E., Leonard G. Rachel J. and Fannie E. Mr. Welch has served as deputy county clerk under S. A. Carrell. He is a Democrat and a strong supporter of prohibition. He and wife are members of the Methodist Episcopal Church South.

Augustus J. White, M. D., is a son of George O. W. and Mary A. (Cole) White, who were born in Massachusetts and New York October 23, 1817, and February 27, 1820, respectively. The father came to Tennessee in 1837 and started the Sycamore Cotton Mills and built the Sycamore Powder Mills. After living alternately in Massachusetts and Tennessee until 1854, he took up a permanent residence in Tennessee and died in Lawrence County April 4, 1886. The mother now resides on the home place. Augustus J. was born in Massachusetts June 26, 1852, and there resided until eight years of age, when he was brought to Tennessee, and has since made the State his home, with the exception of one year spent in California. He has very vivid recollections of the late war, although too young to take part in the same. His early education was obtained in the common schools, but later he was taught by Capt. Thomas H. Paine, present State superintendent of public instruction for Tennessee. He began studying medicine under Dr. James E. Edwards, and later graduated from the medical department of the University of

Tennessee (now Vanderbilt). June 26, 1872, he wedded Lena J. Moss, born in Franklin, Tenn., December 12, 1852, daughter of A. W. Moss, and to them were born five children, three of whom are living: Lena Gertrude, Lyndal Warren and Carrie May Cleveland. Dr. White is a farmer and Democrat, and a successful physician. His wife is a member of the Christian Church.

WAYNE COUNTY.

Thomas F. Acklin is one of the firm of Mays & Acklin, liverymen of Clifton. They established their business April 1, 1886, and keep a full and excellent line of vehicles, the best in town or county. They deal quite extensively in horses and mules, and in connection, in January, 1885, established a retail liquor store, which they have conducted with fair success up to the present time. Thomas F. Acklin is a son of Cleaburn and Martha (McCreley) Acklin, who were born in Tennessee and North Carolina respectively. Thomas F. is a native of Wayne County, born May 15, 1845, and was reared to manhood on a farm. He enlisted in the Confederate Army in 1861, and served in Company F, Forty-eighth Tennessee Infantry for over three years, and in the Twentieth Regiment of Tennessee Cavalry the remainder of the war. From the time of his return home until December, 1882, he tilled the soil, and at the latter date he came to Clifton and has since been engaged in the livery business. Previous to this he kept a hotel in Saltillo for some time. In 1871 he united his fortunes with those of Sarah M. Nunley, and two children have blessed their union: Tempie and James. Mr. Acklin is a Democrat and one of the eminent business men of Clifton.

David R. Adams, a pioneer of Wayne County, Tenn., was born October 17, 1813, son of William and Unity Adams, who were married in their native State (South Carolina), and soon immigrated to Tennessee, where the father farmed and lived for many years. The mother died here December 9, 1832, and six years later the father moved to Missouri, where he died about 1850. He was a Whig in politics. David R. lived with his father until twenty-three years of age, when he united his fortunes with those of Eliza Woodard, a Tennessean, born in 1819, and daughter of Solomon and Elizabeth (Biven) Woodard. To them were born seven children: Martha E. (deceased), William J., Elizabeth A. (deceased), Wiley H., Unity J., George S. and John F. After his marriage Mr. Adams farmed a few years and then moved to Mississippi, but not being satisfied, remained only a few months, when he returned to Tennessee. He resided in different parts of the county until 1852, when he purchased his present farm of 113 acres. The land is in a good state of cultivation and is fairly well improved. When Mr. Adams first moved to Wayne County it was very sparsely settled. He is a member of the Free-Will Baptist Church, and has always been a Republican in politics. He is strictly temperate, and has always evaded lawsuits, never being sued or having to sue but one man in the whole course of his life.

John M. Barnett first saw the light of day in Wayne County, Tenn., in 1834. His parents, John M. and Lovina (Poag) Barnett, were born in Georgia and South Carolina, respectively, and came to Tennessee at an early day and when quite young. The father was a farmer by occupation but also practiced medicine and preached the gospel, being a minister of the Christian Church. He was a Whig and died in Wayne County, in 1834, followed by his wife in 1864. Our subject has always resided on the farm where he was born. It consists of 164 acres of fairly improved land in a good state of cultivation, the principal productions being corn, small grain and stock. In 1859 he was united in marriage to Caroline Skillern, daughter of Anderson and Polly (Spring) Skillern. Mrs. Barnett was born in 1833 and died in 1863, having borne two children: Joseph B. (who died in 1861), and Sarah C. In 1865 Mr. Barnett married Lillie A. Thompson, who was born in 1842, daughter of Jackson and Mary Thompson. This wife died in 1873, leaving one child, Martha J. In 1877 Mr. Barnett took for his third wife Senith Welch, daughter of James and Senith Welch. She was born in 1835, and is a member of the Cumberland Presbyterian Church. Our subject belongs to the Christian Church and is a Republican in politics.

William L. Bell was born in Wayne County in 1844, son of William R. and Elizabeth (Burns) Bell, who were born in North Carolina and Tennessee, respectively. The father came to Tennessee when a young man, and was a tanner by trade, and in connection with this followed farming. He was a Whig in politics, and died in Wayne County in 1863. His wife died in 1844. The father was married four times, his first wife being a Miss Alexander; the second, our subject's mother; the third, Adeline Stockard, and the fourth, Jane Meredith. Our subject was reared on a farm, and at the death of his mother was cared for by his grandmother. From fifteen until nineteen years of age he resided with an uncle. He then enlisted in the Confederate service, and served until the close of the war. He was in many of the principal battles, but was never wounded. He returned home in February, 1865. Shortly after his return he married Martha C. Whitaker, daughter of James and

Delphia Whitaker. She was born in Tennessee in 1840, and is the mother of six children: Conly (deceased), Elizabeth, Samuel, William H., Whitthorne and Charles (deceased). Our subject farmed two years on rented land after his marriage, and in 1868 purchased his present farm of 340 acres. He is a Democrat, and has held the office of deputy sheriff three years, giving good satisfaction.

Joseph G. Berry, a well known citizen of Clifton, Tenn., was born in Hardin County January 22, 1834, son of William and Sarah (Weatherford) Berry, who were born in Georgia and East Tennessee, respectively. The father came to Tennessee with his mother when a boy, and located and afterward married in Hardin County. He died in 1868. Joseph G. was three years of age when his parents came to Wayne County. He was raised on a farm, and in the fall of 1862 enlisted in the Sixth Tennessee Cavalry, United States Army, and was promoted to captain of Company H, and served two years. At the close of the war he engaged in the mercantile business at Waynesboro, and there remained until 1880, when he removed to Clifton, and conducted the hotel at that place very successfully for three years. Since that time he has been connected with the liquor business, farming, and also keeps a hostelry for the traveling public. In 1854 he married Elmyra J. Cypert, who became the mother of the following family: William J., Ada (widow of Isaac H. Old), and Joanna. Mr. Berry is a Republican, and has been a Mason since 1855, and also belongs to the K. of H.

William J. Berry, retail dealer in liquors at Clifton, Tenn., is a son of Joseph G. Berry, whose sketch appears in this work. He was born in Wayne County, Tenn., February 16, 1858, and was reared and educated in the county. In 1876 he engaged in his present business in Waynesboro, and remained there till 1881, when he removed his business to Clifton. He has met with good success in his undertakings, and conducts a strictly first-class saloon. He keeps a fine stock of pure whiskies, wines, beer, etc. October 23, 1877, he married Lou Dora Ramsey. They have two children: Joseph C. and Ralph M. Mr. Berry is a stanch Republican, and was city recorder of Clifton two terms.

Jonathan Frank Biffle was born in Wayne County, Tenn., in 1849. His father, Jonathan Biffle, was a Tennessean, a farmer, and when a young man was deputy sheriff of Wayne County. He served in the Ninth Tennessee Regiment in the late war, under Jake Biffle, and was captured in 1864, while at home on furlough, and taken to Rock Island, Ill., where he was retained a prisoner until his death, January 23, 1864. He left a wife and three children to mourn his loss. His widow, Eliza A. (Hardin) Biffle, married George Walker, of Tennessee, and died July 14, 1885. Our subject, after his father's death, resided with his mother until her second marriage, when she left, giving him possession of the home-farm. He afterward inherited a portion of this farm, and purchased the remainder, in all consisting of 350 acres of fairly improved land. His principal products are corn, small grain and peanuts. Besides this, he owns sixty-four acres of land below his present farm, and a two-thirds interest in 183 acres of timber land. In 1877 he and Mary Clendennin united their fortunes. She is a Tennessean by birth, born in 1858, daughter of Joseph and Bettie Clendennin. Mr. and Mrs. Biffle have four children: Joe E., Jonathan A. (who died in 1881), Nettie E. (who died in 1883) and John W. Mr. Biffle is a Democrat.

Frank Boyd, attorney at law, of Waynesboro, Tenn., was born in Lawrence County, Ohio, on the 30th of July, 1859, being a son of George W. and Ann E. (Songer) Boyd, who were Virginians. The father came to Wayne County, Tenn., in 1808, and located at Wayne Furnace, of which he was superintendent until the business there was suspended. Frank prepared himself for teaching and worked at intervals on the farm in this county. He taught in this and Shelby Counties until 1879. In the meantime he had begun the study of law, and afterward studied under the direction of Howell E. Jackson in the winter of 1879 and spring of 1880. In September, 1880, he entered the Lebanon Law School, from which he graduated in 1881. In August of the same year he came to Waynesboro and engaged in practicing, continuing the same with good success to the present. In November, 1885, he became identified with the drug business of the county, becoming a partner in the same with his brother, George W., at Waynesboro. Mr. Boyd is a Democrat and is a candidate for the attorney-generalship of the Ninth Judicial Circuit. May 22, 1883, he married Laura E., the daughter of A. T. Hassell. Mr. Boyd is one of the rising young lawyers of Wayne County, and a reliable and enterprising young man.

George W. Boyd, druggist of Waynesboro, Tenn., was born in Lawrence County, Ohio, December 9, 1857, son of George W. Boyd, Sr., and came to Wayne County, Tenn., with his parents in 1868. He secured a fair education chiefly by his own efforts and afterward clerked in his father's store. In May, 1883, he came to Waynesboro and engaged in the drug business in company with H. A. Helton. In November, 1885, his brother, Frank Boyd, took Mr. Helton's place in the firm. They keep a stock of drugs and groceries, and control a large share of the trade, in his line, in town and county. They also have the agency for the Domestic sewing machine at this place. He is a Democrat.

Capt. William L. Bromley, postmaster and an early citizen of Waynesboro, Tenn., was born in Wayne County June 26, 1827, and is one of seven children born to the marriage of John Bromley and Edith Hurst, natives, respectively, of Virginia and North Carolina. John Bromley, grandfather of our subject, located in Wayne County in 1818, having located in Giles County the previous year. His son, John, married and reared his family in Wayne County, and followed a farmer's life, being one of the successful agriculturists of his day. He died in the Third District July 26, 1850. The mother lived until March 30, 1884, having attained her seventy-seventh year. William L. spent his early days on his father's farm, and secured but a limited education in the primitive subscription schools of his day. At the age of twenty-two he began tilling the soil on his own responsibility, and continued that occupation until the breaking out of the war, when he enlisted in the Confederate Army, Company I, First Tennessee Cavalry. In 1862 he was chosen captain of Company F, Ninth Tennessee Battalion of Cavalry, and served in this capacity until the close of the war. He then resumed farming, but in 1869 engaged in the general merchandise business as clerk at Flat Woods postoffice. In February, 1876, he came to Waynesboro, where he has since been very successfully engaged in the general merchandise business. The firm is composed of himself and R. C. Martin. In October, 1885, he was made postmaster of Waynesboro, and has been a competent and highly satisfactory office-holder. The captain is an unswerving Democrat in politics, and is a Royal Arch Mason.

John J. Bromley's birth occurred in Tennessee in 1838, son of John and E. Bromley, who were born in Virginia and North Carolina, respectively, and came to Tennessee at an early day. The father was a farmer, and served for several years as deputy sheriff. He was a stanch Democrat and died in 1846, his widow's death occurring in 1881. John J.'s early days were spent on his father's farm. At the age of twenty-two years he began the battle of life for himself, and lived on a farm owned by his father until 1857, when he purchased a portion of this farm, and continued buying out the heirs until he now owns all but one share; 1,200 acres constitute his farm, which is in a good state of cultivation. In 1861 he enlisted in the Confederate Army and served throughout the war. He returned home in the spring of 1865. He is a Democrat in politics. In 1861 he wedded Mary Belsha, daughter of Ewing and Darky (Bromley) Belsha. She was born in Alabama in 1839, and is the mother of six children: William E., Eda C., James A., John L., Richard C. and Thomas C. Mrs. Bromley died July 5, 1875, and September 10, of the same year, he married Sallie Terry, and six children have blessed their union: Charles J., Samuel B. (who died in 1883), Joseph C., Amos H., Mary J. and Emma N.

Cicero Buchanan, M. D., county superintendent of the public schools of Wayne County, Tenn., was born in Giles County, Tenn., April 20, 1842, and is a son of Samuel G. and Sarah E. Buchanan, who were born and reared in Tennessee. Dr. Buchanan was educated at State Springs Academy in Giles County, and his boyhood days were spent on his father's farm. At the breaking out of the late civil war he, in 1861, enlisted in the Third Tennessee Regiment, serving until the close of the war and participating in many of the hardest-fought battles. After Lee's surrender he returned to his home and began the study of medicine under Dr. A. H. Berry, of Lawrenceburg, Tenn., and in 1867 entered the medical department of the University of Nashville, attending one course of lectures. In the fall of 1868 he graduated as an M. D. from the Atlanta (Ga.) Medical College, and in February, 1869, located at Waynesboro, and has since been actively engaged in the practice of his profession. He is regarded as a well-read and reliable physician by his patrons and brother physicians, and has been prosperous both professionally and financially. The Doctor owns about 1,500 acres of land, about 200 acres of which is in a fair state of cultivation. In 1871 Amos and Mary A. Hassell's daughter, Ella A., became his wife. Dr. Buchanan has taken an active part in educational affairs of late years, and in 1882 was elected to the office of county superintendent, and still holds the position. He is one of the Wayne County health officers, is a Democrat and belongs to the F. & A. M.

Jacob B. Burns, one of Wayne County's pioneers, is a son of Samuel L. and Sarah A. Burns, and was born in 1832. His parents were Tennesseans and farmers; the father being an extensive stock raiser, in which business he became quite wealthy. He was sheriff of Wayne County two terms. He died on his farm on Buffalo River (which he purchased in 1837) in 1880. His wife died in 1877. His father, William Burns, was the first man to represent Wayne County in the State Legislature. Pattie E. Johnston became our subject's wife in 1861; she was born in 1843, daughter of John C. Johnston, and became the mother of the following interesting family. Sarah A., Mattie V., Elizabeth J., Mary L., Anna L., Edna (who died in 1876), Lillie J., Carrie K., Lela K. (who died in 1883), Florence B., Willie, Myrtle R., and two infants deceased. At the age of twenty-three our subject began doing for himself on the farm where he now lives, which was given him by his father. It consists of 500 acres, 300 acres of which are in a good state of cultivation. He raises corn, small grain and cotton, and has recently paid considerable attention to stock raising. In 1867 he, in partnership with J. A. Clendennin, opened a mercantile house in the village of Ashland;

but at the end of ten years our subject sold out and engaged in the same business on his farm, continuing about five years. His mercantile life did not prove successful, although he is a man of good business qualifications. He joined the Confederate Army in 1862 and served until 1863, when he was discharged on account of disability. After remaining at home about one year he re-entered the service, remaining about six months, when he again became disabled and did not again enlist. He is a member of the Methodist Episcopal Church South, and is a Democrat. His wife belongs to the Cumberland Presbyterian Church.

Polk D. Burns was born in 1844, in Tennessee. His father, Samuel L. Burns, was a farmer and stock raiser, and lived the greater part of his life in Wayne County, Tenn. He married Sarah A. Baker, and both were born in 1814. They married in 1830, and became the parents of thirteen children, seven of whom are yet living. The father died June 20, 1880, and his widow February 24, 1874. Our subject was married in 1871 to Sallie Kelley, who was born in Tennessee in 1847, and is the daughter of Riley and Sallie Kelley. Mr. and Mrs. Burns became the parents of nine children: Lou E., Sam (died in 1881), Riley K., Thomas T., Bill B., Biffle F., Jennie P. and two infants (deceased) unnamed. Our subject's early days were spent on a farm, and at the age of twenty-six he began doing for himself. He opened a mercantile store in Flatwood in 1868, but at the end of one year sold out and resumed farming. In 1880 he purchased his present farm of 1,000 acres, on which he raises corn, grass and stock. He also owns a one-half interest in 300 acres of land near Ashland, in this county. He served in the Confederate Army in the late war, enlisting in 1862. He served until the close of the war, and surrendered at Jonesboro in May, 1865. He was not wounded nor taken prisoner during his entire service. He is a Mason, and a stanch Democrat in politics, and one of the worthy citizens of the county.

Nathan F. Burns, farmer and native of Wayne County, Tenn., was born August 1, 1856, son of Samuel L. and Sarah A. (Baker) Burns (see sketch of P. D. Burns). From birth he was raised to a farmer's life and now resides on and owns the old homestead. His is the best farm in the county, having been kept in good repair and well taken care of by the father, who was an industrious, enterprising and prosperous farmer. The farm contains 1,375 acres of land and lies on Buffalo River. The products are corn, small grain and stock, the latter receiving Mr. Burns' chief attention. He is a stanch Democrat, and November 7, 1875, he wedded Sallie A. Harbour, daughter of James G. and Esther J. (Lacefield) Harbour. Mrs. Burns was born in Tennessee August 20, 1854, and is the mother of three children: Nathan F., Jr., James S., Jr., and

Miles G. Mr. and Mrs. Burns are members of the Methodist Episcopal Church South, and he may truly be said to be one of the first and best citizens Wayne County can boast of.

Lytle Burns, a wealthy farmer residing in the Fourth District of Wayne County, was born where he now resides May 13, 1858, and is a son of John S. and Rebecca Burns, who were Tennesseans by birth. Lytle is the youngest of their family of eight children, and was reared on the farm and received a liberal education at Waynesboro and Clifton. He has been engaged in agricultural pursuits from boyhood, and has prospered beyond his expectations. Owing to energy and perseverance he is the owner of 1,066 acres of land, about 120 acres of which are well cultivated. In 1880 he was united in marriage to Ida Rankin, daughter of James C. M. and Bettie Rankin, of Wayne County, and their union has been blessed in the birth of four children—two sons and two daughters: James R., Essie M., Margaret E. and an infant son. The family are members of the Primitive Baptist Church, and in politics our subject is a Democrat in politics, and is of Scotch-Irish descent.

William E. Carroll was born in North Carolina in 1827, son of James R. and Mary P. (Hubbard) Carroll. The parents, who were natives of North Carolina, came to Tennessee about 1836, and settled in Marshall County. After residing in different counties they finally settled in Henderson County, where the father died in 1868, and the mother in 1883. After attaining his majority our subject began doing for himself. In 1849 he married Anna Scott, daughter of John M. and Anna Scott. She was born in Wayne County, Tenn., in 1828, and is the mother of eight children: Mary E., born April 2, 1850; William A., born January 25, 1852, and died August 2, 1871; James R., born December 2, 1853; Sarah J., born February 2, 1859; John M., born September 27, 1861; Thomas H., born February 4, 1864; Laura A., born May 14, 1870, and Albert N., born April 8, 1874. Since 1851 Mr. Carroll has lived in Wayne County, and has resided on his present farm of 275 acres since 1866. He purchased it from minor heirs and, owing to the neglect of the administrator to comply with the requirements of law, was compelled to pay for it the second time. He directs his attention to raising corn, small grain and stock, and has accumulated some property by his energy and good management. He and Mrs. Carroll are members of the Christian Church, and in politics he was a Democrat up to the Rebellion, but since that time has been a Republican.

Jackson M. Choat is a native of the State born in 1847, son of Simpson and Sarah Choat, who were also born in Tennessee. The father was a tiller of the soil, and a Democrat in politics. He was a prosperous and honorable citizen, and lived in Wayne County up to the time of his death, which occurred about 1858. His wife died in 1873. Jackson M. Choat resided with his parents until their respective deaths. He and his brother then purchased the home place in partnership. It contains about 700 acres of land, fairly improved, and lies on Buffalo River. He gives his attention to raising corn and peanuts. Mr. Choat is a good neighbor and a worthy citizen, a member of the Masonic fraternity, and a stanch Democrat in politics. In 1879 he married Virgie Hollabaugh, and by her is the father of one child—Isham J. Mrs. Choat is a daughter of Jacob and Rose A. Hollabaugh, and was born in Tennessee in 1863.

George T. Choat is a Wayne County Tennessean, and was born in 1845, son of Simpson and Sarah (Burns) Choat. [See sketch of Jackson M. Choat.] George T. resided with his widowed mother after his father's death, and in 1868 was united in marriage to Margaret E. Graves, daughter of John H. and Sallie Graves. Mrs. Choat was born in Tennessee in 1847, and is the mother of seven children: Henrietta V., William S., Arthur T., Sallie L., May L., V. B. and P. B. In 1864 Mr. Choat enlisted in the Confederate service, serving until the close of the war. He surrendered at Charlotte, N. C., in May, 1865. In 1871 he located on the farm, and purchased it in 1881. It lies on Buffalo River and contains 260 acres of land, 180 acres of which are in a good state of cultivation. Mr. Choat has lived an honorable life, and is one of the worthy and influential citizens of the county. In politics he is a stanch Democrat. His grandfather, Arthur Choat, was a pioneer citizen of Wayne County, having located on Buffalo River when the country was covered with canebrake.

Judge John H. Cole, chairman of the Wayne County Court and native of the county, was born May 17, 1834, son of Bennett and Nancy (Kirwin) Cole, both of whom were born in North Carolina. The father married in his native State and came to Wayne County, Tenn., in 1825, and followed farming and stock raising until his death in 1857. John H.'s boyhood days were spent on his father's farm, and in acquiring such education as could be obtained in the old-fashioned schools of his day. In December, 1860, he married Nancy A. Linn, and engaged in agricultural pursuits. At the breaking out of hostilities between North and South, he suspended work for a time, and in December, 1863, enlisted as a private in Company C, Second Tennessee Federal Mounted Infantry, and served with his regiment in Middle Tennessee until Lee's surrender. He returned home and resumed farming, and that same year was elected clerk of the county court and served by re-election until 1878, with the exception of one term (1869–70). During 1879–80 he served the county in the capacity of superintendent of public schools. He farmed during that time and has continued the same up to the present. In 1881 he was elected magistrate of the Fourth District, and held that position by re-election until January, 1886, when he was elected to his present position of chairman of the county court. Judge Cole's married life has been blessed with twelve children, but four now living: Viola A. (Mrs. J. C. Taylor), Jasper E., Martha V. and Mary F. The Judge is an uncompromising Democrat in politics, although he was a Whig prior to the war. He is a Mason, Royal Arch degree, and a member of the K. of H. He is an adherent of the Christian Church, and is one of Wayne County's competent and just officials.

Thomas N. Copeland, merchant of Clifton, Tenn., and native of Wayne County, first saw the light of day June 29, 1853. He was reared on a farm with his parents, securing a fair education in the common branches. In March, 1881, he left the paternal roof and came to Clifton and engaged in the mercantile business, in which he has continued to the present time, meeting with the success his energy and honesty merited. He keeps a fine stock of general dry goods, besides hats, boots and shoes and gents' furnishing goods. He has a large and lucrative trade, and is one of the leading business men of Clifton. In 1874 he married Florence Ferguson, of Maury County, Tenn., who died November 27, 1885, leaving three children: Mildred Camilla, Osceolla and Lorenzo. Mr. Copeland is a stanch Republican in his political views, and is a member of the K. of H., and the Cumberland Presbyterian Church. His parents, Joseph M. and Sarah W. (Cypert) Copeland, are natives and residents of the county.

Nathaniel T. Cook, M. D., of Wayne County, was born in 1850, and is a son of John L. and Mary A. (Johnson) Cook, who were natives of this State, the father being a farmer by occupation. He served in the quartermaster's department of the Confederate Army, enlisting in 1863 and serving until the close of the war. He was a Democrat and died in Wayne County in 1876. Our subject assisted his parents until he attained his majority, when he began the battle of life for himself and engaged in the grocery and livery business in the town of Clifton. About eighteen months later there was a decline in stock and he at once closed out his business, and in partnership with his uncle, N. W. Johnson, purchased a two-thirds interest in the dry goods establishment of Dr. Selph, and shortly after purchased the Doctor's interest. In 1876 our subject sold out and retired to his father's farm, which he managed three years. He and his brother then erected a steam saw-mill on the latter's farm. He gave this up in 1883 and began practicing medicine, having spent a great deal of time studying that science, and became a partner with his brother, James T. Cook, M. D., of Flatwood, and they are doing a good work. He is a member of the I. O. O. F. and K. of H., and is a Democrat, having cast his first presidential vote for Horace Greeley. In 1870 he married Pinia R. Fuson, daughter of Bethel and Sophronia Fusan. They have four children: John B. (who died in infancy), Heber J., Edner E. and an infant not named.

William M. Cook, mayor of Clifton, and a prominent business man of the town, was born in Wayne County March 23, 1849, son of John L. and Mary Ann (Johnson) Cook, both of whom were natives of Wayne County. William M. was reared on a farm and secured a limited education in his boyhood days, and continued farming exclusively until twenty years of age. He then traded in stock until his marriage, at the age of twenty-two, with Almyra I. Montague. He then resumed farming and followed that and stock trading until 1882, when he engaged in steam saw-milling in the county, at which he has continued ever since. In December, 1884, he moved to Clifton, and the following March engaged in the general merchandise business with G. W. Thompson, continuing the same up to the present time. May 11, 1886, Mrs. Cook died, leaving six living children: Nancy L., Jacob L., Mary, Thomas, Jesse and Nellie. Mr. Cook is a Democrat in politics, and in August, 1885, was elected to the office of mayor of Clifton. He is a Mason and K. of H. and a member of the Cumberland Presbyterian Church, in which faith his wife died.

Capt. Peyton H. Craig, clerk and master of the chancery court at Waynesboro, Tenn., was born in Maury County, Tenn., August 28, 1836, son of William and Amanda (Copeland) Craig, both of whom were born in North Carolina. Johnson Craig, our subject's grandfather, came with his family to Tennessee in December, 1806, and located near Mount Pleasant, where he followed stock raising and farming, and reared a family of fifteen children, and lived to see them all married and with families of their own. He died in Lawrence County about 1845. The father was reared in Maury County and married in Williamson County. In 1853 he moved to Missouri, and died in Laclede County in 1869. The mother died in Maury County, Tenn., when Peyton H. was an infant two weeks old, leaving three other children. The father raised a family of five daughters by his second marriage. Our subject was reared on his great-uncle's (William Blackwood) farm, and secured a good academic education. He prepared himself for teaching, which occupation he began at the age of seventeen years. In July, 1862, he abandoned domestic pursuits and enlisted as a private in Company A, Ninth Tennessee Cavalry, Confederate States Army. In 1863 he organized a company and attached it to the Twentieth Tennessee Cavalry (Col. George H. Nixon), and served as its captain until near the close of the war. He was captured at Ashland by the Federals shortly before the surrender, but was soon paroled. He farmed in Wayne County, and also taught school during the fall and winter months, and in 1873 was appointed clerk and master under Chancellor Nixon, and has served continuously, by reappointment, to the present time. It may be said to his credit that he has discharged the duties of this most important office in a highly satisfactory and efficient manner. In 1859 he wedded Martha A. Mitchell, who died in October, 1871, leaving four children: Mary A. (Mrs. G. W. Jackson), Laura B. (wife of Dr. S. A. Smith), Sallie B. and Wilton. The Captain's second wife, Laura W. Ramsey, died in March, 1875, after less than two years of married life, leaving one child, now deceased. In 1882 he married his present wife, Miss J. Harvey, of Lawrenceburg, who has borne him one son—William Harvey. Capt. Craig is a Democrat, and takes an active interest in political affairs, not only in his county, but in the judicial circuit and State at large. He was, however, an old line Whig, as were his father and grandfather. He is a Mason of Royal Arch and Council degree, being Grand Marshal of the Grand Lodge of Tennessee. He is Secretary of the Grand Convocation of Past Masters of the State, and is High Priest of the local chapter, and Master of the lodge at Waynesboro. He is also a member of the K. of H., and he and wife are church members.

Jonathan Crews, a prominent citizen of Wayne County, Tenn., was born in North Carolina in 1825. His parents, William and Malisent (Hicks) Crews, were natives of the same State, and came to Tennessee about 1830. The father was a farmer, a member of the Hardshell Baptist Church, and a Whig in politics, and during the late war stood firm for the Union. His death occurred in 1871, and his wife's in 1877. Our subject made his parents' home his home until attaining his majority, when he was married to Frances Morrow, a daughter of Archibald and Martha (Parker) Morrow. Mrs. Crews was born in this State in 1827, and is the mother of nine children: Martha A., Malisent, William, Mary E., Nancy J. (deceased in 1886), Eletha C. (deceased in 1861), Sarah F., Archie F. (deceased in 1862) and Gustina. Mr. Crews was a resident of Lawrence County until 1864, when he came to Wayne County and resided on several different farms until 1881, when he purchased his present farm of 80 acres, on which he located and has lived to the present time. He and Mrs. Crews are members of the Hard-shell Baptist Church.

Armstead H. Cunningham, the leading merchant at Forty Eight, Tenn., was born in this State in 1850, and is the son of John R. and Grace

(Kimmens) Cunningham, of Tennessee birth. The father was a farmer by occupation, a member of the Free-Will Baptist Church, a Democrat in politics, and lived in Hickman County until his death, which occurred about 1874. Our subject's juvenile days were spent on a farm. He lived with his father until twenty-one years of age, when he began life for himself, teaching and clerking. In 1874 he purchased Samuel H. Williams' stock of goods at Centreville, Tenn., and did business in that place three years, one year being devoted to the hotel and livery business. He lost considerable property by fire, but, altogether, his career in that place was a success financially. For the next two years he was connected with the commission house of Mellen, Brown & Co., of Cincinnati, Ohio, and in 1876 was married to Laura E. Clagett, daughter of Horatio and Elizabeth (Montgomery) Clagett. Mrs. Cunningham was born in Tennessee, in 1855, and immediately after her marriage she and Mr. Cunningham took an extended tour East, visiting New York, Pittsburgh, the Centennial Exposition and Niagara Falls. After their return Mr. Cunningham engaged in the mercantile business in Forty Eight, where he has since been successfully engaged. He is also postmaster of the town, and he and wife are members of the Christian Church. They have four children: John H., Southern S., Walker M. and James R. A remarkable feature of the family is that from the fourth generation there has never been a female child born into the family. They are of English descent.

John R. Davis, Sr., is a Tennessean, born in 1823. His parents, Anderson and Annie Davis, were born in Virginia and North Carolina, respectively, and came to Tennessee with their parents when young. The father was a farmer and a pioneer citizen of the county, and departed this life in 1873. His wife died four years later. Our subject lived with his parents until twenty-one years of age, at which time he was united in marriage to Jemima Hill, daughter of Thomas and Elizabeth (Felkins) Hill. She was born in Tennessee in 1825, and is the mother of ten children: Annie C., Nancy E., Henry E., Mary J., John J. J., Joseph A., Catherine O., an infant (deceased, not named), Parlee (deceased), and Anderson (deceased). Since his marriage Mr. Davis has farmed in different portions of the county and in Missouri, being in the latter place about four years. In 1878 he purchased the farm, of 188 acres, on which he now lives. It lies about nine miles from the county seat, and is in a good state of cultivation. In 1883 he erected a water-power, saw and grist-mill on his farm, the same having proved quite successful. He has held the office of justice of the peace since 1868, and is a Democrat. He and Mrs. Davis are members of the Christian Church.

William C. Davis first saw the light of day in Maury County, Tenn., in 1838, and is a son of Henry and Elizabeth Davis, who were born in Tennessee. The father was a farmer, and died about 1850. His wife died about five years later. Our subject remained with his parents until their respective deaths, when he resided two years with an uncle, and emigrated to Missouri. After remaining there two years he returned to Tennessee, and has been engaged in farming ever since. In 1859 he was married to Annie M. Davis, a daughter of Anderson and Annie Davis. She was born in Wayne County in 1859, and is the mother of eight children: John A., Lowly I., Cecil K., George W., Salathiel C., William O., Charles H. and Mary A. In 1877 Mr. Davis moved to his present farm, which contains 225 acres, and lies on Beech Creek. Besides this he owns 400 acres of land adjoining this, that is fair land. Mr. Davis and wife are members of the Free-Will Baptist Church, and he is a stanch Democrat in politics.

William J. Dickerson, merchant of Waynesboro, Tenn., and a native of the county, was born August 6, 1861, son of James M. and Sarah A. (Arnett) Dickerson, who were born in Wayne County. The father was a successful stock trader and farmer, and resided in the Fifth District. He was a Republican in politics, and during the late war served in the Union Army as major of the Second Regiment of Tennessee Mounted Infantry, and was United States revenue assessor at Columbia, Tenn., for four years after the war. He died June 30, 1878. William J. was reared and educated in the county and followed farming, stock raising and sawmilling in the Fifth District until November, 1885, when he removed to Waynesboro, and engaged in the dry goods and general merchandise business in company with Huckaba Bros., and has remained with them to the present time, contributing largely to the success of this well known firm. April 3, 1884, he married Mary E. Hamm, of Wayne County. They have one child, Bessie C. Mr. Dickerson is a Republican.

Columbus F. Dixon, was born in Wayne County, Tenn., in 1828, and is a son of John and Elizabeth (Boyd) Dixon, who were born in North Carolina, and came to Tennessee with their parents when quite young. The father was a farmer and distiller, and was very prosperous, supporting a family of seventeen children. His wife died November 23, 1863, and he took for his second wife Mary Foster, who was the mother of five of the children. Mr. Dixon died in Wayne County July 16, 1877. When twenty-four years old our subject married Sarah A. Springer, who was born in Tennessee, in 1836, and a daughter of Jonas and Annie Springer, and twelve children have blessed their union: Jonas S., John, Elizabeth A. (deceased), Mary J., Andrew J. (deceased), James M. (deceased),

Robert M. (deceased), William F., Amanda P., Martha R. and Ella (deceased). Mr. Dixon owns 369 acres of land, on which he has lived thirty-seven years; 150 acres are well improved and well tilled, besides this, he owns two other tracts of land consisting of 118 and 454 acres, respectively. He has filled the office of constable, and is a man who has lived an exemplary life. He and wife are members of the Methodist Episcopal Church, and he is a stanch Republican, and sided with the Union cause during the late war.

Thomas S. Evins, M. D., a prominent physician of Wayne County, was born in Tennessee in 1846, and is the son of William A. and Eliza (Bobo) Evins, who were also Tennesseans. The father was a merchant and farmer, a Democrat and a member of the Missionary Baptist Church. He died January 15, 1856, followed by his widow, in 1870. Thomas S. was united in marriage to Minerva J. Gullick in 1875. She is a daughter of Jonathan A. and Frances C. (Baker) Gullick. Her father is a prosperous farmer, and belongs to the Democratic party. He and wife are members of the Cumberland Presbyterian Church. Mrs. Evins was born in 1846, and is the mother of two children: Frank, born March 3, 1876, died March 3, 1878, and Thomas J., born September 22, 1877. October 8, 1877, Mrs. Evins died. Our subject was educated in the best schools of Bedford County, and lived with his parents until their respective deaths, when he began reading medicine under Dr. H. P. Ferguson, and remained with him about one year. He obtained two courses of lectures in 1870–71 in the Louisville Medical College, after which he located at Wayne Furnace, and after practicing there until 1874 he entered Vanderbilt University, of Nashville, and attended the course of 1874–75, graduating in the latter year. From that time until his marriage he practiced in Waynesboro. Since that time he has resided on his father-in-law's farm. He is a Chapter Mason and has always been a stanch Democrat in politics.

Isaac H. Gobbel is one of eleven children and was born in Wayne County, Tenn., in 1833, son of John and Ruhama Gobbel, who were born in North Carolina, and came to Tennessee about 1820. They lived in different counties in Tennessee until 1853, when they located on a farm in Wayne County, and died in 1871 and 1866, respectively. They were church members and the father was a Democrat. After working for his father until twenty years of age, Isaac H., our subject, engaged in tilling the soil on his own responsibility. In 1852 he married Eliza Murphy, who was born in balmy Alabama, in 1837, daughter of George Murphy. Of the eleven children born to Mr. and Mrs. Gobbel all are living, except John W., the eldest, who died in 1882. The rest are William R., Sarah C., Nancy C., Isaac H., Mary, Rebecca, Paraletha, Martha J., Joseph E. and

Benjamin P. In 1862 Mr. Gobbel joined the Federal Army and served until Lee's surrender. He was captured in 1863, while at home on a visit, but after being in captivity one month, made his escape and returned to the army. In 1873 he purchased the farm on which he now lives, consisting of 198 acres of fairly improved land. He is a stanch Republican, and he and his wife are members of the Methodist Episcopal Church South. Mr. Gobbel has lived in this vicinity all his life, and is a good neighbor and an honest and prosperous citizen.

John Grimes is a Williamson County Tennessean, born in 1811, son of William and Sallie (Little) Grimes. The father was born in South Carolina, and came to Tennessee when quite young, locating in Nashville. He was a farmer and one of the Rangers who, during the war of 1812, assisted in keeping the Indians within their boundary, and for his services drew a land warrant. He was a Whig, and a member of the church from early manhood. His wife died in 1817, and he then married Martha (Akins) Roah. She died in 1841, and the father in 1855. At the early age of sixteen our subject began doing for himself. He did farm work for several years, and made his first purchase of land on Hardin Creek. After living on this, and another farm which he had purchased, he removed to Arkansas; but returned after a short time. In 1860 he purchased the farm on which he now resides, containing 800 acres, 100 acres being in a fine state of cultivation. He has served the people as magistrate almost continuously since 1836, making a good and efficient officer. He is a Republican, and was a strong Union man during the late Rebellion, furnishing three sons for the Federal Army. In 1836 he married Elizabeth M. Stubblefield, daughter of Peter and Sallie (Harris) Stubblefield. Mrs. Grimes was born in Georgia in 1817, and is the mother of thirteen children: William P., who died in 1838; Sarah A. E., who died in 1859; James G.; Robert N., who died in 1863; John M.; Martha E.; Mary J.; Amanda C.; Millard F.; Henry C., who died in 1882; Benjamin F.; Eliza F., and an infant deceased, not named. Mr. Grimes is a member of the Missionary Baptist Church, and his wife of the Methodist Church. The Grimes family is of Irish descent.

Harold A. Grimes, of the firm of Hughes & Grimes, is a Wayne County Tennessean, born October 16, 1853, son of Elihu S. and Nancy Malissa (Keaton) Grimes, who were born in this county. Wilson Grimes, our subject's grandfather, was one of the very earliest settlers of the county. Harold A. was reared on a farm in this county. His father dying in 1855, he was obliged to begin earning his own living early in life. In 1870 he began mercantile life as a salesman, but soon relinquished this occupation to complete his education. He attended and taught school until 1873, and the following year went to Texas and clerked in a mercantile establishment in Dennison three years, and the same year returned home and married Emma L. McDougal, of Savannah, Tenn., who died four months after their marriage. In 1879 Mr. Grimes removed to Clifton and followed clerking until 1882, when he accepted a position as traveling salesman for a wholesale dry goods house in Nashville, remaining such about six months. He then accepted a similar position with a boot and shoe firm, of that city, at which he continued until January, 1885, when he engaged in his present business, as above stated, and has contributed largely to the success of this well known firm. March 20, 1884, he married his present wife, Annie O. Chappell. They have one child, Bettie Elsie. Mr. Grimes is a Democrat, and he and wife are members of the K. & L. of H. He is president of the Clifton Temperance Alliance, and a member of the Cumberland Presbyterian Church.

Robert A. Haggard, attorney at law of Waynesboro, Tenn., is a native of Wayne County and a son of James Haggard, Esq., whose sketch appears in this work. Robert A. was educated in the common schools and was reared on a farm. At the age of twenty-one he became a disciple of Blackstone, with the view of making law a profession, and entered the law department of the State University of Iowa in 1880, and graduated in June, 1881, with the degree of LL. B. He returned home and began practicing in October, 1881, and has continued to the present time, with good success. November 29, 1883, he married Annie C. Norman, a native of Lawrence County. They have one child named Nona. Mr. Haggard is a Republican in his political views, and is candidate on that ticket for county court clerk, subject to the August (1886) election. He is among the successful and enterprising young lawyers of the county, and bids fair to rank among the first in his profession in the State.

Egbert T. Hartwell, of the firm of Hartwell Bros., of Delphos, Ohio, and Clifton, Tenn., manufacturers of handles, neck-yokes, singletrees, etc., was born in Denmark, of the Empire State, January 26, 1846, and is the son of Morris and Louisa (Taylor) Hartwell, who were born in New York and Ohio, respectively. Egbert T. was reared on a farm and received a liberal education in the common schools of New York. After attaining his majority he began life for himself, and after visiting various parts of the West, located at Delphos, Ohio, in 1872, and engaged in his present business there, remaining until 1881, when he came to Clifton, Tenn., and started his present business, which is a branch factory of the one in Delphos, Ohio. Mr. Hartwell was married, October 4, 1882, to Laura A. Taylor, a daughter of William H. and Melissa

Taylor, of Chardon, Ohio. Mr. and Mrs. Hartwell have one son, Charles E., born October 7, 1883. They are members of high standing in the church, and our subject is a member of the F. & A. M. fraternity and is a Democrat in his political views, and of English descent.

Amos T. Hassell is a son of Enoch and Joanna (Ensley) Hassell, and was born in Tyrell County, N. C., August 15, 1814. His parents were also natives of North Carolina. His father came to Tennessee in 1834, locating in Perry County (now Decatur County), where he followed farming, being a justice of the peace until his death, which occurred about the beginning of the war. He had been quite a distinguished politician in former years, and represented Tyrrell County in the North Carolina Legislature. Amos T. Hassell came to Tennessee with his father and at the age of twenty-one left home to do for himself, having little or no education. Later he acquired a good business education by his own exertions, and soon after leaving the paternal roof he began life as a clerk and soon engaged in the mercantile business for himself at Carrollville. In 1844 he came to Waynesboro and continued the same business until 1860, when he sold out and repaired to his farm in the Fourth District until 1871, when he returned to town and built his present large and commodious hotel and business house, and conducted both in his usual successful manner. In August, 1885, he retired from the management of the hotel, but still conducts his mercantile establishment. Mr. Hassell was engaged quite extensively in the mule trade, both before and after the war, and also managed a tannery, saddlery and shoe manufactory. He has in all probability contributed more to the business industries and prosperity of Wayne County than any other one citizen. April 30, 1846, he married Mary Ann Biffel, a sister of Col. Jacob Biffel. She died in 1860 leaving three children: Ella Ann (wife of Dr. Buchanan), Mary C. (Mrs. J. W. Montague), and Joanna (Mrs. John F. Montague). August 22, 1861, he married Mrs. Eliza Jane (Heron) Jones. They have one daughter, Laura E., the wife of Frank Boyd. Mr. Hassell is and always has been an unswerving Democrat in politics, and cast his first presidential vote for Van Buren. He served six years as clerk and master under Chancellor Stephen Provat before and up to the war, and also under Judge R. H. Rose after the war. He is a Mason, Royal Arch and Council degrees, and is one of the leading and enterprising business men of Wayne County.

Henry A. Helton, clerk of the circuit and criminal courts at Waynesboro, Tenn., was born in Wayne County on the 11th of January, 1846, son of Daniel and Elizabeth (Morgan) Helton, natives, respectively, of North and South Carolina. Jesse Helton, our subject's grandfather, came to Tennessee with his family about 1819 or 1820 and located on the head waters of Indian Creek, in Wayne County. He was a hatter by trade, also a mill-wright, and gave the most of his attention to the latter occupation. He was one of the successful men of his day, and died in Hardin County about the beginning of the late war. Our subject's father spent the greater part of his life in Wayne County and is now residing a short distance south of Waynesboro. Henry A. received a common school education in his boyhood days, and in December, 1862, enlisted in the Federal Army in Company F, Sixth Regiment Tennessee Cavalry, serving until the close of the war. In 1867 he engaged in the liquor business in Waynesboro, but at the end of two years converted the business into a family grocery and general merchandise store, which he conducted until 1872. Since that time he has been almost constantly engaged in the mercantile and drug business, being a member of the firm of Turman, Helton & Co. Mr. Helton was a Republican from the time of the war up to the Kuklux troubles in this section, in 1870, and postmaster here three years under Grant's administration. He was elected register of the county in 1869, serving until 1873. May 18, 1876, he was appointed by Judge T. P. Bateman to the office of clerk of the circuit and criminal courts to fill a vacancy, and the following August was elected to the office, and has filled it very efficiently, by re-election, up to the present time. January 21, 1869, he married Samantha C. Christie, and four children have blessed their union: Lemuel L., Walter A., Charles J. and Serepta. Mr. Helton is a Royal Arch Mason and a member of the K. of H. He is a member of the Cumberland Presbyterian Church, and his wife of the Methodist Episcopal Church.

Jacob Hollabaugh, a pioneer citizen of Wayne County, Tenn., was born in 1822, son of George and Catherine Hollabaugh, who were born in North Carolina, and came to Tennessee about 1818, locating in Perry County, where the father resided until his death in 1824. The mother died in 1856. Jacob resided with his widowed mother until after his marriage, which occurred in 1842, to Rosanna Harvey, daughter of James and Rachel Harvey. She was born in Tennessee in 1824, and became the mother of the following family: Mary J., James C., Rachel A., Elizabeth C., George T., John T., Frederick W., Buchanan B., Madison J., Isham G. Harris, Midda V., Joseph B., Luther W. and Jacob S. Elizabeth C., John T. and Joseph B. are dead. Our subject resided on the home farm until 1864, when he sold out and purchased the farm on which he is now residing, consisting of 314 acres, well improved. He has a fine variety of various fruits, and gives considerable attention to bee culture. He has always been industrious, and accordingly has prospered.

He and wife joined the Methodist Episcopal Church South in 1842. Mr. Hollabaugh is a Mason, and has always been a stanch Democrat in politics, and cast his first presidential vote for James K. Polk.

James P. Hollis is a son of William and Sarah (Moore) Hollis, who were born in Tennessee in 1802 and 1809 respectively. The father was a farmer and located in Wayne County in 1804. His wife, who bore him four children, died in 1834, and he then wedded Sarah Kilburn, who was born in 1814, and who became the mother of five children. She died in 1854, and his third wife, Jane Yaw, bore him five children. He lived in Wayne County until his death in 1875. His father, James Hollis, was born in 1759, and married his second wife, Sarah Choete, in 1794, she being born in 1772. He was a soldier in the Revolutionary war, and was a prosperous farmer of Wayne County. He died in 1844. Our subject, James P., lived with his father until 1853, when he married Sarah R. Dixon, daughter of John and Elizabeth (Boyd) Dixon. She was born in 1835, and is the mother of fourteen children: John D., Sarah E. (who died in 1856), William P. (who died in 1859), Mary J., Aaron M., Martha F., Nancy P., Joseph B., Columbus F., James M., Ada R., Fountain J., Arthur T., and one infant deceased, not named. Mr. Hollis has a good farm of 170 acres, on which he raises principally corn. He has held the office of deputy sheriff, constable, and in 1870 was elected justice of the peace, and yet holds the office. He is a Mason and Republican, and he and Mrs. Hollis are members of the Baptist Church.

James A. Holt's birth occurred in Tennessee in 1852, and he is a son of Israel and Mary J. (Davis) Holt, who were also Tennesseans. The father was a farmer, and served in the Confederate Army during the late war. He died in Wayne County in 1866. James A. Holt's early days were spent on his father's farm, and after the latter's death he made his home with his widowed mother until his marriage, in 1876, when he began life for himself as a farmer. In 1875 he began merchandising on Beech Creek, and has been quite successful. His store is superior to those generally kept in the country, and is liberally patronized by the surrounding neighborhood. The farm on which he lives was inherited by his wife from her father's estate, and consists of about 250 acres. In 1882 he was elected justice of the peace, and has faithfully discharged the duties of this office up to the present time. In 1882 he erected a cotton-gin on his farm, and has kept it in good working order. He is a Democrat, and his first presidential vote was cast for S. J. Tilden. He is a member of the Methodist Episcopal Church South, and was married, in 1876, to Louisa J. Tumbo, daughter of Hugh and Mary Tumbo. Mrs. Holt was born in Tennessee in 1860, and is the mother of three children: Hugh I., Dora Lee, and an infant deceased, not named.

Thomas J. Huckaba, clerk of the Wayne County (Tenn.) court, and native of the county, was born March 15, 1851, and is one of seven surviving members of a family of thirteen children, born to the marriage of George E. Huckaba and Rhoda Y. Rainey. Thomas J. secured a common school education, which he much improved, however, in later years, by much desultory study and reading, and constant contact with business and official life. At the age of twenty years he began life for himself, and worked at manual labor as a wood chopper until his twenty-fourth year, when he began farming on rented ground, and in 1878 he and his brother purchased a tract of land in the Fifth District. They improved this somewhat, and from time to time purchased other lands, until our subject soon owned a one-half interest in 400 acres of land. In August of this year he was elected to the office of county court clerk, which he has filled continuously, by re-election, to the present time. During this time Mr. Huckaba has retained an interest in farming. In November, 1883, he, in company with his brothers, William F. and John F., and a friend, Louis A. Hardin, established a general merchandise store in Waynesboro, which is now successfully conducted under the firm name of Huckaba Bros. & Co. They began business with a very limited capital, but by industry, strict business integrity and close attention to business, have succeeded in establishing a good and paying business. He and his brothers, mentioned above, and William J. Dickerson now compose the firm. December 25, 1881, he married Mildred S. Hamm, of Wayne County. To them were born two children: Robert (deceased) and Clarence H. Mr. Huckaba has always been a stanch Republican, and he and wife are consistent members of the Missionary Baptist Church. John F. Huckaba, member of the above-mentioned firm, was born in Bedford County, Tenn., April 25, 1845. He was reared on a farm in Wayne County, and secured a limited early education. In 1863 he enlisted in the Federal Army, serving as private in Company H, Second Tennessee Mounted Infantry. He had his left hand seriously and permanently wounded before the company was mustered in, and was rejected on this account, and served, in all, but a few months. Until October, 1883, he farmed, then engaged with his brothers in his present business, and has contributed largely to its success. December 8, 1867, he married Mary Ann Morrison, and five children are the result of their union: Fannie E., James A., George M., Mary E. and Emerson. Mr. Huckaba and wife are members of the Missionary Baptist Church, and he is a Republican in his political views.

Hughes & Grimes, merchants, of Clifton, Tenn., began business in 1885. The business was established by T. R. Hughes in 1854, and was conducted by him, in connection with his brothers and various partners, until his death, November 21, 1883. From that time up to 1885 the firm was known as T. S. Hughes & Co., and at that date became known as Hughes & Grimes. They keep a fine stock of fancy and staple dry goods, clothing, notions, boots and shoes, hats, gents' furnishing goods, groceries, hardware, queensware, tinware, furniture, agricultural implements, seeds, etc., and control a very large trade in town and county. Thomas S. Hughes, of the above named firm, was born in Wayne County August 30, 1862, and is a son of Frank and Elizabeth B. (Tinnon) Hughes, who were born in Virginia and Tennessee, respectively. The father came to Tennessee in 1855, and was engaged in mercantile business until his death, February 10, 1872. The mother died March 15, 1878. Thomas S. was brought up in the mercantile business with his uncle, T. R. Hughes, after his father's death. He secured a good literary education, attending the University of Tennessee at Knoxville. In March, 1883, he engaged in his present business and has shared the success of this well known firm. He is proprietor of the warehouse at Clifton, and does a large commission business, receiving and forwarding all the goods handled on the river. He is a Democrat, a member of the K. of H. and K. & L. of H., and belongs to the Cumberland Presbyterian Church. January 8, 1885, he married Bettie Speer, of Hardin County.

William Hurt, the leading merchant of Flat Woods, Tenn., was born in Carroll County, Tenn., in 1841, son of Robert M. and Emily (Dickson) Hurt, who were born in Virginia and Tennessee, respectively. The father became a resident of Tennessee at the age of nine years, and was a farmer and merchant by occupation. He is a member of the Missionary Baptist Church, and a Democrat. After his wife's death, in 1856, he married Martha E. Woods, widow of W. H. Woods. Both reside in Carroll County. At the age of twenty our subject enlisted in the Confederate Army, and was captured at Missionary Ridge and taken to Rock Island, Ill., where he was retained until the close of the war. He fought in all the principal battles up to the time of his capture, receiving only a slight wound at Murfreesboro. After his return home he began merchandising with two partners at Trezevant, Carroll Co., Tenn., but the firm dissolved at the end of six years. Mr. Hurt was elected county trustee by the county court, to fill an unexpired term. He spent two years in Obion County farming, and for several years afterward was engaged in different pursuits. In 1882 he and George W. Harris, of Louisville, Ky., opened a general merchandise store at Flat Wood, and are now doing a thriving business. He is a Mason, a member of the Missionary Baptist Church and a Democrat, and was married, in 1865, to Mary E.

Woods, daughter of William and Martha E. Woods. She was born in 1843, and became the mother of one child, Robert. Mrs. Hurt died in 1868, and in 1884 Mr. Hurt married Ada Whittaker, daughter of John C. and Susan Whittaker. She was born in 1866, and is the mother of one child, Roe.

John Jackson is a son of John and Polly (Walker) Jackson, and was born in Tennessee in 1821. He assisted in tilling his father's farm until twenty-four years of age, when he married, in 1845, Susan T. Skillern, and began doing for himself. Mrs. Jackson was born in Tennessee in 1822, daughter of Anderson and Polly (Spring) Skillern, and is the mother of eight children: David S., John A., Mary E., William J., Sarah C., George W., and two infants, deceased. Mr. Jackson has lived in his present neighborhood all his life, and is an honorable and prosperous citizen. His farm consists of about 420 acres of land in a good state of cultivation, the principal products being corn, small grain, clover and stock. Mr. Jackson has served as county trustee one term, and as constable and justice of the peace many years. His wife is a member of the Methodist Episcopal Church South, and he is a Mason and Democrat. His father and mother were natives of North Carolina and Tennessee, respectively. The former was a farmer and was with Jackson in the Creek war, and was a Whig in politics. His wife died in 1822, and he took for his second wife Polly Adams. He moved to Wayne County in 1822, and here died in 1855. His second wife died in 1866.

David S. Jackson is a Wayne County Tennessean, born in 1847, son of John and Susan (Skillern) Jackson, both of whom were natives of Tennessee. John Jackson was a tiller of the soil, and for two terms served as county trustee, holding minor offices in the county also. He was a successful stock trader, and has always been a stanch Democrat. He and Mrs. Jackson are members of the Methodist Episcopal Church South. David S. resided with his parents until twenty-five years of age, when he married and began carving out his own fortune on the farm of 152 acres where he now lives, the principal productions of which are corn, grass and stock. In September, 1864, he enlisted in the Ninth Tennessee Cavalry, Confederate States Army, under Col. Biffle, and served until Hood's raid into Tennessee, when he was captured, while on a visit home, and retained at Nashville about fifteen days. He took the oath of allegiance and was allowed to return home. He participated in all the battles fought during Hood's raid, the principal one being at Franklin. He belongs to the Democratic party, and is a member of the Masonic fraternity. Mahala R. Merriman, daughter of Eli and Rachel Merriman, became his wife December 24, 1875. She was born in 1848.

Squire Allen P. Luna is a Marshall County Tennessean, born on the 13th of August, 1842, son of Robert and Martha Luna, natives of Tennessee. Allen P. was educated in the common schools of Marshall County, and in early life followed the free and independent life of a farmer's boy. March 11, 1866, he united his fortunes with those of Nancy J. Cummins, daughter of George W. and Sarah Cummins, of Tennessee. Our subject moved to Lawrence County and settled at his present place of residence in 1876. He has since devoted the greater part of his attention to the grocery and general merchandise business. He is also postmaster at Chisem postoffice, and in 1882 was elected squire in the Sixth District of Lawrence County, and has filled that position very efficiently to the present time. Mr. and Mrs. Luna became the parents of the following interesting family of children: Sallie M., Henry D., Hattie V., Cora D., Nora B., Mary P., Delbert R. and Almino. Our subject is a Democrat in his political views, and is of French-Irish descent.

Richard C. Martin, a prominent farmer and merchant of Wayne County, Tenn., is a native of North Carolina, born March 22, 1830, son of James and Nancy (Cantrell) Martin, both of whom were born in North Carolina. The father came to Tennessee in 1831, and followed farming for a livelihood, and prospered in his undertakings. He died in 1843, and his wife in 1840. Our subject resided with his parents until their respective deaths, and he and his brothers and sisters continued to till the home farm. In 1855 he came to Wayne County and sold goods at Flat Wood, on Buffalo River, and remained there until 1869. He then purchased his present farm on Indian Creek, and farmed and raised stock for about five years, at which time he rented his farm and moved to Waynesboro and became a partner in the dry goods, grocery and hardware firm of Bromley & Martin. Since 1881 he has managed his farm of 360 acres with good success. His marriage with Mary A. Burns was consummated in 1860. Of their three children, two are living: Mary E. (Mrs. C. H. Boyd) and Ora M. Mrs. Martin died in January, 1880. Mr. Martin is a Democrat and is classed among Wayne County's most enterprising and successful farmers.

James E. M. McAnally is a son of Elisha R. McAnally, who was born in North Carolina, and who was a gunsmith and farmer by occupation. He married Feriba Bowdon, of Georgia, and they together reared a family of twelve children, and accumulated some property. He and Mrs. McAnally were members of the Christian Church, and he was a Whig in politics, and sided with the Union during the late Rebellion. His wife died in 1865, and he in 1873. Our subject's birth occurred in Wayne County in 1830. He began farming for himself at the age of twenty-five years, and after living in different localities in the county, finally, in 1870, purchased his present farm of 160 acres. Besides this, he owns about 500 acres in different localities in the county, and devotes the most of his land to the production of corn, small grain and peanuts. In 1855 he united his fortunes with those of Fannie Robnett, daughter of John and Nancy (Staggs) Robnett. She was born in 1834 and is the mother of eight children: Tolbert F., Houston, Ellender, Louisa, Esther, Margaret, Timothy R., and an infant deceased, not named. Mr. McAnally and his wife are members of the Christian Church, and he has always been a firm Republican in politics.

LeRoy McGee was born in 1825, in Wayne County, Tenn., son of Micager and Betsey McGee. The father was a farmer and blacksmith, and although he began life poor in purse, he accumulated considerable property. The mother died about 1840, and the father then married Margaret Wisdom. He died about 1854. Our subject began doing for himself at the age of eighteen, and at the age of twenty married Martha Clayton, born in 1826, daughter of Hardy and Fannie Clayton, and by her is the father of eight children: Frances E., Mary J., William C., Susan (who died in 1885), Margaret S. (who died in 1883), James H., Rachel A. E. and Leroy S. Since his marriage Mr. McGee has resided on the farm given him by his father. It contains 848 acres of land, 200 acres being the original gift. The rest of the land he has accumulated by his own exertions. His farm is well supplied with water and is very productive, being on Factory Creek. During the late Rebellion Mr. McGee sided with the Union cause, and has since been a loyal, honorable and prosperous citizen. His children have all married except the youngest son, who still remains at home.

Elihu D. McGlamery, register of Wayne County, Tenn., was born in this county January 14, 1838, son of John and Catherine (Brinker) McGlamery, who were born in Georgia and Virginia, respectively. The father came to Tennessee when a young man, about 1816, and lived for a short time in Lincoln County, then moved to Madison County, Ala., and in 1819 came to Wayne County, Tenn., where he raised a family of four sons and six daughters, and followed farming here until his death, in December, 1857. Our subject's school days were somewhat limited. He early learned the carpenter's trade and in October, 1863, enlisted in the Federal Army, serving in Company B, Second Regiment Tennessee Volunteer Mounted Infantry, first as private. He was promoted to first lieutenant, serving in this capacity until he was mustered out after one year's service. He resumed carpentering and also farmed in the Twelfth District until 1870, when he removed to Waynesboro, and in 1874–76 served as deputy sheriff. In August, 1868, he was elected sheriff of the county, and filled this office very efficiently and satisfactorily two terms, when he was elected to his present office, filling this position in an equally satisfactory manner. He has recently been engaged in contracting and building in Waynesboro. October 29, 1857, he married Nancy D. Turman, of Bedford County. Mr. McGlamery is a stanch Republican in politics, and is a member of the K. of H.

James H. McLemore's birth occurred in Halifax County, N. C., in 1826, and he came to Tennessee in 1844, with his mother and step-father. His own father, Joel H. McLemore, was a tailor by trade, and followed that occupation for many years. He died on a farm to which he had retired in 1835. His widow, Betsey (Pullen) McLemore, then married John Whitaker, and after coming to Tennessee died in 1858. Our subject was married February 1, 1849, to Sallie A. Whitaker, daughter of James C. and Delphia (Lyon) Whitaker. She was born in North Carolina in 1828, and came to Tennessee with her parents in 1844, and is the mother of ten children: Virginia W., Richard M., James W. (who died September 13, 1858), Mary E. (who died June 11, 1886), Delphia D., Anna, Sallie H., Robert L. (who died October 14, 1867), John Pullen and Nora. Our subject lived with his father in North Carolina until the latter's death. He acquired a good education, and after his mother's second marriage continued to reside with her until 1849, when he began life for himself. He purchased his present farm in 1847 and has ever since been a tiller of the soil. His farm consists of 412 acres of well improved and exceptionally fertile land in a good state of cultivation. He and wife are church members, and he is a Mason and a stanch Democrat.

Thomas Meredith was born on the 9th of July, 1804, son of Frederick and Mary (Fulton) Meredith, who were born in North Carolina and Virginia, respectively, and came to Tennessee in 1800. They were married the same year and became the parents of eight children, two of whom are yet living. The father was a farmer and located first in East Tennessee, and afterward lived in this State and Kentucky until 1816, when he located in Wayne County, on Buffalo River, and there died in 1826. His wife died in 1863. Up to 1824 our subject resided with his father. At that date he married Mary A. Rasbury, daughter of Lovick and Jane Rasbury. She was born in Georgia in 1805, and came to Tennessee when quite young. She became the mother of three daughters and seven sons. Three of the children are dead. Mrs. Meredith died May 20, 1872, and on the 20th of May, 1877, Mr. Meredith married Mary A. Benham, who was born in Tennessee in 1829, the daughter of William and Elizabeth Benham. Mr. Meredith has been a life-long farmer, and in his young days was very active and powerful, being always ready to assist his neighbors in log rolling, etc. He built a portion of the house, in which he now lives, about fifty years ago, hewed the logs and used the old whipsaw in making joist and other necessary articles. He purchased his present home-farm of 120 acres in 1837, and continued to purchase land from time to time until his real estate amounted to 2,000 acres. During the war he lost, in slaves and security debts, nearly all the property he had accumulated. He has been magistrate of the county for over half a century and has been trustee two terms. He also served as deputy sheriff for six successive years. He has been a life-long Democrat, and furnished five sons for the Confederate Army. He has been a member of the Hardshell Baptist Church for over fifty years. His son, Lovick R. Meredith, was born in Wayne County, in 1827. He remained with his parents until twenty-seven years of age, when he married Anna B. E. Matthews, who was born in Tennessee in 1832, daughter of William Matthews, and immediately began life for himself, working at the following callings: merchandising, stock trading, milling and farming, the latter occupying the principal part of his attention. He is a Democrat, and has served as constable of his district. He enlisted in the Confederate Army in 1862, and served until the final surrender, participating in many of the principal battles. In 1857 he located on his present farm of 1,000 acres, having, besides this, 500 acres in different tracts. He is a Mason, an honorable and well known citizen, and a Prohibitionist. His children are Mary E., Leonidas T., Ledru R., William W., Lenora E., Deborah O. and Belle M.

James F. Meredith is also a son of Thomas Meredith, and was born in Wayne County in 1832. His early days were spent on his father's farm, and at the age of twenty years he married Mary A. Grimes, who was born in Tennessee in 1836, daughter of Henry and Mary A. (Stockard) Grimes. To James and Mrs. Meredith were born the following family: Lydia A. M. F. (who died in 1868), Jane E. B., Alice E., James F. T., Ula A., Annie E. (who died in 1868) and Joseph L. In November, 1885, Mrs. Meredith died. In 1856 Mr. Meredith purchased and located on his present farm of 900 acres on Buffalo River. Besides this he owns 1,600 acres partially improved, on the north side of that river. At the beginning of the late war he enlisted in the Confederate service, but did not take an active part until 1862, when he enlisted in Biffle's regiment, but owing to sickness could serve only a few months. He then returned home, and has since farmed, being very successful in that calling. He has always been a stanch Democrat in politics.

James H. Merriman is a native of Wayne County, born in 1834, son of Eli and Rachel (Tankersley) Merriman. The father was born in Tennessee, and was a farmer by occupation and a Whig in politics. He came to Wayne County in 1816, and lived until his death in 1851. The mother is yet residing in the district, and is seventy-six years of age. After the father's death our subject resided with his mother until thirty-four years of age, when he began farming for himself. In 1861 he enlisted in the Confederate service, and served throughout the war, not receiving a wound during his entire service. He returned home in May, 1865. In 1869 he purchased his present farm, consisting of 320 acres. He is a Democrat in his political views, and belongs to the Masonic fraternity, Lodge No. 127. In 1868 he married Frances E. A. Shields, daughter of J. T. and Martha D. (Old) Shields. She was born in Tennessee in 1850, and became the mother of eleven children: Martha E., James R., Joseph E. (who died in 1881), Thomas F., John C., Rachel C., David H., Virginia A., Walter N., Cynthia R. and Clare B. Mr. Shields is a member of the Christian Church, and his wife of the Cumberland Presbyterian Church.

John F. Montague, one of Wayne County's prominent farmers and stock raisers, was born in that county July 13, 1851. He was educated in the Clifton Masonic Academy, in Wayne County, and when about eighteen years of age he and his brother, William Y., began keeping drugs in Clifton. In 1871 he sold out that business and commenced the study of law, and graduated from the Cumberland University in 1873. He then located at Waynesboro, and practiced his profession with much success until 1883, when he abandoned his legal practice and moved on his present farm of 600 acres. About 150 acres of the land are in a fine state of cultivation. Besides this property he is the owner of a fine tract of bottom land on the Tennessee River, in Hardin County. He has given considerable attention to stock raising since locating on his farm, and, owing to his industrous habits and good business qualifications, has acquired a fine patrimony. He belongs to the Democratic party and F. & A. M. fraternity. To his marriage with Joanna Hassell, in 1875, the following children were born: Amos H., Mary Anna E., Edna C., Frank and Joanna. Mr. Montague is of French descent.

James L. Morgan is a son of Pleasant and Jane Morgan, who were born in North Carolina and Alabama respectively. The father is a farmer, and also follows blacksmithing. He is a member of the Missionary Baptist Church, and in politics he is a Republican, and stood firm for the Union during the late war. Our subject was born in Wayne County, Tenn., in 1841, and remained with his father until 1862, when he enlisted in Company A, Tenth Tennessee Regiment of the Federal Army, and remained in the field until the close of the war. He returned home in July, 1865, and remained with his father until he was married to Mrs. Mary (Miller) Girard, daughter of Micager and Mary· Miller. Mrs. Morgan was born in Alabama in 1839, and by her first marriage is the mother of two children: Charles T. and Lula B. She and Mr. Morgan are the parents of three children: Viola B., Lillie H. and Dieudonie R. Mr. Morgan's farm, which he purchased in 1867, consists of 140 acres of fairly improved land. The principal products are corn, grass, peanuts and small grain. Mr. Morgan located on this farm in 1872. He was constable of his district a short time, is a Republican in politics, and cast his first presidential vote for U. S. Grant. He is a member of the Missionary Baptist Church.

Hon. Jonathan Morris, a prominent citizen of this county, was born in Logan County, of the Blue-grass State, in 1815, son of William and Rebecca (Grimes) Morris, who were born in Tennessee and moved to Kentucky about 1814, remaining only a few years, when they returned to Tennessee. The father was a farmer, and served in the war of 1812, participating in the battle of New Orleans. He was a Whig, and died about 1850. His widow was a member of the Methodist Episcopal Church South, and died a few years later than her husband. Our subject resided on the old homestead until he attained his twenty-first birthday, when he began fighting the battle of life for himself, and in a few years was elected deputy sheriff of the county and held the office three years. He also held the office of county court clerk for four years, and in 1843 was elected to the State Legislature. Since the war he has served as State senator two years and has filled the office of county judge one term. He was elected to the office of county superintendent of public instruction and filled that position very creditably for two years. Mr. Morris has devoted the greater part of his life to public duties, but of late years (since 1857) has retired to his farm of 1,200 acres (which he has owned for several years), lying between Green River and Chalk Creek. Adjoining this farm he has about 3,000 acres of fertile and well watered land, making as fine a stock farm as there is in Tennessee. He has several different farms in different localities in the county, which he is desirous of selling. Besides this large amount of real estate, he owns several grist and saw-mills. Since the war he has lost about $20,000 worth of property by fire. Mr. Morris was married, in 1844, to Nancy J. Montague, daughter of Abraham and Clarissa Montague. She was born in Wayne County July 5, 1823, and is the mother of the following children: Martha R., born January 5, 1847, died November 3, 1863; Wayne, born August 24, 1852; James E. H., born August 31, 1855, died

March 26, 1881; Clarissa F., born September 20, 1859, died March 25, 1886; Thomas F., born February 10, 1861, died October 6, 1884, and an infant, deceased. March 7, 1883, Mrs. Morris died. She was a Methodist in belief. Mr. Morris has been a member of the Methodist Episcopal Church South since 1840. He is a Mason, member of Lodge No. 127, and is a stanch Democrat in politics. He has been a very successful financier, and is one of the worthy and honest citizens of the county.

Hon. Merida Morrison is a Tennessean, born in 1827, son of Edward and Lucy Morrison. The father was a wagon-maker by trade, but owned and lived on a farm. He was in the war of 1812, and after his death his second wife drew a pension. The mother died in 1847 and the father married Elizabeth Butler, and died in 1866. His second wife died in 1885. Our subject assisted his father in the shop and on the farm until his marriage, and since that time has devoted the most of his attention to farming. He purchased his present farm of 385 acres of land, and devotes it principally to the raising of stock. He served the people many years as justice of the peace, and in 1869 was elected to the State Legislature and served one term. In 1845 Mr. Morrison married Miss Lydia Hardin. She was born in Alabama in 1828, and came with her parents to Tennessee when quite young. She is the mother of the following children: Margaret A., William D., Mary A., Martha A., Sofina E., Nancy J., John F., Merida (who died in 1868), Joseph C., and an infant deceased. Mr. Morrison and his wife are members of the Missionary Baptist Church.

William D. Morrisson was born in Tennessee in 1850, son of Merida and Lydia (Hardin) Morrison, whose sketch appears in the work. Our subject's early days were spent on a farm. He made his home with his parents until twenty-three years of age, when he, in partnership with his brother-in-law, purchased the farm on which he now resides. Two years later he became sole possessor. This farm lies on both sides of Green River and contains 286 acres of fairly improved land. Mr. Morrisson is a Democrat and Prohibitionist, and in 1882 was elected justice of the peace and yet holds the office. In 1875 he was married to Lizzie Burns, daughter of Samuel L. and Sallie Burns. She was born in Tennessee in 1853, and is the mother of four children: William S., Sallie, Kate and Mildred. Mr. Morrisson joined the Baptist Church at the age of seventeen. His wife is a member of the Methodist Episcopal Church South.

John J. Nichols, merchant of Clifton, Tenn., is a Perry County Tennessean, born July 2, 1855; son of John J. and Martha J. (Buckner) Nichols. Our subject's Grandfather Nichols came from North Carolina to Tennessee at an early day, and located in Hardin County. His son,

John J., was born in North Carolina, but spent the greater part of his life in Perry County, following mercantile pursuits and the stave business, until his death, when our subject was but two years old. The mother died in 1868, thus leaving our subject to do for himself at an early age. He secured a fair education, and when about eighteen years of age, engaged in the mercantile business as clerk. In 1879 he came to Clifton and clerked until 1882, when he engaged in the family grocery business. In May, 1884, he removed to his present quarters, and added dry goods and general merchandise to his stock, and now carries a full and select line of goods. Besides this he handles a line of agricultural implements and wagons, being agent for the Harrison wagon. He is a Democrat, and is considered a reliable business man of the town. In 1876 he married Rutha J. Harbour, of Hardin County. They have one child, Edna Belle.

James A. Nutt is a native of Wayne County, Tenn., born in 1842, son of Maben A. and Rebecca (Montgomery) Nutt. Maben A. was a farmer and shoe-maker and a minister of the gospel of the Old Baptist persuasion. He raised a family of ten children, and in 1869 came to Wayne County, where he accumulated some property and died October 4, 1873. The mother died in 1884. After the father's death, James lived with and near his mother until her death. He inherited a portion of the old home place, and is the owner of 350 acres of well cultivated land. In 1872 he and Sarah Davasier were united in marriage. She is a daughter of Green and Malinda Davasier, and was born in Tennessee about 1854. David A., Pleasant G., Anna Lee, Maggie, William and an infant daughter (deceased) are the children born to their union. In 1862 Mr. Nutt enlisted in the Confederate service, Capt. Whiteside's company, and remained in service until Hood's raid in Tennessee, when he was wounded at Nashville and taken to the hospital, where he remained a short time. He was at Atlanta, Jackson, Missionary Ridge and many other battles, and was always at the post of duty. He is a stanch Democrat in politics.

Andrew C. Rasbury, a pioneer of Wayne County, Tenn., was born in 1816, son of Lovick and Jane (Campbell) Rasbury, who were North Carolinians. They came to Tennessee in 1814, and settled on the farm where our subject now lives, in 1816. The father died in 1858 and his widow in 1875, being ninety-eight years of age. Our subject has lived on the home farm since one year old. It consists of 525 acres of fairly improved land, 135 acres being in a high state of cultivation. In 1843 he married Jane Voorhies, daughter of David and Elizabeth Voorhies. Mrs. Rasbury was born in Tennessee in 1820, and is the mother of the following eight children: John C. (an infant, deceased, not named),

Mary A., Elizabeth J., Alonzo M., Eudoxia R., Surilda A. and Lovick D. Three of the children are dead. Mr. Rasbury served in the Confederate Army four months, and lost considerable property during that conflict. He served as constable for a short time, and also as deputy sheriff. He is an enterprising citizen and a good and prosperous farmer. He belongs to the Democratic party.

Lott G. Rasbury was born in Tennessee in 1811, and is a son of Lovick Rasbury. [See sketch of A. C. Rasbury.] He has followed the free and independent life of a farmer from boyhood, and was married at the age of twenty-three and began doing for himself, but continued to reside on his father's farm. He wedded Elizabeth Phillips, daughter of Samuel and Sarah Phillips. Mrs. Rasbury was born in 1813 and died in 1835, leaving one child—Sarah J. After his wife's demise our subject returned to his father's house, and made that his home until 1843, when he married Rebecca, daughter of John and Elizabeth (Grimes) Renham. Mrs. Rasbury was born in this State in 1812, and is the mother of seven children: Elizabeth (who died in 1875), Lydia C., Mary, Martha A., William L., Rebecca E. and John A. (who died in infancy). Mr. Rasbury has confined himself to farming and stock raising from early boyhood, and has prospered well in his undertakings, owning in all about 790 acres of land. He has served the people as magistrate of his district for fourteen years, and has made a good and efficient officer. He took up arms during the Rebellion in behalf of the Confederacy, but was only in actual service about three weeks, when he supplied a substitute and returned home. He is a Democrat and a member of the Primitive Baptist Church.

W. T. Ricketts was born in Wayne County, Tenn., in 1841, son of Samuel S. and Mary (Roper) Ricketts, who were born in North Carolina and Tennessee, respectively. The father became a wealthy merchant of Clifton, and was a member of the Cumberland Presbyterian Church. He was a Whig, and died in 1863. His wife died twelve years earlier. The father's second wife was Mary J. Walker. Our subject was married, in 1866, to Nancy L. Montague, daughter of John and Nancy Montague. She was born in Tennessee in 1846, and is the mother of eight children: Della M., John S., Milton (who died October 15, 1873), Frank, Joseph, Mary, Tennessee R. and Nancy. Mrs. Ricketts died July 21, 1882, and November 13, of that year, he married Melissa Montague, sister of his first wife. She was born about 1842, and is the mother of one child, James T. At the age of ten years our subject moved to Clifton with his father, where he remained until 1879, when he purchased and moved on his present farm of 275 acres of land on Buffalo River. He gives his principal attention to raising corn and peanuts, and is extensively known in the county. He is a member of the Cumberland Presbyterian Church, and in May, 1861, enlisted in the Confederate Army, in the First Tennessee Regiment, but was discharged on account of disability. He re-enlisted in the Ninth Tennessee Regiment, and was captured in Wayne County in July, 1863, and was retained until the close of the war. He has been magistrate of the Clifton District for several years, also postmaster of Flat Wood. He is a Democrat.

John Robnett, a pioneer of Wayne County, Tenn., was born in the Palmetto State in 1804, and is a son of John and Margaret (Nesbitt) Robnett, natives of Delaware and South Carolina, respectively. They came to Tennessee in 1816, and were the second family that located in Wayne County. The father farmed until his death, which occurred about 1824. His wife died in 1819. The father took for his second wife a lady by the name of Farris, who died in 1831. John Robnett, our subject, resided with his step-mother two years after his father's death, when he moved on his present farm of 1300 acres. In 1828 he married Nancy Staggs, daughter of Joseph and Fannie (Nesbitt) Staggs, and their union has been blessed in the birth of ten children: Joseph N., John, Cynthia P., Fannie, James, Margaret, Jane, Jeremiah, Neal S. and Ellender. Mr. Robnett is now eighty-two years old, but bids fair to live many years yet. He vividly remembers many incidents of pioneer life, and the hardships, with which the early settlers were obliged to contend, in the settlement of the county. In politics he is a stanch Republican, and furnished two sons for the Union Army. His wife is a member of the Christian Church.

James T. Shields is a native of Maury County, Tenn., born in 1825, son of William B. and Mary D. (Ramsey) Shields, born in Georgia and North Carolina, respectively. The father was a farmer, a member of the Cumberland Presbyterian Church, and a Democrat. He came to Wayne County in 1851, and here died in 1872. His wife died in 1860. Our subject was married, in 1847, to Martha D. Old, a daughter of Henry S. and Eglantine (Stone) Old. She was born in Tennessee in 1830, and is the mother of three children: Mary E. (deceased), Francis E. A. and Virginia I. Mrs. Shields died in May, 1884. Our subject remained at home and assisted his father on the farm until twenty years of age. After his marriage he located in the northern portion of Giles County, where he remained three years, and then moved to Wayne County. In 1863 he located on the farm of 500 acres where he now lives. He became a member of the Cumberland Presbyterian Church in 1865, and is a Mason of Lodge No. 127. He is a stanch Democrat in politics.

Charles W. Shipman, sheriff, and native of Wayne County, Tenn., was born on the 17th of March, 1838. He was educated in the common schools of his native county, and in 1863 enlisted in the Federal Army, in the Second Tennessee Regiment of Mounted Infantry, as a private, but was soon commissioned first lieutenant, and was afterward made captain of Company D in the same regiment. After the final surrender he returned to Hardin County, and was elected sheriff of that county in 1866, and held the office two terms. In 1870 he moved to his farm on Indian Creek, where he followed agricultural pursuits antil 1875. He then located at his present place of residence, where he owns 200 acres of land, 100 acres being well cultivated. Mr. Shipman started in life with no other capital than that bestowed upon him by nature, but has surmounted many hardships and difficulties, and is now well-to-do in worldly goods. In 1880 he was elected trustee of Wayne County, and held the office until 1884, when he was elected county sheriff, and yet holds the office. He is a stanch Republican in his political views, and belongs to the K. of H. and F. & A. M. fraternities. Jane E. Arrendell became his wife January 17, 1867, and the following family of children were born to them: William H., Henry T., Eddie, Jesse T., Ida E., Ola M., Charles and Pantha U. Mrs. Shipman's parents were Erastus and Mary Arrendell, and our subject's parents were Edward and Elizabeth (Thompson) Shipman.

Matthew J. Sims is a son of Robert and Frances (Merritt) Sims, and was born in North Carolina June 9, 1816. [See sketch of A. M. Sims for parents' history.] After attaining his majority he began doing for himself. His early education was such as could be obtained in the rude and primitive log schoolhouses of his boyhood days. He followed farming and school-teaching for ten or twelve years, and in 1840 purchased a large farm on Indian Creek, where he farmed and raised stock until 1865. After the close of the war he established his general merchandise store at Waynesboro, and has continued with good success up to the present time. In 1865 he was appointed clerk of the Wayne County Circuit Court, and held that office ten years. In 1837 he united his fortune with that of Dorothy Greeson, of Bedford County, Tenn., and their union has been blessed in the birth of ten children, eight of whom are living: Shields, Elizabeth (Mrs. J. McWilliams), Z. Taylor, H. C., Winfield S., Dorothy A. (Mrs. John Turman), Mahulda C. and Malinda T. Mr. Sims is a stanch Republican, and was clerk of the circuit court a number years, and also held the office of magistrate, and is one of the old and strictly honorable citizens of the county.

Shields Sims was born in Wayne County, Tenn., December 18, 1838, son of Matthew J. and Dorothy (Greeson) Sims, natives of North Carolina and Tennessee, respectively. The father was one of the early settlers of Giles County and a farmer by occupation. Since the war he has been engaged in the mercantile and tannery business in connection with farming. He is seventy years old and his wife is sixty-nine years of age. Shields Sims was reared on a farm and secured a good common education. At the age of twenty-one he began doing for himself, and in 1863 enlisted in Company H, Second Tennessee Mounted Infantry, Union Army, and served as first sergeant. After his return home, in 1865, he resumed farming, and soon established a tan-yard, which he managed four years, and then purchased his present farm of 290 acres on Falls Branch of Indian Creek. Besides this he owns 300 acres and has an interest in 1,60 acres near his home. He has farmed and raised stock on his present farm since 1870 and has met with good success. In 1859 he married Edith M. C. Youngblood, daughter of Josiah Youngblood, who was born in Rutherford County September 29, 1818, and a son of William and Edith (Reed) Youngblood. William was among the early settlers of Rutherford County. He was a farmer and died in 1844; his wife died in 1875. Josiah has farmed for himself since 1837, and the same year he wedded Mary Horton, who died in 1879, leaving two living children, Edith M. C. and M. Elizabeth. Mr. Youngblood is a Republican, and a member of the Primitive Baptist Church. Mr. and Mrs. Sims became the parents of eight children, seven of whom are living: Jeannette J. (Mrs. W. T. Nowlings), Mary M. (Mrs. James Nowland), Dorothy J., Matthew J., Sarah E., John S. and Francis. Mr. Sims is a Republican, was magistrate of his district six years, and is now one of the board of school commissioners. He and family are members of the Baptist Church, and he has been a Mason since 1868 and joined the Union League in 1866.

Henry Clay Sims, trustee of Wayne County, Tenn., was born on the 15th of November, 1844, son of Matthew J. Sims, of Waynesboro. Henry C. secured the ordinary common schooling in his boyhood days, and in 1863 enlisted in Company H, Second Tennessee Federal Mounted Infantry, serving as a private in the late war until its close. He was conscripted by the Confederates in 1862 and taken to Libby prison, but managed to make his escape and joined the Union Army. Since the close of the war, up to the present time, he has farmed in Wayne County, and has been fairly successful. He is a stanch Republican in his political views, and as such was elected to the county trustee's office in August, 1884, and has discharged the duties of his office to the universal satisfaction of all. He was re-elected to the office in August, 1886. August 5,

1865, the nuptials of his marriage with Jemima C. Copeland, of Wayne County, were celebrated. They have three children: Mahulda Isaphene, Dorothy W. and Mabel. Mr. Sims is a member of the Masonic fraternity, and he and Mrs. Sims are worthy members and workers in the Methodist Episcopal Church.

Abraham M. Sims was born in Wayne County, Tenn., June 13, 1834, son of Robert and Frances (Merritt) Sims, who were born in North Carolina. The father was one of the early settlers of Giles County, Tenn., coming to that county about 1819. He helped to clear and settle the country and was a successful farmer. He moved to Wayne County in 1834, and died in March, 1842. The mother died in 1871. Our subject made his home with his parents until he was seventeen years of age, and after his father's death conducted the home-farm for his mother and sisters. In 1863 he enlisted in the Tenth Tennessee Infantry, and served as high private until September, when he was mustered out on account of bad health. He resumed farming, and in 1868 purchased his present place of 150 acres and is doing well financially. Mr. Sims has earned his property by the sweat of his brow, and now enjoys his home. In 1875 he married Hannah Stockberry, a native of Anderson County, Tenn. They have had four children born to them, three of whom are living: Joseph, Robert M. and Mary O. Mr. Sims belongs to the Republican party and has been magistrate of his district for eight years. Himself and family are members of the Missionary Baptist Church, and he has been a member of the Masonic fraternity eighteen years and was a member of the Union League a short time after the war. Mr. Sims is one of Wayne County's successful farmers and stock raisers, and is recognized as a moral and upright citizen.

Samuel A. Smith, M. D., of Waynesboro, Tenn., and a native of the county, was born on the 3d of September, 1857, son of John and Catherine (Kemper) Smith, who were born in Virginia. The father, who was born in 1814, came to Wayne County when he was a young man, and setled on a farm on Buffalo River, in the Third District, where he married and reared a family of five sons and one daughter. He died March 12, 1871. Samuel A. was reared on his father's farm and secured a limited early education. He began the study of medicine in 1881, and attended the medical department of Vanderbilt University during the sessions of 1882 and 1883, graduating in the latter year. He began practicing in the Sixth District of Wayne County, in June, 1883, but removed to Waynesboro in June, 1886, where he has since been successfully engaged in the practice of his profession. December 25, 1884, he married Laura B., daughter of Capt. P. H. Craig, and by her is the father of one child named Jessie. Dr. Smith is a Democrat and one of the leading practitioners of Wayne County.

John Stockard (deceased) was born in Wayne County, Tenn., in 1819, and was a farmer by occupation, and quite an extensive dealer in stock. He was magistrate of the Sixth District for many years, and discharged the duties of that office honorably and creditably. He was a member of the Cumberland Presbyterian Church, and a stanch Democrat in politics, and furnished four sons to the Confederacy. His first wife was Eliza Craig, who bore him nine children: William N., James L., John M., Mary J., Augustus Z. (deceased), Samuel H. (deceased), Thomas A., Leroy V. and Isom C. His wife died in 1860, and in 1863 he led to the hymeneal altar Mary E. Priest, daughter of Abram and Nancy Priest. Mrs. Stockard was born in Tennessee September 24, 1838, and is the mother of seven children: Cora A., Charles F., Lena, Eula, Bettie D., Edgar and Mosella, who died February 24, 1878. In 1880 Mr. Stockard purchased the farm of several hundred acres of fairly improved land on which his widow now lives. He died in November, 1883, and Mrs. Stockard has since successfully managed and controlled the home place. She is a member of the Methodist Episcopal Church South.

Willis S. Stone is a Tennessean, born in 1840, son of Samuel E. Stone, who was born in Virginia and came to Tennessee when a young man; he followed the mercantile business, first in Wilson County, and afterward in Jackson County, where he resided until his death, in 1854. He was sober, industrious, and very popular among his friends. His widow married Daniel W. Hawes, and both reside in Gainsboro, Jackson Co., Tenn. Willis S. was reared in Gainsboro, and there resided until 1858, when he came to Flatwood and began clerking in the mercantile house of James Matthews, remaining with him until 1861, when he enlisted in the Eighth Tennessee Infantry under Col. Alfred S. Fulton. He was captured at Missionary Ridge and taken to Johnson's Island, and there retained until the close of the war. He was at Perryville, Murfreesboro, and many other battles of note. In April, 1866, he married Ruth T. Pillow, daughter of Alvin G. and Mary (Holt) Pillow. Mrs. Stone was born in Tennessee in 1842, and is the mother of six children: Samuel H., Mary P., Joel A., Ruth, Bransford and John P. In December, 1865, Mr. Stone opened a mercantile store at Flat Wood, and did a successful business for about ten years. In 1883 he purchased his farm of 200 acres, with 90 acres adjoining. He is a Mason, and was elected county trustee. His many years of public life have made him very popular and well known. He is a stanch Democrat in politics.

Christopher C. Stribling, a prominent business man of Clifton, Tenn., and a native of Lawrence County, was born November 24, 1844, son of Andrew H. and Sarah E. (Elton) Stribling, natives of the Palmetto and Keystone States, respectively. The father was born in 1816, and came to Tennessee with his father, John Stribling, in 1834. John, who was an own cousin of Commodore Cornelius K. Stribling, surveyed Lawrence County, and in 1851 removed to Wayne County, where he died in 1882, being the oldest citizen of the county and the oldest Mason in the United States. Andrew H. Stribling married and raised his family in Lawrence County. He was twice married, his second wife being Rachel Clayton. Three children were born to each marriage. At the close of the war he removed to Wayne County, where he farmed, and died in 1884. Christopher C. resided with his parents on a farm and secured a fair English education. At the age of seventeen he enlisted in the Federal Army and served first with Company F, Twelfth Regiment Iowa Volunteer Infantry. He, with his regiment, was captured at Shiloh, and after a two months' imprisonment, was exchanged and discharged in August, 1862. He re-enlisted soon after in Company A, Second Tennessee Mounted Infantry, and served as second lieutenant of his company a part of two years. In 1864 he joined Company E, Eighth Tennessee Mounted Infantry, having helped raise the company, and served as regimental and post quartermaster until the close of the war. He located in Wayne County, and acted as deputy sheriff two years, under Maj. Dickerson. He was elected county court clerk, and after serving part of a four years' term, resigned, on account of the ill health of his family, and later engaged in the drug and mercantile business, continuing at Waynesboro until 1875. In 1874 he established the Wayne *Citizen*, which he conducted successfully until the latter part of 1875, when he moved to Clifton and successfully conducted the same until 1885. In January, 1886, he began keeping drugs and general merchandise, in partnership with T. S. Hassell, and has since continued. He is and always has been a stanch Republican in politics. He is a Mason, Royal Arch degree, and a member of the K. of H. and K. & L. of H. In 1866 Mr. Stribling married Emma I. Cypert, who died in 1875. In 1877 he married his present wife, Amelia A. Waites. They have three children: Thomas H., Monetta L. and Pattie S. Just after the war Mr. Stribling, in company with Col. Owen Hane, was engaged in prosecuting claims against the United States, being under the celebrated John O'Neal, who afterward became famous as commander of the Irish-American Fenians.

Carns M. Tinnon a well-to-do citizen of Clifton, Tenn., was born in Giles County, Tenn., November 15, 1828, son of John and Jane (Davidson) Tinnon, who were born, respectively, in Illinois and the Palmetto State. Our subject's juvenile days were spent in Giles and Lawrence Counties, the family removing to Lawrence County when Carns M. was but twelve years of age. Early in life he began learning the blacksmith's trade and followed that occupation in connection with farming, in Lawrence County, until October, 1871, when he came to Waynesboro and engaged exclusively in blacksmithing, in which he has been very successful. He is a Democrat in political views, but was formerly an old line Whig, and is considered one of the eminent and successful business men of Wayne County.

William Turman was born in Bedford County, Tenn., November 16, 1839, son of John C. and Mary A. (Parker) Turman, natives, respectively, of Georgia and Tennessee. John C. Turman came with his father to Tennessee in 1807, when he was but five years old. They located in Bedford County, and here he was reared, married and raised his family. He came to Wayne County in the fall of 1855, locating on a farm, but later came to Waynesboro, where he died May 4, 1881. He was a Democrat before, and a Republican after the war, being elected to the office of county trustee, but would not serve. He was a consistent member of the Baptist Church, as was his wife, who died June 11, 1857. William was reared a farmer's boy and was educated in the common schools. In 1863 he enlisted in the Federal Army as a private, in the Second Tennessee Mounted Infantry, but was never mustered in on account of physical disability, but served with the regiment one year. In the fall of 1867 he came to Waynesboro and engaged in the mercantile and liquor business, in which he has remained continuously to the present time. He has given farming considerable attention and owns 600 acres of good farming land. He is connected with the saw-milling interests of the county and has added largely to the wealth and prosperity of the county. His residence in Waynesboro is the finest in the county. In 1872, he married Ione Cypert, and four children have blessed their union: Camilla, William B., Sarah and Benjamin D. Mr. Turman is a Republican in politics and a prominent business man of the county.

John Turman, a member of the well-known firm of Turman, Helton & Co., of Waynesboro, Tenn., was born in Bedford County, October 18, 1848, son of John C. and Mary A. (Parker) Turman. [See sketch of William Turman.] His early life was spent on a farm and in acquiring a common school education. In 1869 he began merchandising at Martin's Mills, and remained there a year and a half. He then came to Waynesboro and engaged in a similar business here, carrying on the same up to the present time. He has been more than ordinarily successful, financially, and is one of the reliable business men of the county. He is a Republican and has taken quite an active part in the political affairs of the county. December 12, 1877, he married Dorothy A. Sims, of Wayne County; They have four children: John, Lizzie, James and Benjamin.

Ambrose M. Turnbow was born in the State of Tennessee, in 1853, son of S. H. and Martha Turnbow, who were also natives of the State. The father was an agriculturist, and held different offices in the county for many years. He died in 1875, and his widow in 1878. Ambrose M. assisted his father on the farm, and at the age of twenty-one became the architect of his own fortunes and engaged in farming. In 1874 he was united in marriage to Mary Carroll, who was born in Tennessee, in 1856, and is the mother of five children: William, James W., John, Delia, and an infant not named. In 1880 Mr. Turnbow purchased his present farm, which contains about 500 acres of fairly improved land, on which he raises corn, cotton and stock. He inherited the sum of $300 from his father's estate. He started in life a poor boy, but by energy, honesty and perseverance has accumulated considerable property, and is justly styled a leading citizen. He is a stanch Republican in politics.

Andrew Williams, a pioneer of Wayne County and a native of the State of Tennessee, was born in 1826. His father, William Williams, was a farmer and distiller, utilizing the products of his farm. His wife died in Wayne County, in 1863, and he in 1844. Up to the age of eighteen, Andrew Williams resided on his father's farm. After his marriage to Violet A. King, July 4, 1844, he began doing for himself. His wife was born in Tennessee about 1816, and was a daughter of Joseph and Catherine King. She died in 1870, and in 1873 he married Mrs. Jane E. (Meredith) Bell, widow of William R. Bell, who was born in North Carolina and came to Tennessee when a young man. He was a tanner by trade and followed this successfully until 1850, when he purchased the farm of 800 acres on which Mr. and Mrs. Williams now live. He was always quite successful in his business ventures, and departed this life in 1865, leaving four children: Thomas A., Joseph R., Lovick R. Bell, and an infant deceased, not named. Mrs. Williams was born in Tennessee in 1825, a daughter of Thomas and Mary A. (Rasbury) Meredith. After Mr. Williams' first marriage he lived on his father's farm until 1875, when he located on his present farm. He has retired from active life and gives his attention to deer and fox hunting. He has been an energetic and prosperous man through life, and is a stanch Democrat in politics.

J. & M. Youngblood are merchants of Clifton, Tenn., and established their business in September, 1885. They carry a large stock of staple and fancy dry goods, hats, boots and shoes, groceries and general merchandise. Matthew Youngblood, manager of the business, was born in Wayne County, Tenn., May 6, 1856, son of John William and Margaret (Sims) Youngblood, who were born in Wayne County also. The father was a successful farmer and merchant, and in 1874 removed to Missouri, where he died December 6, 1874. Our subject was reared in his native county and secured a fair education. At the age of twenty-five he began clerking in Waynesboro, and after one year's service there came to Clifton, and was salesman until 1883. He then engaged in the mercantile business in Linden, Perry Co., Tenn., continuing until they established their present business in Clifton. His twin brother Joseph, who is one of the firm, has been a successful traveling salesman for a Louisville grocery firm since 1881. He is a Republican, and has contributed largely to the success of the firm.

PERRY COUNTY.

San Martin Barnett, farmer, blacksmith and manufacturer, was born in Benton County, Tenn., June 1, 1839, the eldest of five children of Mansfield C. and Mary (Barnett) Barnett, and is of English and French descent. His parents were born in Humphreys County, Tenn., in 1812, and 1810, and died in 1863 and 1853, respectively. The father resided in Perry County the greater part of his life. Our subject resided on the farm and attended the common schools, and after this learned the blacksmith's trade, which he has followed, in connection with farming, up to the present time. He owns 104 acres of land and is comfortably situated in life. During the late war he enlisted in the Fifth Regiment Tennessee Infantry, Confederate States Army, and served under Col. W. E. Travis. He participated in the battles of Shiloh and Murfreesboro, where he acquitted himself as a gallant and trustworthy soldier. He was finally discharged (1863) after a service of over two years for disability. He belongs to the Masonic fraternity, and is a liberal thinker in religion, and an active Democrat in politics. He is unmarried.

Barnabas Beasley, one of Perry County's pioneer citizens, was born in North Carolina, on the 18th of May, 1812. His father, John P. Beasley, was born in the same State as himself and married Lucy Ellis, also of North Carolina. Out of their family of seven children, only four are living. They came to Tennessee in 1815, and located on Stone River, in

Rutherford County, where they resided two years, and then took up their abode in Williamson County. John P. died in 1848, and his wife in 1851. Our subject resided with his parents until their respective deaths, and in 1852 came to Perry County, locating at his present home. His farm consists of 675 acres on Coon Creek, and Mr. Beasley may be considered a prosperous and substantial citizen of the county. He has always been identified with the Democratic party, but has never aspired to office. He is unmarried.

Isaac N. Black, M. D., of Linden, Perry Co., Tenn., is a son of Isaac N. and Susan A. (Williamson) Black, who were born in Virginia, and were early settlers of Giles County, Tenn., where they were married. The father was a farmer, and died in 1844. The mother afterward married Joel B. Drake, and bore him four children. She died in Lawrence County in 1861. Our subject made his home with his paternal grandmother until the war, when he enlisted in the Third Tennessee Confederate Infantry, and served with this regiment until the close of the war. He was promoted to lieutenant in 1862, and participated in the battles of Fort Donelson, Chickasaw Bayou, Port Hudson, Raymond, Jackson, Chickamauga (where he was severely wounded), Resaca (wounded there also), Franklin and Bentonville, being slightly wounded at the last two battles. After his return from the army he entered the State Spring Academy, Giles County, and attended the sessions of 1867 and 1868 in the University of Nashville, and the summer of 1868 was spent at the State Medical College of Georgia. In 1868–69 he graduated at Nashville, and has since successfully practiced his profession at Linden, and has also carried on farming since 1875. May 5, 1870, he wedded Julia M. Brashear, of Perry County, and daughter of Thomas Brashear. They have two children: Lula L. and Alma M. Dr. Black is a member of the F. & A. M.

A. J. Blackwell, merchant, of Lobelville, Tenn., was born October 11, 1861, in Hickman County, Tenn. He was reared on his father's farm, and, after attaining his twenty-second birthday, farmed two years on his own responsibility, and in the spring of 1885 embarked in the mercantile business at Lobelville, Perry County, and still continues the same with good success. He carries a general stock of hardware, queensware and glassware, groceries, dry goods, etc., the stock amounting to about $1,500. Mr. Blackwell's education has been obtained principally in the common schools of the county. In the spring of 1885 he and his brother, W. J., came into possession of the home, on which his store building is located, on his share, a tract of fifty acres, which contains iron ore. His parents, Jackson and Mary (Rise) Blackwell, are still living. They were married in this State, and have lived the most of their lives in Hickman County, following farming.

Bailey P. Bone, brother of L. B. Bone (whose sketch appears in this work), was born in the county in which he resides, December 6, 1839. At the age of twenty-eight years he became the architect of his own fortunes, and chose the free and independent life of a farmer as his occupation through life. He took for his companion through life Fessona Crowell, who was born in Humphreys County. At the breaking out of hostilities between North and South, December 25, 1861, he enlisted in the Fifty-third Tennessee Infantry, and remained with this regiment until August, 1863, when he returned home. At the time of his marriage he located on the old homestead, now owned by his brother, Leander, and after one year's residence there moved to Humphreys County, locating near Duck River, where he remained two years, and then returned to Perry County, and has since resided on his present farm. He also owns a farm in Humphreys County, and a river bottom farm in Perry County. He and wife are members of the Christian Church, and are the parents of the following children: William Leander, Polly Ann, John (deceased) and Arthur Garfield.

William O. Britt, a prominent and successful farmer and merchant, of Perry County, Tenn., was born in Humphreys County, January 24, 1819, and is the eldest of eight children of Anderson S. and Mary (Wilkes) Britt, and of Welsh-English extraction. The father was born in Virginia, in 1789, and came to Tennessee at an early period, settling in Sumner County about 1808. He served in the war of 1812, and was in the battles of Horse Shoe, Talladega and the bombardment of Pensacola. He removed to Arkansas in 1846, and died in one year after his removal. His wife was born in Virginia, in 1799, and died in Perry County, Tenn., in January, 1862. The grandfather of our subject, Obed Britt, served with distinction in the Revolutionary war. He was at the Guilford Court House and Yorktown, and was wounded at Waxhaw by a sabre. For his valuable services and gallantry he was given a pension for life. At the age of twenty-one William O. began business as salesman with J. M. and C. Pettigrew, at Perryville, Tenn. August 7, 1844, he wedded Mary M. Britt (who was born in Tom's Creek, July 30, 1822, daughter of William S. Britt), and their union has resulted in the birth of the following children: James H., Julia A., John D., William A., Jennie, Thomas C., Edward H., Robert L., Mollie A. and George S. Only five of these children are living. Mrs. Britt died September 9, 1884, while visiting her daughter in Waverly, Tenn. Mr. Britt is a Democrat and a member of the Methodist Episcopal Church South. He owns 6,500 acres of land, 3,000 acres of which are Tennessee River bottom lands. He is at present erecting a new residence which promises to be commodious and substantial.

John W. Burns was born in Williamson County, Tenn., March 10, 1842, son of George and Nancy (Wilkey) Burns, who were Tennesseans and were married in Williamson County. They came to Perry County in 1859, and there the father tilled the soil until his death in 1878. At the breaking out of the war our subject enlisted in the Forty-second Tennessee Infantry, C. S. A., and served two years. He was at Fort Donelson, Jackson, and several battles of minor note. After returning home he assisted his father on the farm until 1867, when he was united in marriage to Toby Greer, a native of this county. In 1880 Mr. Burns purchased his present farm, on which they located and are at present residing. The farm, consisting of 400 acres of fertile land, lies between Beardstown and Lobelville. To Mr. and Mrs. Burns twelve children have been born, ten of whom are still living. Mr. Burns has always been identified with the Democratic party.

Andrew D. Craig is a son of Andrew Craig, who was born in East Tennessee in 1787, and is said to have been the first male white child born between the Holston River and the Cumberland Mountains. In 1835 he married Martha D. Hardeman, of Williamson County, and in 1843 they came to Perry County, and here the father died in 1862, followed by the mother's death in 1863. The father was a soldier in the war of 1812, and was a minister in the Baptist Church, and afterward in the Christian Church. Andrew D. Craig, our subject, was born December 15, 1838, and made the paternal roof his home until the breaking out of the war between North and South, when he enlisted in the Fifty-third Tennessee Confederate Infantry, and, after the fall of Fort Donelson, was transferred to the Tenth Tennessee Cavalry and remained in the service until Lee's surrender. December 22, 1859, he wedded America Greer, and of seven children born to them six are living. Mrs. Craig died October 17, 1874, and January 24, 1875, he married Adelia Carroll, who bore him six children, four now living. Mr. Craig served as county trustee six years from March, 1870, and as county sheriff four years from August, 1872. Farming is his chief occupation, and he and family are members of the Christian Church.

A. P. Craig, merchant and farmer of Perry County, Tenn., was born on the 2d of March, 1851. His father, G. B. Craig, was born in 1821, and moved to Hickman County, Tenn., when young, and then to Perry County. He has made farming his chief business through life, and is still living. The mother, formerly Miss Julia Caruthers, died in October, 1878. In 1874 our subject began merchandising at Cedar Creek Landing, and has continued the business at that place ever since. January 1, 1879, he married Molly C. McDonald, who was a native of Perry County, and their marriage has been blessed in the birth of three daughters: Julia V., Ruby M. and Bessie. In 1882 Mr. Craig came into possession of the farm where he now lives, consisting of over 700 acres, on the left bank of Buffalo River. Mr. Craig is a member of the F. & A. M., and Mrs. Craig is identified with the Christian Church.

Andrew C. Cude is the only living child of ten children born to Horner and Temperance (Lomax) Cude. The father was born in 1795, in Grainger County, and came to Middle Tennessee when ten years old. He first married Nancy Gordon, who bore him one child. She died, and he then married our subject's mother, who was a native of Georgia. He farmed in Hickman County until October, 1824, and then came to Perry County, locating on the farm now owned by our subject. He died in June, 1858, followed by his wife several years afterward. Up to the time of our subject's marriage with Martha Crudup, which took place in 1845, he resided with his parents. His wife died the same year they were married, and in 1847 he married Caroline Crudup, who died in March, 1863. Four of the five children born to them are still living. Mr. Cude took for this third wife Indiana King, in 1863. Nine children were born to their union, seven of whom are living. In 1853 he moved to the Lone Star State, where he resided until 1857, engaged in farming and stock raising. Since the latter date he has owned and resided on the fine farm of 500 acres said to be at one time the site of an Indian town. In 1864 he enlisted in the Ninth Tennessee Cavalry, and served until after the battle of Nashville, when he returned home, and has since followed the occupations of farming and stock raising. He and wife are members of the Methodist Episcopal Church South, and he belongs to the F. & A. M.

Mrs. Nancy J. Dickson is a native of Bedford County, Tenn., and was born on Duck River August 6, 1833. She is the second of five children born to the marriage of Leroy Blackburn and Elizabeth C. Cooper, and is of Irish extraction. Her father and mother were born in Bedford County, Tenn., April 22, 1812, and February 20, 1811, respectively. Mrs. Dickson, when about six years of age, moved with her parents to Hickman County, where she remained twelve years and then came to Perry County, where she has since resided.. The father moved to Arkansas when comparatively a young man, and remained four years. After his wife's death, April 30, 1857, he returned to Tennessee, and manages the plantation of his daughter, Mrs. Dickson, in a very successful manner. Mrs. Dickson was married in Perry County December 19,

1852, to Albert B. Dickson. To this union there have been no children born, but by adoption Mrs. Dickson has one son, Bethel Tipton Blackburn, born February 18, 1873. Our subject is a member of the Daughters degree of F. & A. M. and also of the Methodist Episcopal Church South. She owns 365 acres of good land, on which she raises the cereals and grasses to some extent, but devotes the most of her land to the production of peanuts. Abundant evidences have been found on her farm of iron ore and also coal, the latter having been satisfactorily tested. Mrs. Dickson's father is an old line Democrat, and a member of the Primitive Baptist Church.

James M. Dodson, proprietor of the Dodson House, at Linden, Perry Co., Tenn., was born in Hickman County in 1835, and is a son of Marshall and Emily (Brown) Dodson, who were born in the Old Dominion, and were brought to Tennessee by their respective parents when quite young. They were married in Williamson County, and soon after moved to Hickman County, where they remained until 1851, when they came to Perry County, where they resided the remainder of their lives. The father died in May, 1863. His widow resided with our subject until her death in July, 1883. At the age of twenty-two James M. united his fortune with that of Martha Jane Harris, who was born in Perry County and is a daughter of David R. Harris. Our subject farmed until the breaking out of hostilities between the North and South, when he enlisted in Company E, Sixth Tennessee Federal Cavalry, and was afterward transferred to Company G, of the same regiment, and served until the close of the war. In 1866 he was elected sheriff of Perry County, serving two years, and then resumed farming. In December, 1872, he moved to Linden and has since kept a first-class hotel. To him and his wife eleven children were born, seven of whom are still living. Mr. Dodson is a member of the K. of H., and his wife is identified with the Methodist Church.

Elias Dodson was born in Hickman County, Tenn., December 29, 1836, one of eight children born to the marriage of Marshall Dodson and Emily Brown. At the age of eighteen our subject acted as overseer of a plantation in Gibson County a few months, then returned home, where he remained until the commencement of the war; then joined the Sixth Tennessee Federal Cavalry, and remained with that regiment until the fall of 1864, when he returned home, and has since followed agricultural pursuits, locating on his present farm about 1869. October 8, 1856, Mr. Dodson married Virginia Shelton, a native of Williamson County, and to their union thirteen children were born, eight of whom are still living. The mother died November 12, 1882, and December 31, 1882, Mr. Dodson married Nancy A. Newton and by her is the father of two children: Unity Lucy Robert Sarah Mat and Clabe B. Mr. Dodson is a member of the K. of H., and he and wife are members of the Christian Church.

Allen W. Dodson is a native of Perry County, Tenn., born October 12, 1851, and is one of four children (two living) of Claiborne B. and Nancy (Norris) Dodson, who came from Hickman to Perry County in 1850. The father was a farmer, and died in 1873. His widow, who is now seventy-two years old, resides with our subject. May 29, 1877, Allen W. Dodson took for his companion through life, Mrs. Mary Dansby, *nee* Maxwell, who was born and reared in Perry County. Mr. Dodson began the mercantile business in Lobelville, and carried a good general stock of goods amounting to about $3,000. In February, 1885, he purchased the farm where he now lives, consisting of 195 acres. He also owns 520 acres near Buffalo River. Mrs. Dodson is a member of the Methodist Episcopal Church South, and Mr. Dodson belongs to the K. of H., and in politics favors Democratic principles.

George H. Dudley is a son of William and Patsey (Petty) Dudley, who were born, reared and married in Hickman County, Tenn. They spent their lives in their native county, and followed farming until their respective deaths. Our subject was born in Hickman County February 10, 1847, and resided with his father until the latter's death. He was twelve years of age at that time. His mother died when he was six years old, and his father took a second wife. To the first marriage eight children were born, two surviving; and to the latter marriage four were born, three of whom are yet living. After his father's death, George H. resided with an uncle until twenty years of age. He then went to Williamson County, where he remained one year, and then returned to Hickman County, and after a two years' residence there, came to Perry County, where he owns about 200 acres of land near Buffalo River. In politics Mr. Dudley is a Democrat. In February, 1873, he married Charlotte Greer, and of the seven children born to them six are living.

Thomas C. Edwards is one of nine children born to the marriage of John A. Edwards and Mary Wilburn, natives respectively of Hickman and Perry Counties, Tenn. They were married in the latter county, where they resided until 1872, and then moved to Hickman County, where the father died and the mother still lives. The father was a Baptist minister. Thomas C. Edwards was born in Perry County January 1, 1848. He resided under the paternal roof until August 17, 1871, when he married Mary Jean Burns, a native of Perry County. In 1879 he came into possession of the farm on which he is at present residing, consisting of 250 acres on the west bank of Buffalo River, near Lobelville,

Mr. Edwards has a very fine strong spring of freestone water near his house, which issues from the side of a steep ridge. Politically he is identified with the Democratic party.

John T. Edwards, merchant of Beardstown, Tenn., and member of the firm of Shepard & Edwards, was born July 7, 1857. At the age of twenty years he began teaching the "young idea" in Hickman County, and at the end of two years accepted a position as salesman in a general merchandise store in Beardstown, continuing six months, when he embarked in merchandising in Dixon, Dixon Co., Tenn., and remained one year. He then continued the same business in Hickman County, and in February, 1882, began business in his present location in partnership with E. H. Shepard. They keep a general stock of goods amounting to about $5,000. September 18, 1879, Mr. Edwards united his fortunes with those of Sallie Shepard, a native of Perry County. To them were born the following family of children: Lorenzo E., Flora Mabel and Edith Lois. Mr. Edward's parents are William H. and Nancy (Wilburn) Edwards, who were natives and farmers of Tennessee. Of their ten children eight are living.

Thomas O. Gray is a well-to-do farmer of Perry County, Tenn., and was born September 3, 1850, in Stewart County, and is one of ten children, five of whom are living, born to the marriage of Martin J. Gray and Louisa Arnold, who were born in Virginia and North Carolina, respectively. and were early settlers of Bedford County, Tenn. They were married in the latter county, but soon moved to Stewart County, where they farmed several years, and came to Perry County in 1852, locating near Standing Rock, a perpendicular bluff 300 feet high on the west bank of Buffalo Creek. The mother died March 14, 1884, followed by the father August 14, 1884. After attaining his majority our subject located on a farm in Humphreys County, where he remained until 1881, when he came to this county and purchased a farm of 140 acres, and here has since resided. He was married to Sarah Owens, and five children have blessed their union: William Martin, Jesse Franklin, Walter Edward, Margaret Emily and Madison Lee. Mr. and Mrs. Gray are members of the Baptist Church.

M. J. Gray, M. D., is a brother of T. O. Gray, whose sketch appears above. He was born in Perry County, Tenn., December 8, 1852, and resided with his parents until their respective deaths. His early days were spent on the farm and in attending the common schools, where he secured a fair education. He purchased the home farm, and December 17, 1874, he united his fortunes with those of Sarah Sophronia Horner, who was born in Perry County, Tenn., and the following are the children born to their union: Russell Horner, Edward Martin, Gertrude Polinia and Bertie. Mr. Gray attended the medical department of the Vanderbilt University during the sessions of 1877-78. He then practiced his profession one year, and in 1879-80 he again attended medical sessions and graduated with the title of M. D. He has since practiced in connection with his farming, and the best of success has attended his efforts.

William N. Greer, of Perry County, was born in July, 1840, in Davidson County, Tenn. He assisted his parents on the farm until 1859, when he went to Arkansas and Missouri, where he spent two years. In 1862 he enlisted in the First Arkansas Battery, and served until the cessation of hostilities. He then returned to Perry County, Tenn., and in January, 1867, he and Amanda Dodson were united in the holy bonds of matrimony. Mrs. Greer was born in Perry County, and became the mother of seven children, six of whom are still living. She died February 22, 1883, and in January, 1886, Mr. Greer united his fortunes with those of Mrs. Huldah (Dille) Kline. Mr. Greer is an F. & A. M., and is independent in his political views, voting rather for the man than the party. His parents, Henry and Harriette (Henry) Greer, were Davidson County Tennesseans. They came to Perry County about 1847, and located on Buffalo River near the present town of Linden. They became the parents of eleven children, seven of whom are living. The father was a farmer, and was tax collector of Perry County in 1850; served as justice of the peace of his district, and died in 1882; the mother died in 1852.

R. A. Guthrie, farmer, and native of Perry County, Tenn., was born on the 28th of November, 1836, and is one of three children born to Andrew H. and Jane (Kirkpatrick) Guthrie, who were born in North Carolina and Sumner County, Tenn., respectively. They were married in the latter place, and came to Perry County about 1835. They followed farming for a livelihood and continued the same until the father's death, in 1864. Our subject's early days were spent on his father's farm. At the commencement of the war he joined the Sixth Tennessee Federal Cavalry, but was soon detailed home to raise a company for the Second Tennessee Mounted Infantry (Federal) and served as captain of that company until the close of the war, being discharged at Nashville in May, 1865. He then returned home and has since been an energetic tiller of the soil, locating on his present farm in 1874. In 1869 he married Mrs. Nancy J. Dodson, *nee* Webb, and their marriage has been blessed in the birth of two children: James M. and Mollie A. (deceased). The mother of these children died February 1, 1880. Mr. Guthrie then married Eliza Sims, in November, 1880. They have two children: Bessie L. and Flary. Mr. Guthrie is a member of the F. & A. M., and he and his wife are members of the Methodist Church.

Robert Houssels, a farmer and successful and prominent leather manufacturer, was born in Rhine (Prussia) Germany, near Cologne, February 18, 1834. He was the youngest of eleven children of John P. and Margaret (Weber) Houssels. Our subject immigrated to America at the age of seventeen and landed in New York; was reared in a rural village and received his preparatory education in the common schools of his fatherland, and finally completed the same in the Mulheim High School. He was apprenticed to the tanner's trade after completing his education, and served three years for his board. He then worked for wages for five years, in Cincinnati, St. Louis and other places, and in 1856 he began tanning in Perry County, Tenn., on his own responsibility, and has succeeded far beyond his expectations, being the owner of 25,000 acres of land, on which he has an iron furance, not now in use. The home place consists of 100 acres, and on this land is his fine steam tannery and his beautiful home residence. October 28, 1860, he wedded Docia Young, born February 4, 1843, daughter of Samuel Young. They have eight children: John H., Robert S., Julia E., Jennie, Bismarck, Rosina R., Minnie R. and Norma. Mr. Houssels is somewhat conservative in politics, but rather favors Democratic principles. He is a member of the Masonic fraternity and a man of liberal and generous disposition, and is always ready to do his part in furthering enterprises for the public good. Mrs. Houssels and some of the children are members of the Methodist Episcopal Church South.

John H. Houssels, proprietor of the Linden Trade Palace, was born November 23, 1861, in Perry County, Tenn., and is one of seven children born to Robert and Docia (Young) Houssels. The parents, who are both still living, were born in Germany, and Perry County, Tenn., respectively. The father came to Tennessee when about twenty years old, and worked as a day laborer. By frugality, industry and good business management he has amassed considerable property. He built up and now controls the tanning industry of the county, owning the large steam tanneries near Mouse Tail Landing, in Perry County. At the age of sixteen our subject accepted a clerkship in a Linden store, in which his father had an interest, and there continued until 1880. He dealt in stock about one year, and then engaged in the wholesale hide and leather business in Evansville, Ind., under the firm name of Houssels & Klein. They disposed of their business at the end of about one year, and our subject returned to Linden and purchased Houssels & Webb's stock of general merchandise, but a year later sold to G. L. Harris & Son, after which he engaged in the peanut and live stock trade until the fall of 1884. He visited Texas during the winter of that year and the summer of 1885, then returned, and again embarked in merchandising, moving into his present commodious business room in January, 1886. His stock amounts to about $8,000. June 20, 1881, Mr. Houssels wedded Gussie Humphreys, of Franklin County, Ark., and two children have blessed their union: Robert Clyde and Claud McIlroy. In 1886 he became a candidate for trustee of Perry County against J. P. Beasley, who had served two terms, having no opposition in his election. It was generally conceded it would be impossible to defeat him, as he had made a strictly first-class officer; therefore our subject's entering the lists against him was quite an undertaking for a boy like himself. The race was quite exciting and resulted in the election of Mr. Houssels by fifty-five majority.

C. Johnson was born April 8, 1811, and is one of nine children of William and Mary (Britt) Johnson, who were born and married in Virginia, and came to Tennessee in 1810, locating in Wilson County. The father was an agriculturist, and died in 1841. His widow died in 1857. Our subject remained at home until fourteen years of age, and having learned the tanner's trade, he worked at the same in Williamson, Davidson and Hickman Counties until 1861, and then located where he now resides. In 1836 he married Mary Isabella White, and eight children were born to them, all of whom are dead. Their mother also died in 1870. Mr. Johnson is a member of the Methodist Episcopal Church South. His grandson, C. Allan Brown, resides with him. He is one of three surviving members of a family of five children born to George W. and Mary (Johnson) Brown, and was born in 1861. His father was a Methodist Episcopal minister for some time, but owing to throat trouble he was obliged to give up that calling and devoted his time to the practice of medicine. He died in 1881, and the mother in 1874. C. Allan entered the medical department of the Vanderbilt University, attending the sessions of 1883, 1884 and 1885. He located at his grandfather's home, near Beardstown, where he has since practiced. June 8, 1886, he wedded Bessie Houssels, the accomplished daughter of Robert Houssels, one of Perry County's most influential and prominent citizens. The Doctor and his wife are church members.

Benjamin C. Kittrell, farmer and merchant, of Farmers Valley, Tenn., was born on the 24th of February, 1832, in Hickman County. Previous to his twenty-first birthday, he resided and assisted his father on the home farm, but after that period he began doing for himself. He taught school until the war, when he enlisted in the First Tennessee Confederate Cavalry, and served faithfully and well until the close of the war. Since that time he has farmed, and is the owner of 500 acres of good land, on which are several old Indian mounds. In November, 1860, he and Martha J. Dowdy united their fortunes, and ten children have been born to their union, nine of whom are still living. Mr. Kittrell and family are members of the Christian Church, and he is a member of the F. & A. M. His father, George Kittrell, was born in North Carolina in 1797, and came to Tennessee in 1807, and after residing in Williamson County a short time, moved to Lewis County previous to the war of 1812. He served in the conflict under Gen. Jackson. He married Betsey Rutherford (our subject's mother), of Sumner County, Tenn., and they came to Perry County in 1858, locating at Farmers Valley. The mother died in Maury County, in 1865, and Mr. Kittrell then sold his farm and went also to Maury County, where he died in 1868.

Elkanah A. Land first saw the light of day in Hickman County, Tenn., March 28, 1827, was a son of Cooper B. and Hannah (Anderson) Land, and one of their eleven children. Cooper Land and his wife are Tennesseans by birth, born in 1806 and 1802 respectively, and since 1841 have been residents and farmers of Perry County. The mother died in 1868. In 1844 our subject began doing for himself, and June 6, of that year married Nancy Barber, of Perry County. They have four children: William R., Mary F., Elizabeth J. and Nancy H. Mr. Land learned the blacksmith's trade in 1847, and followed it in connection with farming for about fourteen years. He came into possession of his present farm of 600 acres in 1844. In October, 1862, he was ordained minister of the Christian Church, and has since been the chief expounder of the gospel in Perry County. He organized all the churches of his denomination in the county, and has also been instrumental in organizing many churches in the adjoining counties. He has administered the ordinance of baptism to about 2,000 persons.

Green C. Ledbetter, a successful planter of Perry County, Tenn., was born April 12, 1824, and was the seventh of twelve children of Henry and Anna (Phillips) Ledbetter, and is of Irish descent. His father, a native of North Carolina, was born about 1788, and was reared and married in his native State. Within a few years after his marriage he immigrated to Tennessee and settled in Lincoln County, where he lived until 1837, when he moved to Perry County and established himself on Lick Creek, where he continued to reside until his death, May 14, 1860. The mother was born in North Carolina about 1789, and died at the old homestead August 12, 1870. Our subject received a limited education, and has made farming his chief business through life. He was married, in Perry County, to Eliza Elizabeth Terry, daughter of Jason Terry. Of their nine children eight are living: Mary A. L., Sarah E., Jane, Nancy M., Eliza, Columbus W., Sion R. and Henry. The mother of this family was born in North Carolina, and was brought by her parents to Tennessee when a small child. They afterward moved to Perry County. Our subject is a stanch Republican, with very conservative, liberal and intelligent views on the political questions of the day. Mr. Ledbetter was a member of the Methodist Episcopal Church, and during its separation he was taken, without his consent, into the Southern wing, although he preferred remaining with the old church. He owns 1,500 acres of land, on which is valuable iron ore, and also abundant evidences of coal, with splendid timber and numerous springs of pure water, which flow the year around.

John N. Ledbetter, one of Perry County's prominent farmers, was born in Lincoln County (afterward Marshall County), November 30, 1825, and is one of twelve children, seven now living, born to Henry and Anna (Phillips) Ledbetter, who were born in North Carolina. They were married in their native State and soon after came to Tennessee, locating in Lincoln County. In February, 1849, they took up their permanent residence in Perry County, where they resided until their respective deaths in 1860 and 1870. Our subject lived with his father and mother until his marriage to Millie Elizabeth Tate, which took place December 16, 1866. He then made his home with his mother three years longer, then moved to a farm which he had purchased on Lick Creek, where he remained ten years, and then located on his present farm of over 500 acres near Lobelville. Mr. and Mrs. Ledbetter are the parents of two children: Martha Ann and John Henry. Mr. Ledbetter belongs to the Republican party, and he and wife are members of the Methodist Episcopal Church South.

H. M. Ledbetter, a Lincoln County Tennessean, first saw the light of day December 18, 1830. He was the youngest of a large family of children born to the marriage of Henry and Anna (Phillips) Ledbetter. [For history of parents, see biography of Green C. Ledbetter.] Our subject was reared on a farm and secured a limited education, owing to the meager facilities of that day; but through steady application has acquired a fine business education, and is one of the intelligent and respected citizens of his locality. After attaining his majority, Mr. Ledbetter began farming for himself, and has made that business his chief calling through life. He and his brothers were strongly opposed to secession, and used their votes and influence to keep the State in the Union, and under this condition of affairs were placed in positions often more unpleasant and more dangerous than army life itself. He is a warm Republican, and was married at the age of twenty-one to Mary E. Vaughn, daughter of William Vaughn. Ten children blessed their union, eight of whom are living: Sarah A. E. (Mrs. T. G. Young), Susan Tennessee (Mrs. A. E. Goblett), Mary J. (Mrs. S. H. Hunt), Henry N., Martha L., Minerva, Matilda and Cora Bell. Their mother was born in Williamson County, Tenn., February 20, 1832. Mr. Ledbetter owns a farm of 800 acres on which he raises large numbers of live stock. His farm is well watered by ever-flowing springs, and some coal beds on them have been sufficiently developed to prove them of great value. The family are members of the Methodist Episcopal Church.

William H. Loggins is a son of Thomas and Elizabeth (Baugus) Loggins, who were born in Montgomery and Humphreys Counties, Tenn., respectively. Both came to Perry County when young, and here they married and spent the remainder of their lives. The father was a farmer, and died in 1871. The mother's death occurred in 1869. Our subject is one of two surviving members of a family of five children, and was born in Perry County, Tenn., September 17, 1857. He resided at home until the family was broken up by his father's death. He was then a farm laborer for eight years, and on November 17, 1879, his marriage with Tennessee Jane Ingram was celebrated. He soon purchased the farm where he now resides, which consists of 384 acres, and soon purchased another farm of 165 acres. To Mr. and Mrs. Loggins four interesting children were born, namely: Docia Elizabeth, deceased; Benjamin Littleton, deceased; Ada Azalie, deceased; and William Thomas, still living. Mr. Loggins is a prosperous farmer, and a man highly esteemed by all who know him.

Capt. Henry H. Long was born in Perry County, Tenn., July 14, 1834, the seventh of twelve children of Hugh W. and Martha A. (Burnett) Long, and of Irish descent. His father and mother were born in Rutherford County, N. C., and Petersburg, Va., September 22, 1798, and September 12, 1799, respectively. The father married in North Carolina, and in 1831 came to Tennessee and purchased 265 acres of land in Perry County. He reared his family in what is now Decatur County, but was then Perry County. He died November 2, 1849, and the mother September 12, 1865. Our subject has always spent his life on a farm. He learned the tanner's trade, but abandoned the business after serving his apprenticeship. His marriage to Eveline Simmons took place in Perry County, March 25, 1854. She is a daughter of Benjamin Simmons, and was born October 10, 1834. They have four children: Sarah A., Frances E., James N. and John W. Mr. Long served in the Federal Army in the Second Tennessee Cavalry under Col. O. N. Haney, and served through the latter part of the late war. After the general surrender he was mustered out at Nashville, Tenn., in May, 1865. He is a stanch Republican, and a conservative and liberal reasoner in politics. He is a Mason, and he and wife are members of the Missionary Baptist

Church. Capt. Long has a fine farm of 453 acres of land and a substantial and commodious residence.

Aaron R. McCage, farmer, and native of the county, was born September 6, 1841, and is one of ten children—six living—born to William B. and Winnie (Potter) McCage, who were both Tennesseans. They were married in Hickman County, and then moved to Lobelville in the early settlement of Perry County. In 1842 they moved to Henderson County, and after a twelve years' residence the family returned to Perry County. The mother died while in West Tennessee, and the father afterward married Mrs. (Crowder) Burchard in 1856, a native of Maury County. The father died August 10, 1874. Aaron R. remained at home until the commencement of the war, when he enlisted in the Fifty-third Tennessee Infantry, and served with it until the fall of Fort Donelson, when he enlisted in the Tenth Tennessee Cavalry, and served until the close. April 5, 1868, he married Martha Jane Burchard, and six children have blessed their union. In 1874 Mr. McCage came into possession of the old homestead, a farm of 200 acres, near the mouth of Lagoon Creek. Just in front of Mr. McCage's residence is a large cave, containing very rich saltpeter veins, but it has never been explored very far. The family are members of the Cumberland Presbyterian Church.

Robert H. Patterson is the eighth of nine children of Robert C. and Malinda W. (Carson) Patterson, and was born on Christmas day, 1838, in Perry County, Tenn. His father was a Virginian, born in 1797, and remained in his native State until twelve years of age. He then came with his father to Tennessee and settled in Bedford County. Here he was reared, educated and married. He moved to Hickman soon after the latter event and, after a two years' residence there, came to Perry County and settled on Tom Creek. His wife was also a Virginian, born in 1800. The father died in 1873 and the mother in 1859. Robert H. received a common school education, and was married, January 17, 1856, to Mary E. Blackburn, daughter of Leroy Blackburn. Mrs. Patterson was born in Bedford County November 29, 1835, and became the mother of six children: Robert L., James W., Malinda E., David C., Emma J. and William L. Our subject served in the Confederate Army in the Tenth Tennessee Cavalry Regiment under Col. N. N. Cox, of Franklin, Tenn. He was captured at the siege of Knoxville, and kept a prisoner at Fort Delaware for thirteen months. Mr. Patterson is a Democrat, and owns 260 acres of good land, on which he cultivates the cereals to some extent and gives considerable attention to stock raising, but makes peanuts his chief market product.

Ezra R. Patterson is one of five children of William and Sarah M.

(Branch) Patterson. He is of Irish lineage and was born in Perry County, Tenn., February 8, 1846. His early days were spent on a farm and in attending the common schools. During the late war he served about nine months in the Ninth Tennessee Cavalry Confederate States Army, under Col. Biffle, and was paroled at Selma, Ala. October 24, 1867, he wedded Martha M. Horner, daughter of John V. Horner, and to their union were born the following children: Emma Elnora, Viola Josephine, Laura Lee, William V., Cora Elizabeth, Robert E., Jesse Harvey and Elbert Foster. Mrs. Patterson was born in Perry County, Tenn., December 7, 1845. Mr. Patterson is a Democrat in his political views, and is the owner of 200 acres of excellent land about thirteen miles from Linden. His farm is devoted chiefly to the production of peanuts, but he also raises the cereals to some extent. His father was born in Perry County, May 25, 1818, and was twice married, our subject being born to his first marriage. He died at his home near Tom Creek, June 15, 1865. His second wife was Sallie Nix, by whom he had six children. Our subject's mother was born on the 15th of December, 1819, and died June 28, 1852.

Charles L. Pearson, native of London, Eng., was born in 1831, and is a son of Henry Robert Pearson and Anne (Harris) Pearson, both natives of England, where the father held the office of chief clerk of the Treasury Department, when he retired after forty-three years continual service. The mother died in 1833, and in 1838 he wedded Charlotte Cousens, who is still living in England. The father died in 1870. At the age of fifteen our subject entered the royal navy of England, and after ten years' service, at the close of the Crimean war, during which he was actively engaged, he retired with the rank of lieutenant. He then came to Niagara, Canada, where he accepted a position as professor of mathematics in the high school, and served one year. He then went to New York and was engaged in the insurance business a few months, after which he followed teaching in Illinois and Iowa until 1860, when he came to Perry County, Tenn., and continued his former occupation until 1865. Since that time his chief occupations have been merchandising and filling various county offices as deputy until 1882, when he was elected clerk of the county court, and still holds the office. March 8, 1865, he married Georgiana P. Brooks, of Williamson County, Tenn., and thirteen children blessed their union, only six now living. The eldest child, George W. Pearson, is a promising young attorney of Linden, and a graduate of Cumberland University. He received his diploma at the age of nineteen, being probably one of the youngest men ever admitted to the bar in Tennessee. Mr. Pearson and family are church members.

Egbert Haywood Shepard's birth occurred in Wilson County, Tenn., October 12, 1825. He is one of eight children, three now living, born to William and Jane (Britewell) Shepard, who were born and married in the Old Dominion, and came to Perry County, Tenn., in 1829 and located on Cane Creek, where they farmed until their respective deaths. At the early age of eighteen our subject was united in marriage to Naomi Wilburn, of Perry County, who died November 17, 1879, having borne six children, five of whom are still living. November 17, 1881, Mr. Shepard wedded Mary Jane Smith, and one child, Samuel Clinton, has blessed their union. In November, 1862, Mr. Shepard enlisted in the Tenth Tennessee Confederate Cavalry, and remained on duty until his capture, while raising a battalion for his regiment. He has since farmed, and has followed merchandising since February, 1882, at Beardstown. In 1849 Mr. Shepard located on his present farm of 1,100 acres, near the junction of Buffalo River and Cane Creek. He was formerly an old line Whig, but since the death of that party has given his support to the Democratic party. In a cave on his farm saltpeter was formerly made.

Thetus W. Sims is a Wayne County Tennessean, born in 1852, one of six surviving members of a family of eight children born to George W. and Jennie (Whitson) Sims, natives of Giles and Hickman Counties, Tenn., respectively. The father's life has been spent on a farm. He removed to Wayne County at an early day and was there married, and resided in that and Hardin Counties until 1877, at which time he moved to the Lone Star State, where he still resides. The mother's death occurred in 1879. Our subject resided with his parents on the farm until twenty-two years of age, when he entered the law department of the Cumberland University, from which institution he graduated in 1876. He then located in Linden, his native town, where he has since made his home. December 26, 1877, he led to the hymeneal altar Nannie H. Kittrell, a native of Maury County, and their union has been blessed in the birth of four children: Edna E., Erskine Kent, Tommie and Bessie.

James L. Sloan was born in Rhea County, Tenn., in 1841, son of James B. and Mary A. (Starrett) Sloan. The father was born in New York and the mother in Virginia. They were married in the latter State and moved to Tennessee, locating in Rhea County, in 1836, where they remained until the father's death in 1845. The mother returned to her former home in Virginia, where she remained until 1854, then returned to Tennessee, and died at her son's residence in Linden October 24, 1885, at the advanced age of eighty-nine years. Our subject remained with his mother until the beginning of the war, when he enlisted in the Eleventh Tennessee Infantry, being second lieutenant of his company until the close of the war. After the first year of the war he was frequently detailed on the ordnance department, being an iron and brass molder by trade. At the close of the war he returned to Nashville, but soon after moved to Centreville, Hickman Co., Tenn., at which place he was admitted to the bar. In 1869 he located at Linden, where he has since enjoyed a large and lucrative practice in Perry and adjoining counties. January 8, 1861, he married Sarah W. Corbitt, of Nashville, and of their ten children, five are living: Walter N., Mary F., Chester L. H., Leonidas W. and James P. Mr. Sloan is a member of the F. & A. M., I. O. O. F., K. of H. and I. O. W. M. He is Post Junior Grand Warden of F. & A. M.

Alvin Tate, farmer, of Perry County, Tenn., was born February 14, 1851, and is one of nine surviving members of a family of twelve children born to Lemuel and Polly Ann (Stricklin) Tate, both natives of Perry County, where they lived and followed farming during the father's life. The father was born September 13, 1822, and the mother February 25, 1825. The former died February 6, 1882. The mother is yet living and makes her home with one her of sons. Alvin Tate, our subject, made his home with his parents until his marriage to Nellie Loveless, which took place March 3, 1872. He farmed the home place until 1880, when he purchased the farm, consisting of 350 acres of land, where he now resides and has been a successful tiller of the soil. To his union with Miss Loveless seven children were born, all of whom are living. Mr. Tate gives his support to the Democratic party, and is one of the prosperous and well respected citizens of the county.

Hon. Jesse Taylor first saw the light of day in Dixon County, Tenn., March 10, 1816, and is the only living member of a family of eleven children born to William and Mary (Bredwell) Taylor. The father was born in South Carolina, and the mother in the Old Dominion. They were married in the Palmetto State, and came to Tennessee at a very early day, locating first in Dickson County, and then coming to Perry County about 1828. They died at the home place, about four miles west of Linden, in August, 1834, and in September, 1839, respectively. Jesse Taylor resided with his parents till the age of eighteen, then married Betsey Wood, and has since followed farming. He served as county court clerk of Perry County two terms, and was elected to the third term, but resigned in November, 1867, having been called upon to represent Perry and Decatur Counties in the General Assembly of Tennessee. He filled the office one term of two years (1867 and 1868). To the marriage above referred to seven children were born—three of whom are still living. Mrs. Taylor died February 14, 1885, and April 14, the same year, Mr. Taylor wedded Mary A. Ledbetter, who was born in Perry County. Mr. Taylor owns a fine farm of 400 acres, and on this farm repose the remains of John T. Tally, an old Revolutionary soldier.

Thomas B. Twilla is a native of Maury County, Tenn., born December 3, 1832, son of William F. and Lucinda (Garner) Twilla, who were born in North Carolina and Tennessee, respectively. They were married and remained in Maury County a few years; thence moved to Hickman County, where their deaths occurred in 1861 and 1862, respectively. Thomas B. resided under the paternal roof until 1857, when he took for his helpmeet through life, Catherine Owens, to which union four children were born: John H., Elizabeth, James W. and Anna. Mrs. Twilla died in 1871, and a year later Mr. Twilla married Mrs. Sarah E. (Niblett) Roberts. Of eight children born to them six are living. Since 1878 Mr. Twilla has been a resident of Perry County. One of his farms adjoins Lobelville on the south, and contains 380 acres, and is the site of what is known as the Indian Spring, so called from supposed Indian works, which exist in the vicinity. In 1884 he moved to his farm of 130 acres north of Lobelville. On this farm is a fine cave spring. Mr. and Mrs. Twilla are members of the Christian Church.

John L. Vaughan, a prominent farmer of Perry County, Tenn., was born in Marshall County, Miss., January 21, 1847, and is one of four surviving members of a family of eight children born to William and Melissa (Craig) Vaughan. The father was born in Virginia and came to Williamson County, Tenn., where he married our subject's mother, then moved to Marshall County, Miss., where he became overseer of a plantation. About 1848 or 1849 he moved to Perry County, Tenn., where he followed farming until his death in 1865. The mother died in about 1850. After the father's death our subject followed the harness-maker's trade in Franklin, Tenn., for five years; then engaged in the livery business and farmed in the county about five years longer. In 1875 he began farming in Perry County, buying his present home farm in 1880. His farm consists of 500 acres of land on Buffalo River. Mr. Vaughan is a Democrat, and September 26, 1877, was married to Martha Steward, who was born in Decatur County and is the mother of three children: Myrtle Estelle, Minnie A. and Sallie M.

William C. Webb was born in the county where he now lives in 1840, the only living child of a family of seven children of John L. and Polly A. (McAnally) Webb. The father was born in North Carolina in May, 1811, and with his parents, John and Elizabeth Webb, came to Tennessee about 1820. Here he married and farmed. He was sheriff of the county a number of years, and died in January, 1884. The mother died about 1874. William C. Webb attended the commercial college in St. Louis, Mo., during the session of 1859–60, and from the latter date and until the breaking out of the war was engaged in the mercantile business. He enlisted in the Sixth Tennessee Federal Cavalry as a private, and served until the close of the war, and was discharged as captain of Company G, of his regiment. On his return home he was elected sheriff of Perry County, which position he resigned after two months' service, and resumed his former occupation of merchandising, following it in Decatur County twelve months. He then returned to Perry County, and in 1867 was appointed collector of revenues for the Sixth Congressional District, comprising twelve counties, and held the position two years. In 1873 he erected his fine merchant, grist, planing and saw-mill on the sources of Buffalo River, one mile from Linden, and is doing a good business. In 1860 he married Martha A. Dodson, of Perry County, and to their union twelve children were born, seven of whom are living. In 1883 Mr. Webb was appointed chancery court clerk of the county, and is filling the office faithfully and efficiently. He and family are members of the Christian Church, and he is a member of the K. of H. and F. & A. M. He is a Prohibitionist, casting the only vote in the county for St. John in 1884.

William T. Weems is a son of Augustus and Susan (Tatom) Weems, and is of Scotch descent. Both parents were born in Dickson County, Tenn., the former in 1818 and the latter in 1824. The father has been a resident of Perry County since 1823. William T., our subject, is the eldest of eight children, and was born in Perry County October 18, 1849. His early days were spent on the farm and in attending the common schools. In connection with his farming he follows the blacksmith's trade, which he learned when young, and is doing fairly well, from a financial standpoint. He owns sixty acres of land, and grain is the principal production. Mr. Weems was married in Perry County, Tenn., February 4, 1869, to Mary J. Lewis, daughter of J. D. Lewis, a farmer and blacksmith. They have three children: Ella Eugenie, Jesse A. and George F. Mrs. Weems was born in Perry County, on Deer Creek, March 8, 1851. Mr. Weems is a stanch Republican and a member of the Masonic fraternity, Dunaway Lodge, No. 440. He and wife are members of the Methodist Episcopal Church South.

Judge Thomas Whitwell, born in Hickman County, Tenn., August 23, 1826, is one of five surviving children born to Pleasant and Margaret (Anderson) Whitwell, both natives of Barren County, Ky. They and their parents were early immigrants to Tennessee, coming to Hickman County in 1823, and were married in Dickson County and came to Perry County in 1837. The father died December 20, 1875, and the mother in July, 1877. Pleasant Whitwell was Perry County's first county court clerk, after the county was divided in 1846, serving two terms of four years each, to 1854. November 25, 1847, our subject was united in marriage to Malissa C. Ward, who was born in Perry County, and to their union were born a family of ten children, all of whom are living. In 1879 Mr. Whitwell moved to his present home, a tract of 1,200 acres lying along Hurricane Creek, some of the bluffs of which contain rich deposits of sulphate of iron (copperas). In August, 1870, Mr. Whitwell was elected judge of Perry County, which office he still holds. The Judge is an old member of the F. & A. M. He was re-elected judge August 5, 1886, for eight years, making three terms of eight years each.

John M. Young is a native of Perry County, Tenn., born April 4, 1840, the eldest of five children of Samuel and Elizabeth (Ledbetter) Young, and of Irish extraction. His father, a native of Tennessee, was born in Dickson County in April, 1816, and was brought to Perry County when only two years of age, and here has since resided. He is yet hale and vigorous, and has held the following offices in the county: sheriff, magistrate and trustee. The mother was born in Lincoln County, Tenn., in 1818, and came to Perry County at the age of nineteen. She is still living at the old homestead in fair health and activity. Our subject has always made farming his chief business in life. August 23, 1863, he wedded Sarah E. Ledbetter, who was born September 10, 1834, and daughter of G. C. Ledbetter, whose sketch appears in this work. Mr. and Mrs. Young have five living children: Samuel G., Robert T., William H., John Brownlow and James Walker. Mr. Young is a warm Republican, and he and Mrs. Young are members of the Methodist Episcopal Church. He owns a farm of 300 acres on Buffalo River, on which is erected a commodious and substantial residence. Mr. Young has served two terms as magistrate, and one year as deputy sheriff of the county. He is considered one of the influential men of the county, and, so far as his means will justify, aids all laudable enterprises.

HICKMAN COUNTY.

Jasper A. Bates, chairman of the county court and native of Hickman County, Tenn., was born on Beaver Dam Creek, near Whitfield, Hickman County, January 15, 1848, and is the second of five children born to the marriage of Lewis Bates and Agnes E. Lancaster, who were born in Hickman County in 1825 and 1828, respectively. Jasper A.'s early education was obtained in the common schools. He chose farming for an occupation, and continued the same until 1871, when he removed to Linden, Perry County, and engaged in general merchandising. Two years later he came to Centreville, and here has since resided. In September, 1874, he entered the Lebanon Law School, from which he graduated in 1875, and has since practiced in Centreville. He was elected chairman of the county court in January, 1883, and has since held the office, to the satisfaction of all. He is a Democrat and cast his first presidential vote for Horace Greeley. May 3, 1876, he was married to Cordelia E. Clagett, daughter of William G. Clagett. Mrs. Bates was born in 1851, and four children have been born to her union with Mr. Bates: Florence O., William C., Douglas T. and Owen L. Mr. Bates is a Mason, a prominent man and leading politician of Hickman County. Mrs. Bates is a member of the Methodist Episcopal Church South.

John M. Bates, merchant, and native of Hickman County, Tenn., was born August 22, 1853, son of Lewis and Agnes E. (Lancaster) Bates. He is the fourth of their five children, and his early days were devoted to farm labor. He attended the country schools of Hickman County, and in the winter of 1871 came to Centreville. He was engaged for some time in the wine and liquor business, and for one year sold sewing machines. In 1874 he began the mercantile business in Centreville, continuing the same until 1876, when he was engaged as solicitor for the produce house of King Bros. & Co., Cincinnati, Ohio, and remained with the firm six years, and was then with Mellen, Brown & Co. for one year. He engaged in the mercantile business again in Centreville in 1883, and continued the same up to July 1, 1886. The firm was known as Bates Bros. & Co. At the latter date he sold out his stock of goods and accepted a position as traveling salesman with M. & L. S. Fechheimer & Co., of Cincinnati, Ohio, with Middle Tennessee as his territory. February 22, 1872, he married Anna Wright, of Hickman County. She is a daughter of Simeon C. Wright, and was born May 16, 1855. They have seven children: Alonzo L., William M., Clarence P., Clifford G.,

Simeon L., Fred and another whose name was not learned. Mr. Bates is a Democrat, and he and wife are members of the Methodist Episcopal Church South.

William George Clagett, general merchant, and the oldest member of the Clagett family now living, is a native of Maryland, born in Prince George County, December 7, 1813, son of Horatio and Rebecca Clagett. Our subject is the third of eight children, and came with his parents from Maryland to Tennessee when only four years of age. His early life was spent on a farm, and his services were given his father until 1830, when he came to Centreville and took a position as clerk in the store of Dale & Phillips, and in the spring of 1835 engaged in the mercantile business with Henry R. Fowlkes. Two years later his younger brother, Horatio, bought Mr. Fowlkes' interest, and the firm became known as W. G. & H. Clagett, and has since continued, being the oldest firm in the State. Upon the organization of the First National Bank at Centreville, in 1885, Mr. Clagett was chosen its vice-president, and still holds the position. He was married July 21, 1835, to Theodosia C. Whitfield, who was born in Williamson County, April 1, 1816, daughter of Wilkins and Mary Whitfield, who were Virginians. Mrs. Clagett died October 1, 1839, and our subject married Elizabeth O. Hornbeak February 10, 1842. She was born in the county February 18, 1818, and is a daughter of Eli B. and Sarah Hornbeak. Mr. and Mrs. Clagett became the parents of nine children, four of whom are living: Sarah R., Letty P., Cordelia E. and Theodosia C. Mr. Clagett was a Whig, but is now a Democrat. He was postmaster of Centreville during Van Buren's administration. In 1847 he was elected magistrate and held the position until the close of the war. In 1866 he became clerk of the circuit court, holding the office nine years. He and wife are members of the Methodist Episcopal Church South. Their long and happy union is drawing to a close, and they can look back over a prosperous and well spent life.

Horatio Clagett, president of the First National Bank of Centreville, Tenn., is the fifth child born to the marriage of Horatio Clagett and Rebecca Gantt, who were born in Prince George County, Md., in 1779 and 1786, respectively. In 1816 they came in a wagon from Maryland to Hickman County, Tenn. Here they spent the remainder of their lives in agricultural pursuits. The father died in 1866, and the mother in 1876. Our subject was born January 17, 1819, and at the age of sixteen years went to Franklin, Tenn., and for two years was engaged as a clerk in the store of Robert Charter. He then came to Centreville, and became a partner with his brother, Wm. G. Clagett, in the mercantile business, and has continued up to the present, they, probably, constituting one of the oldest business firms in Tennessee. Upon the organization of the First National Bank, in 1885, he was chosen its president. Previous to the war he was a Whig in politics; since that time he has voted the Democratic ticket. November 1, 1846, he was married to Miss Elizabeth J. Montgomery, of Hickman County, born October 5, 1826, and to them were born the following children: Matilda T., Mary J., Laura E., Anna S., John H., Robert M. and William G. Mr. Clagett is a Mason, and he and Mrs. Clagett are members of the Methodist Episcopal Church South.

Sidney A. Craig is a son of James, and a grandson of Johnson Craig, whose father came directly from Ireland and settled in Orange County, N. C. He was a Revolutionary soldier, and laid large land warrants in Maury County, Tenn., near where Mount Pleasant now is. Johnson Craig, with four brothers, David, John, William and Samuel, came to Tennessee and settled on this land in the fall of 1808. Johnson Craig was born in Orange County, N. C., November 19, 1773, and married Martha Blackwood May 3, 1798, and came to Tennessee in the fall of 1808. He was a successful farmer and stock raiser; was a Whig in politics and was many times solicited to represent his county in the State Legislature, but, having no political aspirations, always declined. He was a member of the Old Presbyterian Church, and was prominently spoken of as "that noblest work of God," an "honest man." He died in October, 1848, in his seventy-fifth year. His wife was born in Orange County, N. C., August 10, 1781. They were married May 3, 1798, and raised fourteen children: David, Margaret, William, John, Eleanor, Elizabeth, Samuel, Johnson, Nancy, Charles, Mary, Isabell, James and Newton. Mrs. Craig was an affectionate wife and mother, and died in October, 1856, and was buried beside her husband in the Hunter Graveyard, near Mount Pleasant. Our subject's maternal great-grandfather, Aaron Voorhies, came from North Carolina, and settled in Maury County, Tenn., where his son, John Voorhies, who was born in North Carolina, was married to Mary Chaffin. He was a soldier of the war of 1812; was a Democrat in politics, and a great admirer of Gen. Jackson, being with him at New Orleans. He was a successful farmer, and died April 24, 1865. To him were born ten children: Angeline, Robert, Rebecca, Aaron, Margaret Malissa, Jasper Newton, Martha, Mary Jane, David and John. Mrs. Voorhies died July 24, 1874. James Craig, father of our subject, was born in Maury County, Tenn., October 10, 1822, and married Margaret Malissa Voorhies July 24, 1844. Margaret M. Voorhies was born October 24, 1825. They raised ten children to be grown: John Johnson, Sidney Anderson, Emily Frances, Elizabeth Jane, Ann Washington, Martha Ella, James

Millard, Joseph Leroy, William Blackwood (deceased) and Walter Peyton. Sidney A. Craig, our immediate subject, was born on Buffalo River, near Pleasant Garden, in Lawrence County, Tenn., January 5, 1847. His early days were spent on the farm, receiving only a common school education. On the 3d of January, 1871, he was married to his cousin, Miss Eliza Ann Craig, daughter of John and Nancy Craig. John Craig, third son of Johnson Craig, was born October 12, 1808, and was married to Nancy Gordon February 11, 1834, and died June 18, 1885. Nancy Craig, *nee* Gordon, was born May 1, 1815, was married to John Craig, and was the mother of seven children: Elizabeth A., Simeon Brantley, John Henry, Martha Ellen, Mary Isabell (deceased), Eliza Ann and Robert Newton. Eliza Ann Craig, wife of S. A. Craig, was born September 18, 1845, and was married January 3, 1871, and was the mother of four children: Ada May, Charley Ross, Nettie Pearl and Eva Campbell (deceased). Mr. Craig followed farming and school-teaching until 1872, clerked in a store during the year of 1873, and in 1874 established a mercantile store at Napier Furnace, and there continued until 1879, when he came to Centreville, and has continued very successfully in the same business. He was formerly a Democrat, but is now a member of the Greenback party. He was made a Mason in 1868, and he and his wife and two oldest children are members of the Methodist Episcopal Church South.

Ephraim A. Dean, ex-sheriff of Hickman County, and proprietor of the Centreville Hotel, is a native of Williamson County, Tenn., born on the 31st of July, 1838. His parents, John and Eliza (Andrews) Dean, were born in South Carolina and Williamson County, Tenn., in 1803 and 1802 respectively. The father's family came from the Palmetto State to Tennessee in the pioneer days of the latter State, and settled in Williamson County in 1844. The father died in Hickman County, in 1874, to which county he had moved in 1843. The mother died in 1878. Our subject was reared on a farm, educated in the country schools, and was a soldier in the late war, serving in Company H, Eleventh Tennessee Infantry, and arose to the rank of second lieutenant. He was a tried and true soldier, and was wounded at the battle of Murfreesboro. From 1866 until 1872 he farmed, and at the latter date was elected sheriff of the county, and re-elected in 1874, and again in 1876. In 1882 he removed to Centreville, where he now resides. In 1883–84 he erected the Centreville Hotel, which is a fine brick building, and cost $10,000. In 1865 Mr. Dean wedded Susan Anderson, who was born May 11, 1842, and has borne him two children: Elmer A. and John H. In politics Mr. Dean is independent. He is one of the best citizens of the county, generous, charitable and a true gentleman. His wife is a member of the Methodist Episcopal Church South.

James H. Erwin, farmer and stock raiser, was born in Maury County, Tenn., July 27, 1830. In youth he served a five-years' apprenticeship at the shoe-maker's trade, and afterward learned and followed the tanner's trade. In 1867 he began farming, and in time became a successful tiller of the soil. He raises large quantities of corn, and his farm is extensively known as the "Land of Egypt." He was united in marriage November 22, 1855, to Ocra Ann Harbison, who was born in Maury County, in 1837, and is the mother of these three children: Sallie P., Lulu and Archie A. Mr. Erwin is a Democrat, a Mason and a member of the K. of H., and he and wife are members of the Cumberland Presbyterian Church. His parents, Theodrick W. and Lucy (Parrish) Erwin, were born in North Carolina and Alabama, in 1800 and 1788 respectively. Our subject's people came from North Carolina to Tennessee at an early period. Theodrick W. Erwin died April 11, 1874, and his wife in 1833.

Samuel L. Graham was born in Rowan County, N. C., November 18, 1812, son of John Graham, who was born in the same State in 1774. He was, for a time, quite prosperous financially, but reverses came, and he died wholly insolvent. His wife's maiden name was Martha Anderson. She lived and died in North Carolina. Samuel L., our subject, is the fourth of six children, and is of Scotch-Irish extraction. His educational advantages in early boyhood were very limited, as the early death of his father, and the insolvency of the estate, made it compulsory for him to make his own way in the world, and accordingly, at the early age of thirteen years, he became the architect of his own fortunes, and began working at the tailor's trade. He came to Tennessee in 1832, settling at Franklin, where he worked at his trade until 1837, and then removed to Columbia, where he followed merchant tailoring until 1844. From that date until 1850 he was in the mercantile business, in Franklin, in partnership with Mr. R. H. Bradley. Mr. Graham came to what was then Davis' mill (now Pinewood) in 1848, and erected a factory and mill, the former being burned in 1871. He reconstructed and completed his present three-story building, which is 50x90 feet, and cost, including machinery, $80,000. The manufactures are standard sheeting and cordage, the manufacture of the former amounting to 2,250 yards per day, and the latter to 800 pounds of rope or cordage per day, giving employment to about 300 persons. In connection with this there is a good grist-mill and 6,000 acres of land, 1,100 acres of which are in good farming condition. Since his arrival in the place he has been engaged in merchandising, and has one of the most beautiful and comfortable country seats in Tennessee. Mr. Graham has been very prosperous financially, and his property has been gained by years of unremitting toil and an energy and perseverance that has known no diminution. He is charitable and generous with his wealth. He and Andrew Johnson were born in the same State, came to Tennessee about the same time, and each had the same occupation in early life. Mr. Johnson chose politics, and Mr. Graham manufacturing and agriculture, and each prospered in his chosen calling. Mr. Graham was a Whig, and a Union man during the war, and is now independent in politics. In 1846 he wedded Frances E., daughter of Capt M. and Nancy Helm, of Columbia, Tenn. She died in 1863, leaving one son, John M. In 1868 Mr. Graham took for his second wife Thomasella Hardaman, daughter of Thomas and Berthenia Hardaman, of Franklin, Tenn. They have two children: Harry H. and Thomasella H. Mrs. Graham died in 1870, and three years later Mr. Graham married Martha J. Clouston, his present wife, who is a daughter of Edward G. and Cenia Clouston, of Franklin, Tenn. Mrs. Graham is a member of the Episcopal Church.

James Franklin Martin was born in Williamson County, Tenn., April 1, 1857, and is the youngest one of seven children born to Benjamin Franklin and Jane D. (Alston) Martin, who were born in Stokes County, Va., November 19, 1820, and Williamson County, Tenn., January 24, 1825, respectively. Our subject's paternal grandparents were Samuel and Sarah (Clement) Martin, who came from Virginia to Tennessee many years ago, and his maternal grandparents were James and Nancy (Swanzy) Alston, who were Carolinians. B. F. Martin, the father, was a Confederate soldier and died at Nolensville, Tenn., in February, 1862. He was the father of seven children: Brice Joseph Alexander, a Confederate soldier at the age of fifteen years, in the late war, and is now living in Texas; Ellen A. (Mrs. Harrison), Sallie A. (Mrs. Clay), Mary J. (Mrs. Jones), Rebecca A. (Mrs. West), one sister who died in infancy, and our subject. The mother is still living and resides in Williamson County. Our subject's early educational advantages were good, and although raised on a farm he gave little attention to agricultural pursuits. November 25, 1872, he entered the *Review and Journal* office, at Franklin, Tenn., to learn the printer's trade, and remained there nearly five years. He then came to Centreville, Hickman County, where he kept a small job printing office for three months, this being the first printing office ever established in the county. January 28, 1878, he issued the first number of the *Hickman Pioneer*, the first and only newspaper published in the county. He has since been its editor and proprietor with the exception of three months in 1882, when the business was leased to a stock company. Mr. Martin is a Democrat, as his father was before him, and on the day he was twenty-one he attended his first political convention; was elected secretary of the same and was appointed delegate to the coming State judicial convention and was made a member and secretary of the Hickman County Democratic Executive Committee. He is a member of the Methodist Episcopal Church South, and belongs to the U. O. of G. C. and K. of H. fraternities. Unlike the majority of young men of the present day, Mr. Martin never swore an oath in his life, never took a drink of liquor as a beverage, never played for money at a game of chance and has never used opium or tobacco in any form. March 28, 1881, Mr. Martin was united in marriage to Mollie Herndon, daughter of Joseph L. and Naomi Elizabeth (Thompson) Herndon. Mrs. Martin is their only child, and was born in La Fayette County, Miss., September 6, 1862. J. L. Herndon died at Port Hudson, La., in August, 1863, while serving in the Southern Army. Our subject has an only child, a son, who bears the family name Brice, born July 10, 1884.

James M. Meacham is a native of Williamson County, Tenn., born June 6, 1838, son of Green and Elizabeth (Cowan) Meacham, and of Scotch-Irish origin. His father was born in Virginia, in 1802, and his mother in North Carolina, in 1808. The family emigrated from Virginia to Tennessee, about 1806, and settled in Williamson County, and there both parents died, the father in 1851 and the mother in 1849. James M. is the sixth of seven children, and spent his youthful days following the pursuits of a farmer's boy. His early school days were limited, but owing to his own exertions he is well informed on the general topics of the day, and is one of the finest business men of Tennessee. He came to Pinewood in 1857, and entered the employ of R. & S. Graham, as salesman in a general merchandise store, and two years later was made book-keeper, and subsequently general manager of the extensive business of S. Graham, at Pinewood, and has been in that gentleman's employ for over twenty-nine years. In 1866 he was united in marriage to Lucy Cameron, of Columbia, Tenn., who died in 1870, leaving two children: Cowan C. and Eddie J. In 1872 Mr. Meacham married Alice Baker, who died in 1873. He remained single until 1880, when he united his fortunes with those of Fannie Baker, of Maury County, Tenn. Two children have blessed their union: Marion B. and Fannie G. Mr. Meacham is an Independent in politics and was a Union man during the late war. He and wife are leading members of the Christian Church and prominent people of the county.

Col. John H. Moore, attorney at law, and native of Centreville, Tenn., was born January 1, 1842, and is a son of Dr. S. B. Moore, a Smith County Tennessean, born in 1809. He removed to Hickman County in 1831, where he became eminent in his profession, and several times represented Hickman County in both houses of the Tennessee General Assembly. He was a leader among men, and died in the county of his adoption in 1869. His father was Armstead Moore, of Irish extraction and a Virginian, born in the latter part of the last century. He came to Tennessee in the pioneer days of the State, and died here in 1843. The mother of our subject was Mary A. (Hambeck) Moore, who was born in Hickman County, in 1815, and came of one of the pioneer families of Tennessee. Her death occurred in Hickman County, in 1856. Our subject is of Irish-Welsh descent. His early life was spent in his native town, and at the age of fourteen he entered Burrett College in Smith County, Tenn., where he remained for some time. In 1859 he entered the United States Naval Academy at Annapolis, Md., and there remained until about the time of the breaking out of the late war. At the bombardment of Fort Sumter he was in Smith County, Tenn., and there he enlisted in Company B, Seventh Tennessee Infantry, Confederate States of America, and upon the organization of the company he was chosen its second lieutenant, and for gallant and meritorious conduct was made first lieutenant, in 1862, and was subsequently made captain, which position he held until the close of the war. He was one of the brave and true soldiers of the Confederate Army, and was very popular with his comrades. After his return home he began reading law, and was licensed to practice in 1866. He is a Democrat and a leader of his party in this portion of Tennessee. In 1876 he was the elector on the Democratic ticket from his Congressional District, and was a candidate for Congress in 1878, but was defeated after one of the most noted political fights ever occurring in his district. He owns extensive iron lands in this county and in Alabama, and is a stockholder in the Standard Charcoal Company, of this county. He was married in 1868 to Margaret C. Williams, daughter of Maj. S. H. and Cordelia Williams, early settlers and prominent people of Maury County. Col. and Mrs. Moore have one daughter, Levisa G. Mr. Moore is a prominent man in Tennessee, and an honorable citizen and true gentleman.

Hon. Orville A. Nixon, clerk and master of the chancery court, is a native of Centreville, Tenn., born May 23, 1834, son of Henry and Cordelia (Pavatt) Nixon, and is of Scotch-Irish and French origin. His father was born in South Carolina March 25, 1798, in Kershaw County, and in 1804 the family came to Wilson County, Tenn., where they resided one year, then removed to Rutherford County, where they remained until

1807, when they took up their abode in Maury County. In 1819 Henry Nixon, O. A. Nixon's father, came to Hickman County, and in 1826 to Centreville. The father of our subject was the early attorney-general of this part of Tennessee, and by profession was a lawyer. He was a soldier under Jackson in the Seminole war, and died December 13, 1833. The mother was a native of Sumner County, Tenn., born February 15, 1812, and died in Centreville in 1854. Orville A. Nixon is the youngest of their family, and the rudiments of his education were obtained in Centreville Male Academy. In 1851 he entered Jackson College, at Columbia, and graduated from that school in 1853. Two years later he began reading law under Judge T. P. Bateman, and was admitted to the bar in 1856, and the same year was appointed clerk and master of the chancery court, and held that position until 1868. In 1884 he was appointed to the same, and is now discharging the duties of that office. Politically he was a Democrat, and voted with that party until 1876, when he became a member of the National party and cast his vote for Peter Cooper. He still adheres to the Greenback principles. In 1878 and 1879 he represented Hickman, Perry and Lewis Counties in the General Assembly, and in 1882–83 he represented Hickman County in the State Legislature. Cora C., Henry, Lizzie, Forest and Thomas are the children born to his marriage with Virginia A. Overton, which took place December 19, 1856. Mrs. Nixon was born in Dixon County, November 18, 1838. The Nixon family have been known in Tennessee for almost a century. They were noted for their energy and enterprise, and our subject is a fair representative of the family. He is a Mason, and has done much for the advancement and prosperity of the county.

Andrew Norris, M. D., is the sixth of seven children born to the marriage of A. W. Norris and Elizabeth Larkin, who were born in Cincinnati, Ohio, March 8, 1791, and Williamson County, Tenn., February 4, 1801, respectively. The father came to Tennessee when a young man and through life followed agricultural pursuits, dying May 29, 1869. The mother died September 20, 1872. Our subject was born in Williamson County November 27, 1839, and his early education was acquired at the Union Academy in his native county, and at a later period he became a student at the Triune Male Academy. He began the study of medicine in 1856 at Middleton, Rutherford County, under the directions of Dr. John L. Webb, and graduated from the medical department of the Nashville University in 1859. In 1860 he located at Fosterville, Tenn., where he continued to reside and practice until the spring of 1861, at which time he enlisted in Company F, Eighteenth Tennessee Volunteer Infantry, Confederate States Army, and was chosen first lieutenant, which position he held until 1862. He then resigned his command and joined the Fourth Tennessee Cavalry, serving until the close of the war. He was captured at the fall of Fort Donelson and held a prisoner for ninety days. In 1865 he came to Hickman County, where he has practiced his profession with the best of success ever since. Since 1870 he has resided in Centreville, and his office is located at Goodrich Station September 21, 1865, he married Mollie E. Walker, born January 25, 1845, and seven children have blessed their union: John, Mackie P., Cora B., Matilda C., William W., Fannie and Bernard. Dr. Norris is a Democrat, formerly a Whig, and he and Mrs. Norris are members of the Christian Church.

Walter S. Nunnelly, merchant, farmer and stock raiser, was born where he now resides April 12, 1851, son of Lawson H. and Elizabeth (Sandels) Nunnelly, and is of English-Irish extraction. Lawson Nunnelly was born in North Carolina October 31, 1801, and immigrated to Tennessee about 1815, and was one of the most energetic and hardest working men of Hickman County. He was known far and wide as the "friend of the poor man." He was very charitable, and his death, which occurred September 7, 1885, was lamented by all. His wife was born in the Emerald Isle June 11, 1841, and came to America in 1843, locating in Knox County, Ohio. She came to Tennessee in 1847, and is a resident of Old Vernon. She is a sister of Prof. John Sandels, who for a number of years was a professor at Kenyon College, Ohio. He was born in Ireland, came to America in 1843, and died in Louisiana in 1878. Our subject is the elder of two children. The other, Annie B. (now Mrs. M. H. Meeks) was married December 31, 1880, and is a resident of Savannah, Tenn. Our subject acquired a fine business and literary education, and owns the old Nunnelly homestead. He owns 1,600 acres of land, and is extensively engaged in rearing stock. He began merchandising at Old Vernon in 1882, and has since continued. January 12, 1875, he married Nettie Phillips, who was born in Hickman County in 1853. They have four children: Elise, Harry, Kate and Annie. Mr. Nunnelly is a Democrat, and he and wife are members of the Episcopal Church.

William H. Phillips, sheriff, and native of Hickman County, was born June 13, 1850, son of William and Susan (McNealy) Phillips, and is of English descent. The father was born in Hickman County, and served as sheriff six years. He represented his county in the State Legislature two terms, and died in 1867, about sixty-three years of age. Our subject's paternal grandfather was William Phillips, who was born in North Carolina and came to Tennessee as early as 1808. He was the first sheriff of Hickman County, and served for sixteen years. He was one of the early settlers of Tennessee. The mother of our subject was born in Hickman County, and died about 1858. William H. is the eldest of four children. He received a practical education, and carried on farming until he was elected sheriff of Hickman County, in August, 1884. In December, 1874, he was united in marriage to Miss Lizzie Primm, and their union was blessed with five children: Clara, Nellie, Fannie, Pollie and Bennie. Mrs. Phillips is a member of the Methodist Episcopal Church South, and her husband votes the Democratic ticket and belongs to the K. of H. fraternity.

Joseph H. Russell, druggist and postmaster at Centreville, Tenn., is a Tennessean by birth, born in Hickman County, Tenn., June 5, 1853, son of F. B. and Hester (English) Russell. He resided on a farm until 1882, when he engaged in the steam-boat business, which he continued for two years. He then came to Centreville, where he has sold drugs since February, 1886. He was commissioned postmaster of Centreville, and was married November 25, 1875, to Mary E. Jones, who died February 8, 1879. Her two children—Leta and Omer—died before she did. His second marriage occurred December 24, 1881, to Nellie Grimes, a native of Hickman County, born in 1858. They have one child—Henry. Mr. Russell is a Democrat, and cast his first presidential vote for Samuel J. Tilden. Mr. and Mrs. Russell are members of the Christian Church, and he is of English origin. Our subject's parents were born in Williamson and Maury Counties, Tenn., respectively. The father was born in 1821, and his parents were from Virginia.

Campbell Slayden, M. D., a leading citizen of Hickman County, Tenn., was born on the 30th of April, 1827, and is a son of William E. and Rosa (Shelton) Slayden. The family are of English origin, and both parents are natives of the Old Dominion. They came to Tennessee about 1813, and settled in Dixon County, where the father followed the mechanic's trade and wagon-making for many years. He died in 1861, and his wife in 1854. The early years of Dr. Slayden were spent on the home farm and in attending the schools of his native county. At the age of twenty-one years he began the study of medicine, and first attended lectures at the old Medical College, of Cincinnati, Ohio, and subsequently entered the medical department of the University of Nashville, from which he graduated in 1852. He located on Harpeth River, in Davidson County, where he practiced for about three years, and the following ten years was a resident of Dixon County. Since that time he has resided in Pinewood, where his professional labors are meeting with well deserved success. He has made his own way in life, and is one of the leading physicians of his part of Tennessee. He is a Democrat and a Mason, and was married in August, 1851, to Emily Jane Anderson, of Davidson County. Seven children have blessed their union: Emma J., Rosa C., Thomas J., Addie, William C., George A. and John P. Dr. and Mrs. Slayden are members of the Christian Church.

Dr. Elisha G. Thompson, general merchant, of Centreville, was born six miles north of the town March 13, 1836, son of Asa and Mary (Carothers) Thompson and of English-Scotch descent. His father was born in North Carolina in 1797, and his mother in Hickman County, Tenn., in 1807. The Thompson family came to Tennessee about 1802, and settled in Robertson County, where they lived until 1805, then they came to what is now Hickman County. Here the grandparents of our subject died. Here, also, the father of Mr. Thompson died in 1875. He was a farmer by occupation. Of ten children born to him our subject is the fifth. He was educated in the country schools, and remained on the farm until nineteen years of age, when he began clerking in a store in Centreville. He began studying medicine in 1857, in the office of A. D. Childress, of Hardin County, Tenn. Two years later he began selling drugs in Wayne County, continuing the same until the breaking out of the war, when he enlisted in Company F, Wayne County Rangers, Second Battalion of Cavalry. He was afterward in the First Tennessee Cavalry, and served as second lieutenant. He was commissioned captain in September, 1861, and held this position until 1862, when he was compelled to resign on account of ill health. He went to Roupe's Valley Iron Works, in Alabama, where he secured the position of post surgeon. In 1865 he returned to Centreville, and here has since resided. In 1868 he began the practice of his profession in this place and continued for twelve years, when he began merchandising. He is a Democrat, and from 1866 until 1874 he was deputy circuit clerk. In 1874 he was elected circuit court clerk and was re-elected in 1878, thus showing his popularity as a citizen and office holder. He is a Royal Arch Mason, and was married in December, 1866, to Catherine Carothers, of Mississippi, who died May 20, 1878, leaving one son, H. Clagett. In 1879 Dr. Thompson married Fannie Phillips, of Holly Springs, Miss. They have one child, Lucy.

John T. Walker, cashier of the First National Bank of Centreville, Tenn., is a native of Hickman County, Tenn., born September 2, 1848, and is of Scotch-Irish descent. His father, James Walker, was a native of North Carolina, born in 1811, and was a farmer and cabinet-maker by occupation, and served in the Seminole and Mexican wars. His death occurred in Hickman County, in 1872. The family came from North Carolina to Tennessee, and settled in Bedford County at an early day, and became prominent and respected citizens of that county. The maiden name of our subject's mother was Mary E. Cooper. She was born in Bedford County, Tenn., in 1827. The subject of our sketch is the second of their eight children. His juvenile days were spent in laboring on a farm and in attending the common schools, where he obtained a good English education. In 1871 he embarked in the general merchandise business at Whitfield, Tenn., and in 1872 began traveling for a Cincinnati (Ohio) business house. In 1875 he went to Nashville, but during this time retained his business interest at Whitfield. Since 1876 he has been a resident of Centreville, and ever since his location in the town has been engaged in the mercantile business. Upon the organization of the First National Bank of this place, he was chosen its cashier and has filled the duties of this position very efficiently and satisfactorily. He is a prominent business man of the county, and is respected alike for his many sterling business qualities and his personal integrity and worth. In 1874 he united his fortunes with those of Miss Mary J. Clagett, of Centreville, daughter of Horatio Clagett. Mr. Walker is a Democrat, and his first presidential vote was cast for Horace Greeley. His wife is a member of the Methodist Episcopal Church South.

S. McE. Wilson, M. D., merchant and physician, was born in Hardeman County, Tenn., March 2, 1838, son of Samuel B. and Tillissee (McElwee) Wilson, and is of Scotch-Irish descent. His parents were natives, respectively, of Kentucky and Tennessee, and born in 1808 and 1815. After residing in Tennessee for some time they removed to Mississippi, and there the father died in 1861, and the mother in 1866. Our subject spent his early days on a farm, and at the age of sixteen entered the Ripley Male Academy at Ripley, Miss., remaining until 1858, when he entered the University of Mississippi. He came to Tennessee in the fall of 1859, and began teaching school near the famous Shiloh Church, and at a later period became principal of Ebenezer Academy, in Humphreys County, Tenn. The war broke out about this time, and he went to Mississippi, and continued teaching until the close of the war and then returned to Tennessee. He began the study of medicine in 1861, while teaching school, and afterward read in the office of Drs. Croxton and McFarland. In 1866 he began practicing in Benton County, and later in Decatur County. In 1869 he removed to Stewart County, and a year later (1870) came to Centreville, and since that time has dealt in drugs and engaged in the active practice of medicine. He married, in 1861, Mary T. Moore, of Humphreys County, and by her he became the father of twelve children, six now living: Eunice, Roffie, Thomas, Jordan, Fannie and Estelle. Dr. Wilson is a Mason, and he and wife are members of the Methodist Episcopal Church South. He is one of the leading men of Centreville, and in 1874 was elected by the county court to fill the unexpired term of David Dean, as county trustee, and in August of the same year was elected by the people as trustee of Hickman County, and was re-elected for three successive terms, holding the office for a period of eight years. He was also postmaster of Centreville five years, and may be said to be a thoroughly self-made man. His first vote was cast for John Bell, of Tennessee, for President, and since that time he has always voted with the Democratic party.

LEWIS COUNTY.

Z. V. Dabbs, a prominent old citizen, residing at Newburg, Lewis Co., Tenn., and a native of the same county was born April 8, 1827, son of John and Winphra Dabbs, who were born in North Carolina and emigrated to Tennessee at an early date, locating in Lewis County. They were married about 1823, and became the parents of the following ten children: William P., Paten G., Z. V., Willis C., Matilda C., Mary J., John C., Richard I., Alsey C. and Winphra E. The father died in 1856, and the mother in 1865. Our subject is the third child born to their union. He was educated in the common schools of Lewis County, and from boyhood until 1877 was engaged in tilling the soil. Owing to failing health at that time, he was compelled to give up farm life, and has since been acting as deputy for the county officials. He has been magistrate of Lewis County for many years, and was first elected to the office in 1849. He has been fairly successful, and is regarded as a prosperous and industrious man. In 1847 he married Lucinda Grinder, daughter of Robert and Elizabeth Grinder, who were natives of North Carolina, and early settlers of Lewis County, Tenn. Mr. and Mrs. Dabbs are the parents of four children: John R., William C., Mary E. and Admira C. Mr. Dabbs is a Democrat, and the family are members of the Cumberland Presbyterian Church.

Samuel L. Massey, recorder of Lewis County, Tenn., and merchant of Newburg, was born in Lawrence County October 12, 1845. His parents, Dr. Richard and Levisa Massey, were married in Lawrence County about 1832, and became the parents of five sons and four daughters: Newton A., Jasper D., Nancy A., Mary A., Richard A., Levisa, William G., Aramatta L. and Samuel L. Richard Massey, Sr., was a prominent physician for over sixty years in Lawrence County. He died

September 25, 1884, and his wife August 22, 1880. Our subject attended the common schools of Lawrence County, and the greater part of his life was spent on a farm. In 1880 he came to Newburg and engaged in the grocery and general merchandise business, where he still remains. In 1882 he was elected county recorder of Lewis County. He has been a very successful business man, and is considered one of the first citizens of the county. He is a Democrat, and in 1867 was married to Emily F. Craig, a daughter of James and Malissa Craig, of Lawrence County. Mr. Massey and wife are members in good standing of the Methodist Episcopal Church South.

James W. Stockard, county court clerk of Lewis County, Tenn., was born in Maury County, Tenn., on the 11th of February, 1819, and is the son of Richard and Elizabeth Stockard, born respectively in North Carolina and Tennessee. They were married about 1812, and had born to their union six daughters and four sons: Eleanor, John J., James W., Elizabeth D., Amanda E., Margaret, Catherine M., Richard V., Sarah A. and Samuel M. The father died in 1850, and the mother in 1833. James W. was their third child, and was educated in the common schools of Maury County. In 1851 he moved to Lewis County, where he purchased land and farmed until 1880. He at that time was elected county court clerk of Lewis County, and has since held the office. In 1844 Mary S. Jennings, daughter of George and Ann Jennings, of Maury County, became his wife. She died June 21, 1854, leaving the following children: John R., Samuel J., William J., Beatrice E. and George H. January 2, 1885, Mr. Stockard married Ursely, widow of William Wilson and daughter of Felta Biffle, of Wayne County. Mr. and Mrs. Stockard became the parents of three sons: Silas M., Joseph A. and Thomas V. This wife died February 4, 1861, and December 17, 1865, Mr. Stockard married Parmelia A. Davidson, widow of Jesse Davidson and daughter of William and Mary Cody. Our subject and wife are members of the Cumberland Presbyterian Church, and politically he is a Democrat.

Index Prepared By:
Colleen Morse Elliott
Fort Worth, Texas

Abernathy, Andrew J. 794
  Elizabeth 845
  Martha 820, 824
  William 845
Acklin, Cleaburn 849
  James 849
  Martha 849
  Sarah M. 849
  Tempie 849
  Thomas F. 849
Adair, Jacob 750
Adams, Daniel 755
  David R. 849
  Eliza 849
  Elizabeth A. 849
  George S. 849
  Hodge 799
  John F. 849
  Martha E. 849
  Polly 871
  Unity J. 849
  Wiley H. 849
  William 849
  William J. 849
Adkison, D. H. 762
  David 750
Akin, J. H. 774
  N. B. 805
  John 764, 803
  Samuel 750, 787
Akins, Martha 864
Alberson, S. V. 784
Alcorn 751
Alexander 751, 850
  Mary Ann 839
  Mary J. 845
  Mc. 839
Alford, W. M. 759
  Bailey 750
  Charles A. 807
  Edward C. 807
  Emma 829
  Emma C. 807
  Fannie 829
  George T. 807
  Isaac W. 807
  James B. 807
  James M. 807, 829
  Joseph H. 807
  Maggie S. 807
  Martha F. 807
  Mary P. 807
  William R. 807
Allen 820
  S. H. 760
  John T. 842
  William B. 759
Allison, Andrew 755
Allsop 751
Alston, James 915
  Jane D. 915
  Nancy 915
Alton 754
Anderson 758
  J. H. S. 805
  W. C. 760
  Chas. 756
  Emily Jane 921
  Erastus 791
  Hannah 900
  James 770, 776, 790
  Jas. 771
  John 779
  Margaret 908
  Martha 914
  Robert 786, 792
  Susan 913
Andrews, Eliza 913

Andrews, Cont.
  Robert L. 799
Angel, John 791
Anthony, John 755
Appleton, James 751
  Mary F. 818
Archer, George 756
  Rachel 847
  Thomas 752, 762
Armstrong 826
  Charles 750
  Hames 750
  Nathan 750
  Samuel 750
Arnett, Sarah A. 862
Arnold, Louisa 896
Arrendell, Erastus 882
  Jane E. 882
  Mary 882
Ashmore, Joshua 750
Atkin, Samuel 787
Atkins, Samuel 779
Atkinson, W. T. 794
Atkisson, Jesse 768
Austin, P. A. 753
  P. G. 753
  Phillip G. 762
Aydlotte 773
Aydelott, Samuel 790
Azbell, Solomon 751
Badgett, Tolitha 818, 831
Bailey, Mildred 821
Baker, Alice 916
  Fannie 916
  Frances C. 863
  John 793
  Larkin 783
  Nettie 835
  Sarah A. 855
  William N. 783
Baldwin, Joseph 751
Barber, Abraham 780
  Allen 779
  Nancy 900
Barham, Hartwell 783
Barker, G. W. 766
Barnett, C. E. 758
  J. M. 766, 767
  S. M. 784
  Caroline 850
  John M. 850
  Joseph B. 850
  Lillie A. 850
  Lovina 850
  Mansfield C. 889
  Martha J. 850
  Mary 889
  San Martin 889
  Sarah C. 850
  Senith 850
  William 765
  Wm. 766, 770, 773, 775
Barnwell 796
Barry 782
Bass 786
Bassham, J. M. 762
  R. L. 760
  Keziah 827
Bastian, Josiah 781
Bastin, Josiah 791
Bate, H. C. 758
Bateman, T. P. 794, 795, 867, 918
Bates 821
  J. A. 794, 796
  J. R. 784
  Agnes E. 910
  Alonzo L. 910

Bates, Cont.
  Anna 910
  Clarence P. 910
  Clifford G. 910
  Cordelia E. 910
  Douglas T. 910
  Florence O. 910
  Fred 911
  Jasper A. 910
  John 790
  John M. 910
  Lewis 910
  Moses 783
  Owen L. 910
  Simeon L. 911
  William C. 910
  William M. 910
Baugus, Elizabeth 902
Baxter, Nathan 794
  Nathaniel 805
Beal, William 795
Beard, George 785
Beasley, J. P. 899
  Barnabas 889
  John P. 889, 890
  Joseph 793
  Lucy 889
Beatty, Thomas H. 806
Beavers, Lydia Ann 825
Beeler, Daniel 752, 755, 758,
  John 750, 752 757
Beery, Robert 790
Belew, Eliza C. 828
Bell, Adeline 850
  Charles 851
  Conly 851
  Elizabeth 850, 851
  Jane 850
  Jane E.888
  John 923
  Martha C. 850
  Samuel 851
  Whitthorne 851
  William H. 851
  William L. 850
  William R. 850, 888
Belsha, Darky 853
  Ewing 853
  Mary 853
Benham, J. M. 773
  Elizabeth 874
  Jasper 774
  Mary A. 874
  William 874
Bennet 750
Bentley 794
  T. L. 825
  Daniel 761
  Lee M. 844
  Matty J. 822
Bently, L. M. 753
Bob (colored) 757
Benton, Thomas H. 790
Berry, A. H. 854
  G. 775
  J. G. 766
  Ada 851
  Elmyra J. 851
  Joanna 851
  Joseph C. 851
  Joseph G. 851
  Lou Dora 851
  Ralph M. 851
  Sarah 851
  William 851
  William J. 851
Berryman, Clayborn 790
Biffel, Jacob 866

Biffle 828, 829
  J. B. 776
  J. I. 768
  J. T. 773
  N. F. 771
  Eliza A. 851
  Feltz 924
  Jacob 764
  Jake 851
  Joe E. 852
  John 765
  John W. 852
  Jonathan 851
  Jonathan A. 852
  Jonathan Frank 851
  Mary 852
  Mary Ann 866
  Nathan 764, 770, 772, 775
  Nettie E. 852
  Ursely 924
  William M. 774
Billingsby, J. 760
Bird 796
  Mary 810
Birgen, James 750
Bishop, Elizabeth 816
  Elizabeth J. 816
  Reden 816
  Rosin L. 790
Biven, Elizabeth 849
Black, Alma M. 890
  Helen M. 845
  Isaac N. 890
  Julia M. 890
  Lula L. 890
  Mark 790
  Susan A. 890
Blackard, Levi 750
Blackburn 785
  Ambrose 802
  Bethel Tipton 894
  John 771, 804, 805
  Leroy 903
  Mary E. 903
Blackwell, A. J. 890
  W. J. 890
  Jackson 890
  Mary 890
Blackwood, Martha 812, 912
  William 859
Bladen, Ed B. 775
Blair, James 770
  Thomas 758
Blakely, Mary A. 842
Bliss 796
Blythe, Chanie A. 830
  Jacob 750, 830
  Jane 830
Bobo, Eliza 863
Bodenhammer, Sarah E. 808
Bone, L. B. 891
  Arthur Garfield 891
  Bailey P. 891
  Fessona 891
  John 891
  Leander 891
  Polly Ann 891
  William Leander 891
Booth, Jerry 790
Borders, Joshua 757
Boshers, Thomas 776
Boswell, A. 760
Bowden, Feriba 872
Bowman, John 806
Boyd 770
  C. H. 872
  G. W. 766, 771
  Ann E. 852
  Elizabeth 862, 868
  Frank 852, 866
  George W. 852
  Laura E. 852, 866
  Mary E. 872

Bradley, R. H. 914
Bradshaw, J. A. 762
Bradstreet, James 750, 755
Braly, Elizabeth A. 828
Bramlett, L. M. 756
Branch, Sarah M. 904
Branden, John 755, 756
Brashear, T. M. 783
  Julia M. 890
  Thomas 890
  Thomas M. 782, 783
Brashers, Jacob 751
  John 751
  Rob. 754
  Robert 752
  William 751
Breckenridge 786
  John C. 821
Bredwell, Mary 906
Breece, Henry 790
Brenn, George 751
Brentley, Daniel 758
Brewer, G. H. 775
  John J. 775
Bridges, J. C. 771
Brien, John S. 794
Briggs, Jesse 794
  William 791
Briley, Joshua 779
  William 784
Brine, J. L. 757, 769
Brinker, Catherine 873
Britewell, Jane 905
Britt, Anderson S. 891
  Edward H. 891
  George S. 891
  James H. 891
  Jennie 891
  John D. 891
  Julia A. 891
  Mary 891, 899
  Mary M. 891
  Mollie A. 891
  Obed 891
  Robert L. 891
  Thomas C. 891
  William A. 891
  William S. 891
  Wm. O. 799, 781, 785, 891
Bromley 771, 872
  J. J. 775
  W. L. 774
  Amos H. 853
  Charles J. 853
  Darky 853
  Eda C. 853
  Edith 853
  Emma N. 853
  James A. 853
  John 750, 853
  John J. 853
  John L. 853
  Joseph C. 853
  Mary 853
  Mary J. 853
  Richard C. 853
  Sallie 853
  Samuel B. 853
  Thomas C. 853
  William E. 853
  William L. 852, 853
Brooks, Georgiana P. 904
  James 750, 755
Brothers, Eliza J. 823
  Robert 823
Brown 861, 910
  Mrs. C. C. 753
  H. H. 783
  H. M. 783
  J. C. 760
  T. G. 768
  W. T. 805
  Allen 764

Brown, Cont.
  Andrew 756
  Aquila 750
  Bessie 899
  C. Allen 899
  Emily 894
  George W. 899
  James H. 783
  John 764
  John C. 825
  John P. 796
  Joseph 779, 781
  Mary 899
  Milton D. 805
  Nat 775
  Thomas G. 768
  Wiley 750
Brownlow 839
  W. J. 760
  James 828
  Martha A. 828
Bryant 750
  W. T. 768
  Charity 812
  Jacob 754
Bryson, Sally 788
Buchanan 758
  C. 771
  M. H. 757
  Alonzo L. 808
  Cicero 854
  Demosthenes 808
  Ella 854
  Ella Ann 866
  Franklin 808
  John 750, 790, 808
  Mary J. 808
  Maxilian A. 755
  Maxmilian H. 752, 757
  Samuel 808
  Samuel G. 808, 854
  Sarah E. 808, 854
  Solon 808
  Walter 808
Buckner 772
  A. P. 805
  S. B. 760
  Martha J. 878
Bullock 796
Bumpass, A. W. 753, 758, 761
  H. J. 784
  Abner 750
  Augustine W. 756
  Gabriel 750, 755
  Hartwell J. 818
  James 750
  Mary A. 818
Bundrant, John W. 768
  Peter 768
Burchard, W. E. 795
  Martha Jane 903
Burkett, J. R. 759
Burlesson, Wm. 750
Burnett, Martha A. 902
Burns 773
  P. D. 855
  S. W. 774
  Anna L. 854
  Biffle F. 855
  Bill B. 855
  Carrie K. 854
  Charles 764
  Chas. 770
  Edna 854
  Elizabeth 850
  Elizabeth J. 854
  Essie M. 856
  Florence B. 854
  George 892
  Ida 856
  Jacob B. 854
  James 753
  James R. 856

Burns, Cont.
  James S. 855
  Jennie P. 855
  John S. 856
  John W. 892
  Lela K. 854
  Leroy 759
  Lillie J. 854
  Lizzie 878
  Lou E. 855
  Lytle 856
  Margaret E. 856
  Mary A. 872
  Mary Jean 895
  Mary L. 854
  Mattie V. 854
  Miles G. 856
  Myrtle R. 854
  Nancy 892
  Nathan F. 855
  Pattie E. 854
  Polk D. 855
  Rebecca 856
  Riley K. 855
  Sallie 855, 878
  Sallie A. 855
  Samuel L. 854, 855, 878
  Sarah 857
  Sarah A. 854, 855
  Thomas T. 855
  Toby 892
  William 854
  Willie 854
  Wm. 765, 770, 772
Burnum, Joshua 795
Busby 758, 767
  N. C. 808
  George H. 808
  James F. 808
  John S. 808
  Paul Jones 808
  Sallie J. 808
  Samuel T. 808
  Stephen J. 808
  Verlinda 808
  William A. 808
  William M. 808
Bushby, S. 753
  Stephen 751
Butler, Elizabeth 878
  Robert 790
Byter, James 751
Cade, Samuel 765
Cahal, T. H. 756
  Jerry H. 769
Campbell 751
  B. F. 788
  J. M. L. 759
  W. B. 759
  W. H. 788
  Adelia 809
  Hugh A. 809
  James 790
  Jane 879
  Lou 809
  Martha C. 788
  Richard 809
Cameron, Lucy 916
Cannon, Carrie E. 809
  Emma C. 809
  Francis M. 809
  Geneva 809
  James E. 809
  James M. 809
  John C. 809
  Mary E. 809
  Shiloh T. 809
  Temperance 809
  Thomas F. 809
  William E. 809
  Wm. 750
Cantrell, Nancy 872
Carlisle, Mary J. 827

Carothers, Catherine 921
  Mary 921
Carr 770
  Robert 750
Carrell, S. A. 753, 758, 848
  Julia A. 810
  Mary Frances 810
  Mary L. 810
  Mary S. A. 843
  Matthew F. 810
  Paris A. 810
  Stephen A. 810, 843
Carroll 771
  S. A., Jr. 841
  Adelia 892
  Albert N. 856
  Anna 856
  James R. 856
  John 805
  John M. 856
  Laura A. 856
  Mary 888
  Mary E. 856
  Mary P. 856
  Sarah J. 856
  Thomas H. 856
  William 806
  William A. 856
  William E. 856
Carrothers, Andrew 791
Carson, Malinda W. 903
Carter, H. C. 784
  David 764
  Dora I. 832
  Eliza M. 827
  Gideon G. 803
  James 827
  Jemima 836
  Kincheon 803
  Mary A. 837
  Washington 766
Caruthers, Andrew 799
  Hykua 782
Cash, Wm. 755
Cathey, Griffith 803
Catron 802
Cauthen, Eliza 830
Cavender, J. A. 762
Cavitt 802
Chadwick, Thomas 755
Chaffin, J. C. 760
  J. L. 760
  Alice L. 816
  Mary 912
  Rob. 756
  Robert 752, 753, 755
  Wm. 753
Chambers, Drury 750
  John 750
Chappell, Annie O. 865
Charter, Robert 796, 911
Cheairs, N. G. 760
Cheat, Aaron 750
  Richard 750
Cherry, Daniel 764
Childress, A. D. 921
  W. T. 776
  Adian D. 807
  Fannie 829
  Jesse 779
  Martha F. 807
  Nancy 807
  Wm. G. 768
Choat 767
  P. B. 857
  V. B. 857
  Aaron 755
  Arthur 857
  Arthur T. 857
  Henrietta V. 857
  George T. 857
  Isham E. 857
  Jackson M. 856, 857

Childress, Cont.
  Little 768, 769
  Margaret E. 857
  May L. 857
  Sallie L. 857
  Sarah 856, 857
  Simpson 856, 857
  Virgie 857
Choat, William S. 857
Choate, T. J. 810
  Andrew Lee 810
  Charles A. 810
  Daniel R. 810
  Eliza J. 810
  Ella T. 810
  James T. 810
  John Rufus 810
  Martha 810
  Mary Ellen 810
  Nancy 810
  Richard 810
Choete, Sarah 868
Christian, J. W. 805
  Thos. T. 805
Christie, Samantha C. 867
Christy, James 750
  Thomas 750
Chromister, Adam 750
  Phillip 750, 752, 756
Churchwell, F. 769
  Richard 764
Clagett, W. G. 794, 796
  Anna S. 912
  Cordelia E. 910, 911
  Elizabeth 861
  Elizabeth J. 912
  Elizabeth O. 911
  Horatio 911, 922, 861
  John H. 794, 912
  Laura E. 861, 912
  Letty P. 911
  Mary J. 912, 922
  Matilda T. 912
  Rebecca 911
  Robert M. 912
  Sarah R. 911
  Theodosia C. 911
  William G. 910, 912
  William George 911
Clark, W. C. 794
  W. P. 799
Clarke 803
Clay, A. G. 769
  Sallie A. 915
Clayton, Boswell 790
  Fannie 873
  Hardy 873
  John 790, 802, 803
  Martha 873
  Rachel 886
Clement, Sarah 915
Clendenen, Joseph 774
  Theodore 773
Clendennin, J. A. 854
  Annie 829
  Bettie 852
  Joseph 852
  Mary 852
Clouston, Cenia 915
  Edward G. 915
  Martha R. 915
Cobb, R. L. 756
Coble 779
Cocke, Adaline F. 811
  Albert H. 811
  Alice 810
  Dade W. 811
  Frances 811
  George W. 811
  Jackson M. 811
  John C. 811
  Lucy Ann 811
  Maria L. 811

Cocke, Cont.
  Mary D. 811
  Peter P. 810, 811
  Taylor F. 811
  Thornton H. 811
  Walker A. 811
  William C. 810
Cody, Mary 924
  Parmelia A. 924
  William 924
Coffee, J. F. 760
Coffman, Nancy 827
Cole, Bennett 857
  Jasper E. 858
  John H. 857
  Mary A. 848
  Nancy 857
  Nancy A. 857
  Martha V. 858
  Mary F. 858
  Viola A. 858
Coleman, W. P. 793
  Abner 783
Colley, T. H. 816
  Maggie B. 816
Collier, A. T. 771
  M. 766
  Matthew 771
Collins, H. 759
  James 764
Colston, Henry 764
Comer, Hannah P. 837
  Jessee 837
  Margaret 837
Comes, J. J. 771
Compton, Nancy 820
Condor 802
Cook 772
  A. P. 771
  I. S. W. 758
  Almyra I. 859
  Ed 760
  Edner E. 859
  Heber J. 859
  Henry 758
  Jacob L. 859
  James T. 859
  Jesse 859
  John B. 859
  John L. 858, 859
  Lizzie 840
  Mary 859
  Mary A. 858, 859
  Nancy L. 859
  Nathaniel T. 858
  Nellie 859
  Pinia R. 859
  Thomas 859
  William M. 859
Cooper 817
  A. G. 805
  R. H. 772
  R. M. 805
  R. T. 806
  Albert G. 803
  Elizabeth C. 893
  John H. 806
  Leroy Blackburn 893
  Mary E. 922
  Nancy J. 893
  Paris 805
  Peter 918
  Robert M. 805
Copeland, T. N. 772
  Amanda 859
  Florence 858
  Jemima C. 884
  Joseph M. 858
  Lorenzo 858
  Mildred Camilla 858
  Osceolla 858
  Reuben 790
  Sarah W. 858

Copeland, Cont.
  Thomas N. 858
  Willis 770
  Wm. 770
Corbitt, Sarah W. 906
Corender, Edward 791
Cornell, Alice 811
  Fred W. 811
  Margaret 811
  Robert B. 811
Coruthers, William H. 793
Cotes, Joshua 779, 780
Cottham, Alfred 775
Cotton, J. T. 774
  S. W. 797
Couch, R. W. 774
  Charity 811
  Charles E. 812
  Emily C. 812
  John A. 811
  Manda E. 812
  Mary E. 812
  Mary J. 811
  Thomas 811
  William 814
  William A. 812
  Zilpha M. 814
Coulert, Archibald 750
Cousens, Charlotte 904
Cowan, Elizabeth 916
Cox, N. N. 786, 847, 903
  Chas. 771
  Nancy C. 814
Craig, A. D. 783
  A. P. 892
  G. B. 892
  P. H. 769, 773, 774, 884
  S. A. 796, 913
  W. C. 754
  Ada May 913
  Adelia 892
  Amanda 859
  America 892
  Andrew D. 892
  Ann Washington 912
  Anna 812
  Bessie 893
  Charles 912
  Charley Ross 913
  David 912
  Eleanor 912
  Eliza 885
  Eliza Ann 913
  Elizabeth 812, 912
  Elizabeth A. 913
  Elizabeth Jane 912
  Emily 812
  Emily F. 924
  Emily Frances 912
  Eva Campbell 913
  Isabell 912
  James 805, 812, 912, 924
  James Millard 912, 913
  John 787, 912, 913
  John Henry 913
  John Johnson 912
  Johnson 812, 859, 912, 913
  Joseph 812
  Joseph Leroy 913
  Julia 892
  Julia V. 893
  Laura B. 860, 884
  Laura W. 860
  Malissa 924
  Margaret 912
  Margaret Malissa 912
  Martha 812, 912
  Martha A. 860
  Martha D. 892
  Martha Ella 912
  Martha Ellen 913
  Mary 912
  Mary A. 860

Craig, Cont.
  Mary Isabell 913
  Mattie 812
  Melissa 812, 907
  Millard 812
  Molly C. 893
  Nancy 912, 913
  Nettie Pearl 913
  Newton 912
  Peyton H. 859
  Robert Newton 913
  Ruby M. 893
  Sallie B. 860
  Samuel 912
  Sidney 812
  Sidney A. 912
  Sidney Anderson 912
  Simeon Brantley 913
  Walter 812
  Walter Peyton 913
  William 859, 912
  William Blackwood 913
  William Harvey 860
  Willie 812
  Wilton 860
Cray, P. H. 776
Crews, Archie F. 860
  Arter Simeon 812
  Arthur 812
  Daniel Webster 813
  Eletha C. 860
  Eliza Emeline 813
  Frances 860
  George Washington 813
  Gustina 860
  Henry Clay 813
  Jeremiah Benjamin 813
  Jonas 812, 813
  Jonathan 860
  Jonathan McClane 813
  Louvisa 812
  Louvisa Amanda 813
  Malisent 860
  Martha A. 860
  Martha Ann 812
  Mary E. 860
  Mary Virginia 812
  Melvina Catherine 813
  Nancy J. 860
  Sarah F. 860
  William 860
  William James 812
  Zachariah F. 813
Crisp, John 750
  Mansil 752
  Maurice 756
Crockett, David 750, 751, 752,
    755, 756, 757
  Patterson 750
Cross, J. W. 828
  Mary A. 828
rosthwait, John 751
Crowder 903
Cromwell, Fessona 891
Croxton 922
Crudup, Caroline 893
  Martha 893
  Robt. 783
Cude, Andrew C. 893
  Caroline 893
  Horner 779, 893
  Indiana 893
  Martha 893
  Nancy 893
  Temperance 893
Culp, H. A. 784
Cummins, George W. 872
  Nancy J. 872
  Sarah 872
Cunningham 750, 751, 796
  A. H. 772
  J. A. 799
  Armstead H. 860

Cunningham, Cont.
  Grace 860
  James R. 861
  John H. 861
  John R. 860
  Laura E. 861
  Solomon P. 752
  Southern S. 861
  Walker M. 861
Curl, William 790, 792
Curtis, Wm. B. 766
Cypert, T. J. 775
  Baker 764
  Elmira J. 851
  Emma I. 886
  Ione 887
  Jesse 764, 765
  Robert 770, 771
  Sarah W. 858
Dabbs, W. C. 804
  Z. V. 923
  Admira C. 923
  Alsey C. 923
  John 923
  John C. 923
  John R. 923
  Lucinda 923
  Mary E. 923
  Mary J. 923
  Matilda C. 923
  Nat. 779
  Paten G. 923
  Richard I. 923
  William C. 923
  William P. 923
  Willis C. 923
  Winphra 923
  Winphra E. 923
Dale 796, 911
Dalton, B. H. 759
  W. C. 750
Daniel, J. B. 783
Dansbee, Thomas 795
Dansby, Mary 895
Darden, Alfred 795
  Henry 795
Davasier, Green 879
  Malinda 879
  Sarah 879
David, N. C. 771
Davidson, Daniel 790
  Jane 886, 887
  Jesse 924
  Parmelia A. 924
Davis 751
  C. B. 753
  W. C. 844
  Anderson 861, 862
  Annie 861, 862
  Annie C. 861
  Annie M. 862
  Catherine O. 861
  Cecil K. 862
  Charles H. 862
  George K. 862
  Henry E. 861
  James 764
  Jasper 768
  Jemima 861
  John A. 862
  John J. J. 861
  John R., Sr. 861
  Joseph A. 861
  Lowly I. 862
  Mary A. 862
  Mary J. 861, 868
  Nancy E. 861
  Parlee 861
  Salathiel C. 862
  William 757
  William C. 862
  William O. 862
  Wm. 753

Day, Henson 752, 755, 756
Dean & Herbert 822
Dean, E. A. 796
  Q. A. 798
  Daniel 794
  David 923
  Eliza 913
  Elmer A. 913
  Ephraim A. 793, 913
  Green B. 805
  John 913
  John H. 913
  Ransom 795
  Robert 790, 792
  Susan 913
  William 791
Deaton, Elias 790, 799
Deavenport 841
  T. D. 758, 760, 761
  T. J. 756
  Amanda Finch 813
  Jennie L. 813
  Mannie F. 813
  Maria P. 813
  Martha M. 813
  Matthew 813
  Thomas 758
  Thomas D. 753, 813
  Thomas E. 814
  William H. 814
  Zuba 813
Deering 761, 774
DeLaney, Margaret 811
DeLobel, Henry 785
Denning, A. P. 776
  J. J. 776
Denny, S. R. 769
Denton, Edward 750
  Joseph 764
  Samuel 779, 780
Depoint, Green 750
Depriest, Jesse 779
Deshozer, A. C. 793, 794
Dickerson 886
  D. I. 775
  J. M. 775
  Bessie C. 862
  James M. 862
  Mary E. 862
  Sarah A. 862
  William J. 862, 869
Dickey, Wm. R. 798
Dickson 772
  J. B. 784
  Albert B. 894
  Emily 870
  Nancy J. 893
  Sarah A. 821
  Thomas 821
Dicus, S. R. 768
Dillahunty 756
  Edmund 794, 805
Dille, Huldah 897
Dixon 774
  Amanda P. 863
  Andrew J. 862
  Columbus F. 862
  Elizabeth 862, 868
  Elizabeth A. 862
  Ella 863
  Ephraim 772
  George H. 760
  James 779, 780, 781, 782, 784
  James M. 862
  John 764, 862, 868
  Jonas S. 862
  Joseph 780, 782
  Martha R. 863
  Mary 862
  Mary J. 862
  Robert M. 863
  Sarah A. 862

Dixon, Cont.
  Sarah R. 868
  Wallace 778
  William F. 863
Dobbins 802
  Alexander T. 814
  Calladonia E. 818
  David 814
  Elizabeth Calladonia 814
  Favor A. 814
  George W. 814
  James P. 814
  John J. 814
  Martha 814
  Martha Camilla 814
  Mary J. 813
  Nancy C. 814
  Robert T. 814
  William P. 814
  Zilpha 814
  Zilpha M. 814
Dodd, S. L. 796
Dodson, C. B. 783
  E. 779
  H. H. 847
  Allen W. 895
  Amanda 897
  Clabe B. 895
  Claiborne B. 895
  Elias 894
  Emily 894
  James E. 783
  James M. 783, 894
  Marshall 894
  Martha A. 908
  Martha Jane 894
  Mary 895
  Nancy 895
  Nancy A. 895
  Nancy J. 897
  Unity Lucy Robert Sarah Mat 895
  Virginia 894
  Willis 765, 790, 799
Doety, Wm. E. 799
Doherty, J. W. 769, 784
  Wm. F. 767
Dollane, Thomas 750
Douglas, J. M. 797
  Wm. E. 797
Dowdy, Martha J. 899
  Thomas 779
Downey, Richard 805
Downing, Joshua 791
Drake, Joel B. 890
  Susan A. 890
Duckworth, ___ 750
Dudley, Charlotte 895
  George H. 895
  Patsey 895
  William 895
Duke, John 764
Duncan 772
  E. T. 788
  M. 750
  Catharine 788
  Elijah 779, 788
  Lizzie 788
  Minnie 788
  Nancy 788
  William 790
  Wm. R. 788
Dunn 758
  David 790
  James 814
  Maria 814
  Sarah T. 815
  Thomas 814
Durham, James 773
  Jas. 769
Dustin & Dunn 815
Dustin 758
  W. H. 758, 814

Dustin, Cont.
 Eli 815
 Ellen 815
 Gertrude E. 815
 Maggie J. 815
 William H. 815
 Willis S. 815
 Wm. H.761
 Zuba 814
Dyal, Patrick 756
Dycus, Edward 802
Eads, Wm. 769
Earnest, Mary 830
 Moses 830
 Sarah F. 830
Easley, E. W. 793
 F. S. 795
 J. D. 793, 795
 Edward W.783
 James D. 796
 John 783, 792
 Millington 792, 793
 Thos. S. 805
East 768
 T. M. 775
 Thomas 776
Eastham, Mildred 839
Eaton, A. J. 759
Edmiston, J. E. 750
 W. A. 762
 Mary P. 807
 Wm. A. 752, 753
Edwards, T. W. 783
 W. A. 783
 W. F. 773
 Edith Lois 896
 Flora Mabel 896
 James E. 848
 John A. 895
 John T. 896
 Lorenzo E. 896
 Mark F. 764
 Mary 895
 Mary Jean 895
 Nancy 896
 Sallie 896
 Thomas C. 895
 Thomas F. 770
 William H. 896
Edwin, J. G. 784
Egleston, Harriett 835
Eldridge, Edwin H.787
Elliott, J. H.759
 James 764, 765
 John 771
Ellis, J. T. 754
 Lucy 889
Elton, Sarah E. 886
English, Amanda 846
 Hester 920
 James 765, 770
Ensley, Joanna 866
Erwin, Archie A. 914
 James H. 914
 Lucy 914
 Lulu 914
 Ocra Ann 914
 Sallie P. 914
 Theodorick W. 914
Escua, J. W. 816
 Alice 816
Estes, Robert 793, 794
Ethridge, John 751
 Thomas 751
Evans, T. J. 783
 T. S. 773
 Ebenezer 757
 Sarah F. 843
 Thomas 779
Evins, Eliza 863
 Frank 863
 Minerva J. 863
 Thomas J. 863

Evins, Cont.
 Thomas S. 863
 William A. 863
Ewing 778
Falls 751
Farmer, Joseph 752, 754
 Richard 755
Farris 881
 J. 760
Fath, Mrs. Mary 758
Fecheimer, L. S. 910
Fechheimer, M. 910
Felkins, Elizabeth 861
Ferguson, H. P. 863
 Florence 858
Fields 833
Fillmore, Zuba 814
Finch, Amanda 813
Finn, Obediah 790
Fisher, M. M. 837
 Eveline 830
 John 754
Flanigan, William H. 804, 805, 806
Flannery, Daniel A. 756
Fleeman, J. W. 815
 Elizabeth J. 816
 Ernest T. 816
 Etta E. 816
 James R. 816
 James William 816
 John T. 816
 Katie W. 816
 Mary Lure 816
 Mattie Liou 816
 Nancy 815
 Sarah E. 816
 Wiley Perry 816
 William 815
Flowers, J. D. 794
 Permelia E.817
 Wm. J.783
Fondren, Martha A. 830
Forbes, James 755
Forsence, James 799
Foster, 750, 751
 J. J. 763
 Albert W. 816
 Alice 816
 Celia 816
 Cora 816
 Daniel M. 816
 Daniel W. 816
 Dora 816
 George W. 816
 James W. 816
 John H. 816
 Julia A. 816
 Maggie B.816
 Martha N.816
 Mary 862
 William 791
 Willie 816
Foulkes, Gabriel 792
Fowler, J. L. 766
 Wm. A.766, 768
Fowlkes 796
 N. F. 793
 Edward 795
 Gabriel 790, 793
 Henry R. 911
Frain, J. W. M. 805
Fraley, Jacob 764, 779
Frank, Thomas 754
Freeman 833
Frierson 786
 L. E. 749
 Samuel D. 794
Fry 796
Fugate, Andrew 751
Fulton, Alfred S. 885
 Mary 874
Fusan, Bethel 859

Fuson, Pinia R.859
 Sophronia 859
Gabel, David 762
 Thomas 762
Gabill, Barney 750
Gains, Edward P. 790
Gallaher 768
 David 764
 David N. 766
Gambel, T. 764
 James H. 764
Gambell, ___ 751
Gambrell, William 773
Gantt, George 798
 Rebecca 911
Gardner, Rufus 791
Garner, A. 775
 W. P. H. 754
 John 751
 Lucinda 907
Garret 750
Garrett, G. H. 764
 L. 760
 Alice L. 816
 Daniel 802
 James W.816
 Joseph 816
 Joseph C. 817
 Levi 790
 Millie E. 816
Garrison, John 750
Gaswell 751
George, S. J. 795
 Solomon J. 793
Gest, John 750
 Joseph 755
Gibbs, J. A. 769
Gibson, A. J. 759
 John 764
Gilbert, Martha 841
Gillespie, Patrick 756
Gilmore, J. M. 761
 Anna 817
 Elizabeth 817
 James M. 817
 John S. 817
 Lillie 817
 Mattie 817
 Narcissa 817
 Permelia E. 817
 Willie D. 817
Girard, Charles T. 877
 Lula B. 877
 Mary 877
Glasscock, Ellen 846
Glasgow 775
Glover, F. 759
Goats, Maggie C. 836
 Nancy 836
 Philip 836
Gobbel, Benjamin P. 864
 Eliza 863
 Isaac H. 863
 John 863
 John W. 863
 Joseph E. 863
 Martha J. 863
 Mary 863
 Nancy C. 863
 Paraletha 863
 Rebecca 863
 Ruhama 863
 Sarah C.863
 William R. 863
Goblett, A. E. 901
 Susan Tennessee 901
Goedeker, George 758
Goff, Amos F. 756
Goggins, Nancy 833
Gooch, 800
 Mary E. 835
Goodman, A. F. 805
 J. 760

Goodman, Cont.
  Ambrose 762
  Drury D. 803
Gordon 790
  Nancy 893
  Powhattan 804
  Thomas 760
Gotthardt, Charles 780
Graham, R. 916
  S. 916
  Charles 783
  Frances E. 915
  Harry H. 915
  John 914
  John M. 915
  Martha 914
  Martha J. 915
  Samuel 797
  Samuel L. 914
  Thomasella 915
  Thomasella H. 915
Graves 773
  John H. 857
  Margaret E. 857
  Sallie 857
Gray 751
  J. M. 760
  M. J. 896
  T. O. 896
  Alex 792
  Bertie 897
  Edward Martin 897
  Gertrude Polinia 897
  Jesse Franklin 896
  Louisa 896
  Madison Lee 896
  Margaret Emily 896
  Martin J. 896
  Russell Horner 897
  Sarah 896
  Sarah Sophronia 896
  Thomas O. 896
  Walter Edward 896
  William Martin 896
Green 754, 772
  O. N. 750
  Edie 836
  Mary L. 836
  Thomas 750, 836
Greer, Amanda 897
  America 892
  Charlotte 895
  Harriette 897
  Henry 897
  Huldah 897
  Toby 892
  William N. 897
Greeson, Dorothy 882, 883
Gregory, J. B. 784
Gresham 754
  George 752, 757
Grey, Alex 792
Griffin, John L. 794
  Oswald 780, 781
Grimes 770, 772, 869, 870
  J. A. 766
  R. W. 805
  Amanda C. 864
  Annie O. 865
  Benjamin F. 864
  Bettie Elsie 865
  Elihu S. 864
  Eliza F. 864
  Elizabeth 880
  Elizabeth M. 864
  Emma L. 865
  Harold A. 864
  Henry 764, 875
  Henry C. 864
  Isaac G. 764
  James E. 774
  James G. 864
  John 864

Grimes, Cont.
  John M. 864
  Lucke 752
  Luke 755
  Martha 864
  Martha E. 864
  Mary A. 875
  Mary J. 864
  Matthew 771
  Millard F. 864
  Nancy Malissa 864
  Nellie 920
  Rebecca 877
  Robert N. 864
  Sallie 864
  Sarah A. E. 864
  William 864
  William P. 864
  Wilson 864
Grimmitt, Benj. 794
Grinder, Elizabeth 923
  Lucinda 923
  Robert 802, 923
Grove, Henson 764
Gullet, James 803
Gullick, Frances C. 864
  Jonathan A. 864
  Minerva J. 863
Guthrie, R. A. 783, 786, 897
  Andrew H. 897
  Bessie L. 897
  Daniel 845
  Eliza 897
  Flary 897
  James M. 897
  Jane 897
  Mollie A. 897
  Nancy J. 897
Hagan, T. N. 762
  Alonzo A. 818
  Andrew A. 818
  Bettie A. 818
  Burgeous B. 818
  Burgeous M. 818
  Calladonia E. 818
  Cecil 818
  Charles M. 818
  Edward W. 818
  Etha J. 818
  Ethel May 818
  Francis M. A. 818
  George W. 818
  Hartwell B. 818
  Henry 818
  James A. 818
  James W. 818
  John A. 817
  John E. 818
  John H. 818
  John W. 818
  Lewis N. 818
  Lurilla A. 818
  Malenia A. 818
  Marcella R. 818
  Marcella T. 818
  Mary A. 818
  Mary E. 818
  Mary F. 818
  Mary T. 818
  Mattie B. 818
  Mattie E. 818
  Minnie B. 818
  Mollie E. 818
  Rebecca 817
  Robert H. 818
  Susan R. 818
  William H. 818
  William J. 818
  Willie 818
Haggard 767, 770
  Annie C. 865
  James 865
  Robert A. 865

Hail 754
  Araminta T. 847
  Ella 819
  John A. 847
  John T. 819
  Laura N. 819
  Margaret E. 819
  Margie A. 819
  Martha 818, 847
  Mary A. 819
  Tolitha 818
  Tolitha E. 819
  William F. 818, 819
Halbert, Mary 827
Hale 808
  W. P. 847
  Eliza S. 820
  John 804
  John A. 831
  Martha 831
  Sarah E. 831
  Tolitha 831
  William 791
Haley, J. W. 805
Halford, James 750
  Joseph 750
Hall, William B. 762
Hambeck, Mary A. 917
Hamilton, J. M. 829
  Isaac 756
Hamm, Henry D. 775
  Mary E. 862
  Mildred S. 869
Hammond, G. W. 814
  Malenia A. 818
  Mary J. 814
  Willis 752
Hammonds, George W. 819
  Jesse Wade 819
  Maria C. 819
  Ursley 819
  Willis 819
Hand, Hugh B. 783
Hane, Owen 886
Haney, O. N. 902
  Owen 775
Hanks, George 755
Hannah, Clinton C. 820
  Eli F. 819
  James H. 820
  John 819
  John W. 820
  Mary 819
  Mary A. 820
  Mary O. 820
  Sallie R. 820
Harbison, Ocra Ann 914
Harbour, Esther J. 855
  James G. 855
  Rutha J. 879
  Sallie A. 855
Hardaman, Berthenia 915
  Thomas 915
  Thomasella 915
Hardee 760
Hardeman, Martha D. 892
Harder, Edmond 784
  Wm. H. 786
Hardin 772
  A. K. 774
  B. S. 773
  Alex. 794
  Benjamin 765, 766, 767
  Eliza A. 851
  Louis A. 869
  Lydia 878
Harmon, Jacob 780, 782
Harper, Wylie V. 798
Harrington, Chas. 771
  Wiley 764
Harris 773, 795
  G. L. 898
  R. C. 764

Harris, Cont.
  Anne 904
  David R. 782, 894
  George W. 870
  Hooten 790
  Madison 783
  Martha Jane 894
  Sallie 864
  William 791
Harrison 758, 844
  W. A. 775
  Charles O'Conner 821
  Daniel G. 820
  Daniel M. 821
  David 820
  David L. 821
  Eliza 820
  Eliza E. 821
  Ellen A. 915
  James K. Polk 821
  Lulu E. 821
  Sarah A. 821
  William T. 821
Hartwell, Charles E. 866
  Egbert T. 865
  Laura A. 865
  Louisa 865
  Morris 865
Harvey, J. 860
  M. B. 845
  R. 758
  R. H. 761
  Holcomb 822
  Isham O. 822
  Isom 821
  James 867
  John H. 822
  John W. 821
  Mary 822
  Matty J. 822
  Mildred 821
  Mildred M. 822
  Rachel 867
  Robert B. 822
  Robert H. 821
  Rosanna 867
  Sarah P. 845
  Thomas G. 764
Harvill, J. H. 793
Hassell, A. T. 766, 769, 770, 772, 852
  T. S. 886
  Amos 854
  Amos T. 866
  Eliza Jane 866
  Ella A. 854
  Ella Ann 866
  Enoch 866
  Joanna 866, 876
  Laura E. 852, 866
  Mary A. 854
  Mary Ann 866
  Mary C. 866
Hatcher 758, 844
Hawes, Daniel W. 885
Hay, Robert 758
Hayes, Jennie P. 845
Hayne, Robert 750
Haynes 751
Hays, Austin 768
  Thomas 755
  Wallace 768
  Wm. H. 768
Hearlson, James 750
  William 750
Helm, M. 915
  Frances E. 915
  Nancy 915
Helton, H. A. 852
  J. W. 769
  Charles J. 867
  Daniel 866
  Eliza Emeline 813

Helton, Cont.
  Elizabeth 866
  Henry A. 866, 867
  James 754, 755, 772
  Jesse 751, 755, 866
  Lemuel L. 867
  Samantha C. 867
  Serepta 867
  Turman 771
  Walter A. 867
Hemphill, R. C. 772
Henderson 781
Henry, Harriette 897
Hensley, Abel T. 806
  Charity 812
  James 802
  James F. 803
  John 805
  Larkin 802
  Mary Virginia 812
  Samuel 802
  Simeon 812
  William 802
Henson, C. J. 753
  John 750
Henton, William 764
Herbert, C. L. 822
  F. C. 822, 823
  S. B. 829
  Martha A. 823
  Peter 823
  Rebecca 823, 829
  Snowden B. 822
Herndon, Joseph L. 916
  Mollie 916
  Naomi Elizabeth 916
Heron, Eliza Jane 866
Herrin, C. J. 824
  Amanda 824
  Amanda F. 820
  Benjamin F. 820
  Blanche 820
  Charles F. 820
  Charles J. 820
  David 790
  Dora J. 820
  Eliza S. 820
  Emma E. 820
  Emma H. 820
  Frank 820
  Horace 820
  James L. 820
  Jennie L. 820
  Joel M. 820
  Joseph 820
  Martha 820, 824
  Marth J. 820
  Mary 820
  Mary J. 820
  May J. 820
  Napoleon B. 820
  Theodore 820
Hickman, Edmund 789, 790, 792
Hicks, Charles 755
  Elijah 790
  Gilbert 790
  Louvisa 812
  Malisent 860
  William 790
Higgs 751
  Wm. 755
Hill 751
  A. 753
  D. H. 761
  J. A. 759
  Abel 754
  Elizabeth 861
  James 755
  Jemima 861
  John 766, 770, 773
  Obedience 770
  Richard 752, 756
  Rob A. 770

Hill, Cont.
  Robert 753
  Thomas 861
  Wm. K. 754
Hillhouse, James 755
  John 752, 755, 756
  Robert 750
Hine 771
Hines, Hester 811
  John 793, 811
  Lucy Ann 811
  William 803
Hinson, N. J. 784
  George 791
  Mervin 790
Hinton, Lucinda 756
Hix, W. A. 784
Hodge, Jane J. 832
  William 787
  Wm. 779
Hogan, J. H. 761
  David 779
Hollabaugh, Buchanan B. 867
  Catherine 867
  Elizabeth C. 867
  Frederick W. 867
  George 867
  George T. 867
  Isham G. Harris 867
  Jacob 857, 867
  Jacob S. 867
  James C. 867
  John T. 867
  Joseph B. 867
  Luther W. 867
  Madison J. 867
  Mary J. 867
  Midda V. 867
  Rachel A. 867
  Rosanna 867
  Rose A. 857
  Virgie 857
Hollabough, George 779
Holland, Jane 830
  Thomas 751
  Tom 758
Holliday, Moses 750
  Stephen 750
Holligan, Jerry 779
Hollis, J. N. 768, 769, 775
  Aaron M. 868
  Ada R. 868
  Arthur T. 868
  Columbus F. 868
  Fountain J. 868
  James 770, 868
  James M. 868
  James P. 868
  Jane 868
  John D. 868
  Joseph B. 868
  Martha F. 868
  Mary J. 868
  Nancy P. 868
  Sarah 868
  Sarah E. 868
  William 868
  William P. 868
Holmes, John 805
  Wm. 780, 781
Holt, D. E. 768
  Dora Lee 868
  Hugh I. 868
  Israel 868
  James A. 868
  Louisa J. 868
  Mary 885
  Mary J. 868
  Wm. 768
Homer 785
Hood, D. K. 771
Hooe, Alice 810
Hooper, Enoch 779, 781

Hoover, Michael 797
Horder, Jerry 790
  William 790
Hornbeak, E. B. 793, 796
  J. W. 793
  P. M. 793, 794
  Eli B. 795, 911
  Elizabeth O. 911
  Robert 796
  Sarah 911
Hornbeck, Eli 790
Horne 758, 844
  W. P. 844
Horner, John 779
  John V. 904
  Martha M. 904
  Sarah Sophronia 896
Horton, James 750
  Mary 883
House, G. W. 771
Houssels, Bessie 899
  Bismarck 898
  Claud McIlroy 899
  Docia 898
  Gussie 899
  Jennie 898
  John H. 898
  John P. 898
  Julia E. 898
  Margaret 898
  Minnie R. 898
  Norma 898
  Robert 781, 898, 899
  Robert Clyde 899
  Robert S. 898
  Rosina R. 898
Houston, John L. 780, 781
Howard, J. W. 768
  Phillip 775
Howney, James M. 794
Hubbard, J. R. 794
  Josiah H. 795
  Mary P. 856
Huckaba 771, 862
  J. B. 775
  Clarence H. 869
  Fannie E. 869
  Emerson 869
  George E. 773, 775, 869
  George M. 869
  James A. 869
  John F. 869
  Mary Ann 869
  Mary E. 869
  Mildred S. 869
  Rhoda Y. 869
  Robert 869
  Thomas J. 869
  William F. 869
Huddleston 796
  John 790, 792
  John W. 793
  Reeves A. 793
Hudson, C. Y. 803, 804
  Adam B. 823
  Amanda J. 823
  Andrew N. 823
  Eliza B. 823
  Eliza J. 823
  Isaac D. 823
  James S. 823
  Jesse J. 823
  Mary C. 823
  Nora E. 823
  Priscilla 823
  Robert M. 823
  William D. 823
  Young M. 823
Hueler, Jacob 758
Hueser, John H. 759
Huffstedler, Jacob 779
Hughes 769, 772, 864
  A. M. 794

Hughes, Cont.
  G. T. 749, 754
  J. R. 766
  T. R. 774, 869, 870
  T. S. 870
  Bettie 870
  Ed. 754
  Elizabeth B. 870
  Frank 870
  George T. 841
  John M. 750
  Thomas S. 870
Hulme, I. N. 783, 786
Humphreys 784
  Gussie 899
  Parry W. 794
  West W. 794
Hunt 754
  J. M. 783
  S. H. 901
  George W. 805
Hunter, John 750, 762
  John S. 804
  H. W. 772
  Horatio C. 793
  Isaac 799
Hurley 750
Hurst 794
  Edith 853
Hurt 773
  Ada 871
  Emily 870
  Martha E. 870
  Mary E. 870
  Robert 871
  Robert M. 870
  Roe 871
  William 870
Hutchinson, C. 750
  Jesse 750
Ingraham, Beasley 750
Ingram, Tennessee Jane 902
Inman, James 790
Irvine 753
  Josephus 750, 752, 755,
    757, 758
Irwin 796
Isaacs, Annie 824
  Seymour 824
  Simon 823
Isham, Geo. 750
Isom, George 756
Jackson, G. W. 860
  J. 771
  Andrew 768
  David S. 871
  George W. 871
  Howell E. 852
  Jesse 756
  John 764, 871
  John A. 871
  Mahala R. 871
  Mary A. 860
  Mary E. 871
  Polly 871
  Sarah C. 871
  Susan T. 871
  William 751
  William J. 871
Jarmon 779
  Wm. 781
Jarrett 758
Jenkins 753
Jennings, Ann 924
  George 924
  Mary S. 924
Jerrett 844
Johnson 771
  A. S. 760
  C. 899
  J. E. 761
  J. H. 760
  N. W. 858

Johnson, Cont.
  W. W. 837
  Albert S. 824
  Amanda 824
  Andrew 824, 915
  Ann Eliza V. 824
  Edna E. 824
  Eldridge H. 824
  Elizabeth Agnes 845
  Emma 824
  Emma M. 824
  Jane 824
  John 802
  John A. 773
  Joseph L. 824
  Josephus S. 824
  Laura 836
  Laura L. 824
  Lewis 764
  Loulie H. 824
  Martha O. 824
  Mary 824, 837, 899
  Mary A. 824, 858, 859
  Mary E. 824
  Mary Isabella 899
  Mary J. 824
  Richard F. 824
  Robert 824, 845
  Robert A. 824
  Robert C. 824
  Wiley B. 824
  William 794, 802, 899
  William W. 824
Johnston, Andrew 805
  John C. 854
  Pattie 854
Joiner, Columbus M. 825
  James 825
  Lucy 825
  Lydia Ann 825
Jones 751, 796
  D. H. 774
  D. J. 766, 776
  D. L. 775
  J. M. 771
  M. S. 798
  Eliza Jane 866
  Henry 790
  John 830
  John A. 798
  John L. 794
  Joseph 790
  Mary A. 830
  Mary E. 920
  Mary J. 915
  Sarah A. 830
Joslin, William 792
  Wm. 794
Joyce, Ella 819
  Henry 819
  Nancy 819
Judd, John 775
Juep, J. B. 751
Keaton, Nancy Malissa 864
Keeton, J. A. 816
  Julia A. 816
Kelley, James 783
  John 838
  Joseph 779
  Malinda C. 828
  Mary T. 838
  Sallie 855
  Susan 838
Kelly, Albert 762
Kelsey, Thomas 762
Keltner, S. G. 760
Kemper, Catherine 884
Kendel, R. W. 775
Kendrick, W. P. 770
  Wm. P. 771
Kennedy 750
  J. B. 829
  Alice 829

Kennedy, Cont.
  Alice L. 826
  Francis H. 752
  John 754, 825
  John B. 825
  John S. 813
  Joseph McClain 826
  Patsy 825
Kennon, Jane 833
Keys 754
  Thomas 755
Kidd, Allen H. 826
  George 826
  Nancy N. 826
Kilburn 751
  Sarah 868
Killpatrick, John W. 803
Kimbel, R. A. 783
Kimble, F. H. 783
Kimbrew, Nancy 819
Kimmens, Grace 860
Kimmins, Joseph 790
Kindle, W. R. 771
King 768, 910
  Alexander 803, 805
  Catherine 888
  Indiana 893
  John 750
  Joseph 888
  Violet A. 888
Kinzer, James H. 783
Kirk, Lewis 761
  Lewis M. 757
Kirkey 802
Kirkpatrick, Jane 897
Kirwin, Nancy 857
Kitchen, George 750
Kittrell, Benjamin C. 899
  Betsey 900
  George 900
  Martha J. 899
  Nannie H. 905
Klein 898
Kline, Huldah 897
Koger, Martha A. 823
  William 823
Kyle, J. L. 768
  James 837
  Reuben 766
Lacefield, Esther J. 855
Lackey, Flora 826
  Ida 827
  Minnie L. 827
  Nannie M. 826
  William K. 826
  William P. 827
Lacy, Stephen 793
Laird, S. R. 771
Lancaster, W. H. 784
  Agnes E. 910
Land, Cooper B. 900
  Elizabeth J. 900
  Elkanah A. 900
  Hannah 900
  Mary F. 900
  Nancy 900
  Nancy H. 900
  William R. 900
Landman, Maria C. 819
  Samuel 819
Lankford, Benjamin 802
Larkin, Elizabeth 918
Larney, A. F. 756
Lawrence 752
Lawson, E. W. 793
Layton, John S. 803
Leahorn, Wm. 750
Leath, Nancy 815
Ledbetter, G. C. 909
  H. M. 901
  J. P. 783, 784
  Anna 900, 901
  Colubmus W. 900

Ledbetter, Cont.
  Cora Bell 902
  Eliza 900
  Eliza Elizabeth 900
  Elizabeth 909
  Green C. 900, 901
  Henry 900, 901
  Henry N. 901
  Jane 900
  John Henry 901
  John N. 901
  Martha Ann 901
  Martha L. 901
  Mary A. 907
  Mary A. L. 900
  Mary E. 901
  Mary J. 901
  Matilda 901, 902
  Millie Elizabeth 901
  Minerva 901
  Nancy M. 900
  Sarah A. E. 901
  Sarah E. 900, 909
  Sion R. 900
  Susan Tennessee 901
Lee, Henry N. 775
Legg, Celestia 827
  David C. 827
  Eliza J. 827
  Emily E. 827
  Emma Clarinda 827
  James A. 827
  Joel E. 827
  Keziah 827
  Mary 827
  Mary J. 827
  Nancy 827
  Rufus E. 827
  Susan S. 827
  Theodocia 827
  William 827
  William W. 827
Leman 758
Lemaster, J. W. 770
Levi, Daniel 750
Lewis, J. D. 908
  J. W. 783
  T. J. 783
  Aaron 780, 782
  John C. 795
  Mary J. 908
  Merriwether 803
Lindsey 751
  A. J. 760
  T. J. 756
  W. W. 760
  Alonzo 760, 818
  Bessie 818
  Dannie 818
  Edward A. 818
  Etha J. 818
  Eugene S. 818
  Ezekiel 761
  Maizy 818
  Nancy 756
  Willie 818
Lindsley, James 805
Lineberry, C. 784
Linn, Nancy A. 857
Little, M. M. 784
  Sallie 864
Littleton, John 773
  Reilley 773
Litts 800
Locke, E. C. 820
  Asenath C. 827, 828
  Cora E. 828
  Eliza M. 827
  Elizabeth A. 828
  Ephraim C. 828
  James W. 827
  John S. 828
  Martha A. 828

Locke, Cont.
  Mary A. 828
  Nancy C. 827
  Nathaniel H. 828
  Rachel 827
  Robert N. 828
  Sallie R. 820
  Sarah F. 828, 835
  Walter 827
  Walter S. 828
  William M. 828
Lockhart, John 750
Loggans, Samuel 764
Loggins, Ada Azalie 902
  Benjamin Littleton 902
  Docia Elizabeth 902
  Elizabeth 902
  Tennessee Jane 902
  Thomas 902
  William H. 902
  William Thomas 902
Lomax, Samuel 790
  Temperance 893
  Thomas 783
Long, H. H. 784
  Eveline 902
  Frances E. 902
  Henry H. 783, 902
  Hugh W. 902
  James N. 902
  John W. 902
  Martha A. 902
  Sarah A. 902
  Wm. 750
Looney, A. M. 845
  Fannie K. 845
Love, David 792
  Matthew 758
Loveless, Nellie 906
Lowe, John 790
Lucas 754, 758
  George 750, 753, 755, 756, 761
  Maria P. 813
  Willis 750, 751
Luker, Mrs. S. D. 758
Lumpkin, Andrew J. 828
  Anna E. 828
  Barney P. 828
  Caladonia 828
  Charles 828
  Eliza 828
  Eliza C. 828
  Gustavus H. 828
  James F. 828
  James M. 828
  Jane Gertrude 828
  John B. 828
  John C. 828
  Katie Jane 828
  Louis N. 828
  Lucius T. 828
  Malinda C. 828
  Margaret L. 828
  Mollie L. 828
  Richard Earl 828
  Robert Lee 828
  Sarah C. 828
  Sarah M. 828
  Telie A. 828
  William G. 828
  William H. 828
  William J. 828
  William S. 828
Luna, Allen P. 872
  Almino 872
  Cora D. 872
  Delbert R. 872
  Hattie V. 872
  Henry D. 872
  Martha 872
  Mary P. 872
  Nancy J. 872

Luna, Cont.
  Nora B. 872
  Robert 872
  Sallie M. 872
Lynn, James 792
  Joseph 792, 793
Lyon, Delphia 874
McAnally, Elisha R. 872
  Ellender 873
  Esther 873
  Fannie 873
  Feriba 872
  Houston 873
  James E. M. 872
  John 750
  Louisa 873
  Margaret 873
  Polly A. 907
  Timothy R. 873
  Tobert F. 873
  William 750
McBride 750
  William L. 762
McCage, Aaron R. 903
  William B. 903
  Winnie 903
McCain 751
McCallister, Wm. 754
McCann, Clere 791
  John 791
McCarn, Daniel G. 768
McCauley 754
McChish, John 750
McClain, E. 758
  Alice 829
  Alice L. 826
  Annie 829
  Elizabeth 829
  Ephraim 829
  John 829
  Samuel 831
  Susan 831
McClanahan, W. P. 817
  Anna 817
McClendon, Nathan 752, 758
McClinden 751
McClintock 754
McClish, John 802
McClure, H. D. 829
  J. H. 769
  Claudie A. 829
  Emma 829
  Fannie S. 829
  Harvey B. 829
  John 766
  Maudie R. 829
  Rebecca 829
McCollum, Flora 826
  James J. 839
  Levi 793, 795
  Medora 839
McComb, Rebecca 823
McConnell 751
  James 755
  Joseph 790
  Joshua 792
  Wm. E. 797
McCoy, Eliza 820
McCracken, Amanda 846
  Calvin 846
  John 752
  Roxanna W. 846
McCrea 749
McCreary, Asenath C. 827
McCreley, Martha 849
McCulley, C. B. 769
  John 764
McCullough, R. A. 771
McDonald, Mary 788
  Molly C. 893
McDool, James 767
McDougal, ___ 768
  A. G. 776

McDougal, Cont.
  Emma L. 865
  John 771, 775, 776
  Mary 831
McElwee, Tillissee 922
McFarlan 796
McFarland 922
McGaw, Wm. 755
McGee, Betsey 873
  Frances E. 873
  James H. 873
  LeRoy 873
  Leroy S. 873
  Margaret 873
  Margaret S. 873
  Martha 873
  Mary J. 873
  Micager 873
  Rachel A. E. 873
  Susan 873
  William C. 873
McGill, John 794
McGlamery, Catherine 873
  Ed 775
  Elihu D. 873
  John 873
  Mary E. 841
  Nancy D. 874
  Mary E. 810
McGown, J. P. 760
McGrew, Celia 816
McGuire, Nancy 807
McIntyre, Daniel 750, 759
  David 750
  Duncan 752, 755
  Hugh C. 754
  John 750
  Nelson 755
McKey, Alice C. 830
  Charles 830
  Charles A. 830
  Dovey E. 830
  Edward T. 830
  Eliza 830
  Elizabeth S. 830
  Eveline 830
  James H. 830
  Luther A. 830
  Martha A. 830
  Pink L. 830
  Rob Roy 830
  Rufus B. 830
  Sarah A. 830
  Sarah F. 830
  Taylor H. 830
McKinney 751
McKnight, William 761
McLaren, A. 750
  R. L. 831
  Andrew 750
  Chanie A. 830
  Charles T. 830
  Daniel 830, 831
  John 831
  John C. 830
  Margaret 819
  Mary 824, 831
  Mary J. 830
  Morgan (colored) 757
  Ruben 762
  Sarah E. 831
  Susan 830, 831
  Susan C. 830
  Theodore D. 830
  William F. 830
McLean 769
  Burgie 832
  Coda 832
  Dora I. 832
  Elizabeth C. 831
  John L. 831
  Rachel C. 832
  Samuel 750

McLean, Cont.
  Samuel D. 831
  Thomas 832
  Walter 832
McLemore, Anna 874
  Betsey 874
  Delphia D. 874
  James H. 874
  James W. 874
  Joel H. 874
  John C. 793, 795
  John Pullen 874
  Mary E. 874
  Nora 874
  Richard M. 874
  Robert L. 874
  Sallie A. 874
  Sallie H. 874
  Virginia W. 874
McMackin, Adelia 809
  Elizabeth 847
  Martha 810
McMasters, Lurilla A. 818
  Zilpha 814
McMillan, James 750
McMillen, Elizabeth 829
McMinn, James R. 794
McNealy, Susan 919
McNickle 779
McWilliams, J. 882
  Elizabeth 882
  Mack, S. D. 775
Mackey, Wm. 755
Maddox, Victoria 839
Mahon, H. W. 770
  Henry 767, 771
  Martin 770
Malone 758, 771
Manley, John 757, 762
Martin 768, 771
  J. F. 797
  J. H., Sr. 798
  M. A. 794
  P. H. 759
  R. C. 853
  Benjamin Franklin 915
  Brice 916
  Brice Joseph Alexander 915
  Ellen A. 915
  James 872
  James Franklin 915
  Jane D. 915
  Mary A. 872
  Mary J. 915
  Mollie 916
  Nancy 872
  Ora M. 872
  Rebecca A. 915
  Richard C. 872
  Sallie A. 915
  Sam H. 775
  Samuel 915
  Sarah 915
  Wash. 798
Mason, Nathan 755
  Warren 750
Massey, S. L. 805
  Aramatta L. 923
  Emily F. 924
  Jasper D. 923
  Levisa 923
  Mary A. 923
  Nancy A. 923
  Newton A. 923
  Richard 923
  Richard A. 923
  Samuel L. 923
  William G. 923
Matthews, B. F. 760, 834
  Anna B. E. 875
  Daniel 775
  David 750
  Elbert 779

Matthews, Cont.
  Jacob 750
  James 802, 885
  William 750, 875
Maxwell, Mary 895
  William S. 783
Mayberry 796
  Frank 773
  Henry 790
Mayfield, Elijah 802
  Samuel 764, 802
Mays 849
  J. M. 749
Meacham, Alice 916
  Cowan C. 916
  Eddie J. 916
  hlizabeth 916
  Fannie 916
  Fannie G. 916
  Green 916
  James M. 916
  Lucy 916
  Marion B. 916
Meaks, M. H. 794
Meeks, M. H.919
  Annie B. 919
Mellen 861,910
Melton, Wm. 750
Meredith 767
  Alice E. 875
  Anna B. E. 875
  Annie E. 875
  Belle M. 875
  Deborah O. 875
  Elizabeth 838, 839
  Frederick 764, 874
  James F. 875
  James F. T. 875
  Jane 850
  Jane E. 888
  Jane E. B. 875
  Jane J. 832
  John 764, 765, 766
  Joseph L. 875
  Ledru R. 875
  Leonra E. 875
  Leonidas T. 875
  Lovick R. 875
  Lydia A. M. F. 875
  Mary 874
  Mary A. 874, 875, 888
  Mary E. 838, 875
  Thomas 758, 874, 875, 888
  Thomas H. 832
  Ula A. 875
  William W. 875
  Wm. 770
Merriman, Clare B. 876
  Cynthia R. 876
  David H. 876
  Eli 871, 876
  Frances E. A. 876
  James H. 875
  James R. 876
  John C. 876
  Joseph E. 876
  Mahala R. 871
  Martha E. 876
  Rachel 871, 876
  Rachel C. 876
  Thomas F. 876
  Virginia A. 876
  Walter N. 876
Merritt, Frances 882, 884
Mester, Anna M. 833
  Frances 833
  George H. 832, 833
  John W. 833
  Kasper 832
  Katie 833
  Louis H. 833
  Mary 832
Metcalf, Felicia L. 833

Metcalf, Cont.
  James M. 833
  Jane 833
  Mary L. 833
  William H. 833
Michels, Henry 797
Milam, Bartley 790
Miller 767
  J. J. 762
  Alex 755
  Alexander 752, 753
  John 750, 751
  John L. 806
  Joseph 761
  Lewis 754, 760
  Mary 877
  Micager 877
Milton, Elijah 750
  Elisha 750
Mitchell 751
  Araminta 836
  David C. 803
  Greenberry 788
  John 764
  Martha A. 860
  Samuel 772
  Thos. 750
Monday, Wm. 754
Montague, A. 766
  J. W. 866
  Abraham 775, 877
  Almyra I. 859
  Amos H. 876
  Clarissa 877
  Edna C. 876
  Frank 876
  Joanna 866, 876
  John 880
  John F. 866, 876, 770
  Mary Anna E. 876
  Mary C. 866
  Melissa 880
  Nancy J. 877
  Nancy L. 880
  William L. 774
  William Y. 876
Montgomery, D. 795
  Elizabeth 861
  Elizabeth J. 912
  John 791
  Rebecca 879
Moore, J. H. 794
  J. M. 768
  S. B. 797, 917
  W. P. 760, 813
  Armstead 917
  Jas. 772
  John H. 916, 917
  Jordan 799
  Levisa G. 917
  Margaret C. 917
  Mary A. 917
  Mary T. 922
  Sarah 868
  William P. 760
  Wm. C. 784
Morgan 751
  L. M. 769
  Daniel 810
  Dieudonie R. 877
  Eliza J. 810
  Elizabeth 866
  James L. 876
  Jane 876
  Lillie H. 877
  Mary 810, 877
  Peter 796
  Pleasant 876
  Viola B. 877
Morris 764
  A. 773
  J. 771
  W. L. 771

Morris, Cont.
  Clarissa F. 878
  Elias 790
  James E. H. 877
  Jonathan 766, 877
  Jordan 770
  Joseph 790
  Martha R. 877
  Nancy J. 877
  Rebecca 877
  Shadrack 803
  Thomas F. 878
  Wayne 877
  William 877
Morrison, J. P. 795
  L. W. 784
  Edward 878
  Elizabeth 878
  John F. 878
  Joseph C. 878
  Kate 878
  Lizzie 878
  Lucy 878
  Lydia 878
  Margaret A. 878
  Martha A.878
  Mary A. 878
  Mary Ann 869
  Merida 878
  Mildred 878
  Nancy J. 878
  Sallie 878
  Sofina E. 878
  William 791
  William D. 878
  William S. 878
Morrow, Archibald 750, 860
  Frances 860
  John 768
  Martha 860
Mosby 767
Moss, A. W. 849
  Lena J. 849
Mulholland, Elizabeth 845
Mullen, Wm. 799
Murphy 830
  J. D. 793
  Absalom 750
  Eliza 863
  George 863
  John 775
  Mark 780, 782
  Mathew 767
Murrell, John A. 767
Murrill, W. T. 793
Murtishaw, B. A. 771
Musgrave, Nancy 751
Napier 802
  Wm. H. 805
Neal, P. A.758
  W. P. 760
  W. W. 758
  Amanda H. 834
  Nancy 833
  Paul A. 834
  Sarah M. 834
  Wiley W. 833
Neely, S. L. 784
Nelson, Alice 841
  Allie 842
  John 841
Nesbitt, Fannie 881
  Margaret 881
Newsom, Green B. 780, 781
Newton, Jesse 779
  John 779
  Nancy A. 895
  Robert 752
  Ursley 819
Niblett, Sarah E. 907
Nichols, J. J.772
  Edna Belle 879
  John H. 878, 879

Nichols, Cont.
  Martha J. 878
  Rutha J. 879
Nicholson, A. O. P. 756
Nicks, John 790
Nieman, Mary 832
Nightengale 803
Nix, Sallie 904
Nixon, G. H. 754, 757, 794
  H. 758
  O. A. 794, 799
  W. F. 761
  W. J. 758
  W. T. 758
  Canty 798
  Cora C. 918
  Cordelia 917
  Elizabeth G. 834
  Forest 918
  George 803
  George H. 759, 769, 805, 834, 860
  Henry 794, 834, 917, 918
  Laura 834
  Orville A. 917, 918
  Thomas 918
  Virginia A. 918
  William T. 834
Noles, Allen J. 805
Norman, Annie C. 865
  Rachel C. 832
Norris, A. W. 918
  Andrew 797, 918
  Bernard 919
  Cora B. 919
  Elizabeth 918
  Fannie 919
  John 919
  Mackie P. 919
  Matilda C. 919
  Mollie E. 919
  Nancy 895
  William W. 919
North, H. 835
  N. M. 835
  Harriett 835
  Ira 835
  Ira, Jr. 835
  Mary E. 835
  Mary I. 835
  Sarah F. 835
  William Lee 835
Nowland, James 883
  Mary M. 883
Nowlings, W. T. 883
  Jeannette J. 883
Null, John 750
Nunley, J. W. 764
  Sarah M. 849
Nunn 781
Nunnelly 796
  Annie B. 919
  Elise 919
  Elizabeth 919
  Harry 919
  Kate 919
  Lawson H. 919
  Nettie 919
  Walter S. 919
Nutt, Anna Lee 879
  David A. 879
  James A. 879
  Maben A. 879
  Maggie 879
  Pleasant G. 879
  Rebecca 879
  Sarah 879
  William 879
Old, Ada 851
  Eglantine 881
  Henry S. 881
  Isaac H. 851
  Martha D. 881

Oliphant, Samuel 790
O'Neal, John 886
Orr, Robert 758
Overton, Virginia A. 918
Owens, Catherine 907
  Sarah 896
Oxford 751
Page, Moses 768
Paine, Harlan 750
  Thomas 750, 761
  Thomas H. 848
Parker, J. B. 758, 843
  John A. 835
  Joshua 835
  Martha 860
  Mary A. 887
  Nettie 835
  Thomas 755
  Wm. 749
Parkes, Elizabeth G. 834
  Laura 834
  Loulie S. 844
  Wm. 754, 761, 762
Parks, Catherine D. 845
  James 845
Parrish, Lucy 914
Parrott, James 756
  Margaret C. 756
Parsons, Miles 750
Patterson, Cora Elizabeth 904
  David C. 903
  Edward 794
  Elbert Foster 904
  Emma Elnora 904
  Emma J. 903
  Ezra R. 903
  James W. 903
  Jesse Harvey 904
  Laura Lee 904
  Malinda E. 903
  Malinda W. 903
  Martha M. 904
  Mary E. 903
  Robert 779
  Robert C. 903
  Robert E. 903
  Robert H. 903
  Robert L. 903
  Sallie 904
  Sarah M. 903
  Viola Josephine 904
  William 779, 903
  William L. 903
  William V. 904
Patton, James 806
Pavatt, Cordelia 917
  Stephen C. 757, 769, 784, 794
Payne, Hardin 753
  Thomas H. 846
  William B. 764
  Wm. B. 766
Pearce, Spencer 750
Pearson, C. L. 783, 784
  Anne 904
  Charles L. 904
  Charlotte 904
  George 784
  George W. 904
  Georgiana P. 904
  Henry Robert 904
Peerey 796
Peery, Buchanan 790
  George 790
  James 790
  Levi 790
Pennicuff 751
  Jacob 756
Pennington, J. J. 762
  Absalom 750
  Daniel 750
  David 750
  Isaac 750, 755
  Jacob 750

Pennington, Cont.
  Moses 750
  William 750
Perkins 750
  Nicholas 756
  Samuel V. 804
Perley, S. 766
Pettigrew, C. 891
  J. M. 891
  George 786
Petty, Patsey 895
Peyton, George J. 798
Phenix, Henry 757
Phenixe 751
Philips 796
Phillips 911
  Amanda 799
  Anna 900, 901
  Bennie 920
  Clara 920
  Elizabeth 880
  Fannie 920, 921
  Lizzie 920
  Nellie 920
  Nettie 919
  Pollie 920
  Samuel 880
  Sarah 880
  Susan 919
  William 792, 793, 919
  William H. 919, 920
Pickard, P. P. 783
Pickens, Andrew 750
  Eliza B. 823
Pierce, H. M. 791
  Aaron A. 836
  Alexander A. 836
  Annie L. 836
  Araminta 836
  Bertie M. 836
  Emmett L. 836
  George W. 836
  Ida G. 836
  Jemima 836
  Laura 836
  Lucy 836
  Lulu E. 836
  Maggie C. 836
  Maggie V. 836
  Mannie M. 836
  Mary L. 836
  Minnie J. 836
  Samuel 762, 836
  Spencer 836
  William A. 836
  William H. 836
Pillow, Alvin G. 885
  Gideon J. 772
  Granville A. 772
  Mary 885
  Ruth T. 885
Plummer, F. A. 805
Poag, Lovina 850
Poley, John 750
Polk, L. J. 772
  W. J. 772
  James K. 757
Pollard, Wm. 769
Pollock 750
Pope, C. A. 765
  Craig W. 764
Porter, G. B. 759
  J. J. 769
Poteet 751
  Sam D. 756
  Samuel D. 752
Potter, Winnie 903
Potts, Mollie E. 818
Powell, A. J. 760
  J. B. 837
  J. M. 837
  M. M. 754, 837
  Andrew 837

Powell, Cont.
  Benjamin 754
  Bettie A. 818
  Calvin T. 837
  George 837
  Hannah P. 837
  John D. 837
  Lillian E. 837
  Malinda 837
  Mary J. 814
  Nannie E. 837
  Sarah L. 837
Pratt, A. J. 759
Prewett 754
  Martin 750, 751
Price 754
  Elizabeth 816
  Ezekiel 838
  Lillie S. 838
  Martha 838
  Mary T. 838
  William J. 838
Priest, Abram 885
  Green D. 750
  Mary E. 885
  Nancy 885
Prim, J. T. 796
  John S. 792
  John T. 798
Primm, Lizzie 920
Prince, Miles 784
Prior, E. 760
Provat, Stephen 866
Puckett, M. H. 793
Pullen, Betsey 874
  Sarah L. 837
  Thomas 763
Putnam, L. M. 759
Quarles, Amon T. 838
  David T. 838
  Elizabeth 838
  "Granny" 788
  Mary E. 838
  Mary J. 808
  Mary T. 838
  Russell A. 838
  William L. 838
Rackley, Phoebe 846
Rainey, Rhoda Y. 869
Rains, A. B. 749
  I. B. 749
  J. A. 783
  John A. 780, 782
Ramsey, R. G. 762
  Laura W. 860
  Lou Dora 851
  Mary D. 881
Randal, Nancy 779
Rankin, Bettie 856
  Ida 856
  James C. M. 856
Rasbury, Alonzo M. 880
  Andrew C. 879
  Elizabeth 880
  Elizabeth J. 880
  Eudoxia R. 880
  Jane 874, 879
  John A. 880
  John C. 879
  Lott G. 880
  Lovick 772, 864, 874, 879, 880
  Lovick D. 880
  Lydia C. 880
  Martha A. 880
  Mary 880
  Mary A. 874, 880, 888
  Rebecca 880
  Rebecca E. 880
  Sarah J. 880
  Surilda A. 880
  William L. 880
Ray, H. J. 773

Ray, Cont.
  John 750, 751
Rayburn, Henry 764, 765, 771
  John 764, 773
Read, S. 764
Reed, Edith 883
Reeves, A. M. 793
  Charles 767
  James 764
  Redden 805
  Redding 803
  Thomas 764, 771, 773
Renfro 767
Renfrow, Peter 764
Renham, Elizabeth 880
  John 880
  Rebecca 880
Reynolds, Hugh R. 837
  James M. 773, 775
  Joe 750
  Joseph B. 794
  Mary A. 837
  Nannie E. 837
  Nehemiah 750
  William 750
Rhoads, James 802
Rhodes, W. 759
Ribble, Alice 811
Rice, H. E. 784
  Isaac 764
  Millie E. 816
Richardson, M. J. 758
  George W. 762
  William 790
Ricketts, S. S. 769, 772
  T. R. 772
  W. T. 880
  Charles 772
  Della M. 880
  Frank 880
  James T. 880
  John S. 880
  John W. 805
  Joseph 880
  Mary 880
  Mary J. 769, 880
  Melissa 880
  Milton 880
  Nancy L. 880
  Samuel S. 880
  Tennessee R. 880
Rickman, B. G. 783, 786
Ridgeford, James 815
Riesenbeck, Anna M. 833
Rise, Mary 890
Roach, Stephen 772
Roachwell, W. 776
Roberts 754
  A. J. 775
  John O. 764, 767, 772
  Sarah E. 907
Robertson 767
  Isaac 764, 773
  Michael 764
Robinson, W. H. 759
  Isaac 769
Robnett, Cynthia P. 881
  Ellender 881
  Fannie 873, 881
  James 881
  Jane 881
  Jeremiah 881
  John 873, 881
  Joseph N. 881
  Margaret 881
  Nancy 873, 881
  Neal S. 881
Roddy 836
Rodgers, George 750
  Jesse 792
Rogers, George 755
Roland, Stephen 750
Roper, James 827

Roper, Cont.
  Keziah 827
  Mary 880
Rose, R. H. 758, 769, 844, 866
  S. E. 752, 844
  W. S. 839
  Alfred H. 839
  Alfred P. 839
  Elizabeth 838, 839
  Mary Ann 839
  Medora 839
  Mildred 839
  Robert 794
  Robert H. 838, 839
  Solon E. 835
  Victoria 839
  William 838, 839
Ross 771
  A. H. 773
  J. L. 775
  W. B. 767
  Henry 755
  Rachel 827
  William B. 764
  Wm. B. 766
Rowels, William P. 758
Rowls, W. P. 844
Rubbert, Margaret 839
Russell 776
  F. B. 920
  J. H. 796
  J. R. 764
  Henry 920
  Hester 920
  James 772
  James R. 764
  Joseph H. 920
  Leta 920
  Mary E. 920
  Nellie 920
  Omer 920
Rust, Lucy 825
Rutherford, Betsey 900
Rutledge, J. H. 769
  Susan 830
Salmon, James 779
Sandels, Elizabeth 919
  John 919
Sanders 768
  J. H. 760
  George 755
Sandroell, Alois 759
Sanford, Edward 772
Schade, Charles C. 840
  Christina 840
  George 839
  Henry 840
  John 758, 839, 840
  Joseph B. 840
  Lizzie 840
  Margaret 839
  Mary C. 840
  Theresa B. 840
Schull, Benjamin 764
  David 764
Scott, J. 768
  R. P. 764
  Anna 856
  James 751, 756, 758, 779
  John M. 856
  William 764
Scully, Maria 814
Seahorn 754
Segmore 754
Selph 858
Sexton, Alice J. 840
  Edward H. 840
  Elizabeth A. 840
  John J. 840
  Lewis A. 840
  Mary E. 840
  William R. 840

Shannon, Gazaway 848
　Jane 848
　Maggie E. 848
Sharp 751
　Edward 802
　Henry 752, 755, 756, 757
　John 802
　John M. 803
　Joshua 802
　Nehemiah 802
　Samuel 802
　Thomas 838
　William 802, 805
Shaw, R. A. 773
　James G. 803
Shegog, Robert 796, 798
Shelton, J. M. 762
　Rosa 920
　Virginia 894
Shepard, E. H. 896
　Egbert Haywood 905
　Jane 905
　Mary Jane 905
　Naomi 905
　Sallie 896
　Samuel Clinton 905
　William 905
Sherrell 773
Sheild, E. J. 838
Shields, J. H. 774
　J. T. 876
　Frances E. A. 876
　Francis E. A. 881
　James T. 881
　Martha D. 876, 881
　Mary D. 881
　Mary E. 881
　Virginia I. 881
　William B. 881
Ship, Joseph 792
　Josiah 790
Shipman, C. W. 775
　Charles 882
　Charles W. 882
　Eddie 882
　Edward 882
　Elizabeth 882
　Henry T. 882
　Ida E. 882
　Jane E. 882
　Jesse T. 882
　Ola M. 882
　Pantha U. 882
　William H. 882
Shirley, John 750
Shoffner, Jane 824
　Martin 824
　Mary 837
　Mary A. 824
Short, Thomas H. 768
Shouse 799
Shy, Lewis 786
Sills, W. C. 762
Simmons, Benjamin 902
　Eveline 902
　Thomas 783
　Wiley 770
　Wm. 751
　Young 802
Simms 758
　J. B. 761
　Daniel 750
　Elizabeth 817
　John B. 841
　Julia A. 810
　Mary E. 810, 841
　Paris L. 810, 841
Simonton, John 755
　Mary 844
Simpson, Hugh 771
Sims, A. M. 882
　H. C. 882
　M. J. 770, 771

Sims, Cont.
　T. W. 784
　Abraham M. 884
　Bessie 905
　Daniel 802
　Dorothy 882, 883
　Dorothy A. 882, 888
　Dorothy J. 883
　Dorothy W. 884
　Edith M. C. 883
　Edna E. 905
　Eliza 897
　Elizabeth 882
　Erskine Kent 905
　Frances 882, 884
　Francis 883
　George W. 905
　Hannah 884
　Henry Clay 883
　Jeannette J. 883
　Jemima C. 884
　Jennie 905
　John S. 883
　Joseph 884
　Mabel 884
　Mahulda C. 882
　Mahulda Isaphene 884
　Malinda T. 882
　Margaret 889
　Mary M. 883
　Mary O. 884
　Matthew J. 882, 883
　Nannie H. 905
　Robert 882, 884
　Robert M. 884
　Sarah E. 883
　Shields 882, 883
　Thetus W. 905
　Tommie 905
　Winfield S. 882
　Z. Taylor 882
Sinclair, Wm. 769
Siser, John 779
Sizemore, Abraham 751
Skillern, D. S. 774
　Anderson 850, 871
　Caroline 850
　Polly 850, 871
　Susan T. 871
　Wm. A. 775
Skipwith 803
Slayden, Addie 921
　Campbell 920
　Emily Jane 921
　Emma J. 921
　George A. 921
　John P. 921
　Rosa 920
　Rosa C. 921
　Sarah A. 809
　Thomas J. 921
　William C. 921
　William E. 920
Sloan, W. N. 785
　Chester L. H. 906
　James B. 905
　James L. 784, 905
　James P. 906
　Leonidas W. 906
　Mary A. 905
　Mary F. 906
　Sarah W. 906
　Walter N. 906
Smith 765
　J. L. 764
　R. H. 794
　S. A. 860
　W. C. 808
　Alice 841
　Allie 842
　Andrew J. 841
　A. Wildie 842
　Benjamin 750

Smith, Cont.
　Calvin T. 841
　Catherine 884
　Daniel 750
　Daniel D. 793
　Eliza 828
　James 841
　James H. 841
　Jessie 885
　John 750, 884
　John L. 769
　John N. 841
　Jonas C. 842
　Laura B. 860, 884
　Louisa 842
　Louisa W. 841
　Martha 841
　Martha J. 841
　Mary Jane 905
　Mary T. 842
　Matilda J. 842
　Mattie B. 818
　Robert N. 842
　Robert O. 804
　Robert W. 842
　Ruth 842
　Sallie J. 808
　Samuel A. 884
　Samuel J. 841
　Sarah C. 842
　Thomas Benton 821
　Warren 783
　William 750, 841, 842
　William R. 841, 842
Smithson, Noble 794, 835
Smotherman, James 769
　Sarah C. 769
Soaper, B. 759
Solinsky, Annie 824
Songer, Ann E. 852
Sowell, H. B. 758
　Amanda H. 834
　Henry B. 842
　Joseph M. 842
　Mary A. 842
Sparkman, J. C. 763
　Delany M. 840
　James G. 840
　Mary E. 840
Spear, Nathan 751
Spears, Edward 772
Speer, Bettie 870
Spence, W. C. 761
Spencer, A. J. 826
　M. E. 826
　Jacob 771
　Nannie M. 826
　Thomas 751
Spiegel, A. L. 835
　Mary I. 835
Spreegle, Asenath C. 828
　James 828
Spring, Polly 850, 871
Springer 758
　N. C. 808
　Aaron 808
　Aaron F. 843
　Alice Leslie 843
　Alix C. 843
　Annie 862
　Caladonia 828
　Emma B. 843
　Jacob 808, 843
　James C. 843
　Jonas 862
　Lillie S. 843
　Malinda C. 843
　Margaret 837
　Mary S. A. 843
　Mollie C. 843
　Robert C. 843
　Ruth 842
　Sallie E. 843

Springer, Cont.
  Sarah A. 862
  Sarah M. 828
Staggs, David 767
  Fannie 881
  James 764
  Joseph 764, 881
  Nancy 873, 881
Stamfield, Jackson 791
Stanfield, A. J. 799
  John F. 796
Stanley, Ferney 779
  Ferry 787
  John 779
Stanly, Isaac W. 779
Starrett, Mary A. 905
Stebastian, S. P. 797
  W. K. 794
  Samuel 793, 796, 797
Steel 750
  David 756
Steele, Alexander 764
Steen 754
Stephens, Elisha 786
Stephenson, John 761
Steward, Martha 907
Stewart, B. G. 793
  J. W. 754
  M. 796
  W. A. 758
  W. T. 752
  Alex. 754, 762
  Alexander 844
  Bart G. 792
  Charles 793, 795
  Daniel M. 843
  David 750
  Jennie L. 844
  John W. 844
  Lazarus 756
  Loulie S. 844
  Parkes Evans 844
  Sarah F. 843
  Thomas 755
  William A. 843
Stockard, J. W. 804, 805
  Adeline 850
  Amanda E. 924
  Augustus Z. 885
  Beatrice E. 924
  Bettie D. 885
  Catherine M. 924
  Charles F. 885
  Cora A. 885
  Edgar 885
  Eleanor 924
  Eliza 885
  Elizabeth 924
  Elizabeth D. 924
  Eula 885
  George H. 924
  Isom C. 885
  James L. 885
  Jamed W. 924
  John 768, 885
  John J. 924
  John M. 885
  John R. 924
  Joseph A. 924
  Lena 885
  Leroy V. 885
  Margaret 924
  Mary A. 875
  Mary E. 885
  Mary J. 885
  Mary S. 924
  Mosella 885
  Parmelia A. 924
  Richard 924
  Richard V. 924
  Samuel H. 885
  Samuel J. 924
  Samuel M. 924

Stockard, Cont.
  Sarah A. 924
  Silas M. 924
  Thomas A. 885
  Thomas V. 924
  Ursely 924
  William J. 924
  William N. 885
Stockberry, Hannah 884
Stone, Barton W. 800
  Bransford 885
  Eglantine 881
  Joel A. 885
  John P. 885
  Mary P. 885
  Noble 750
  Ruth 885
  Ruth T. 885
  Samuel E. 885
  Samuel H. 885
  Solomon 750
  Temperance M. 845
  Thomas 845
  William 793
  Willis S. 885
  Wm. 750
Stoneball, Anderson 765, 772
Story, William C. 806
Straughn, William 755
Strawn, Horace 751
  Wm. 755
Strayhom, Josiah K. 803
Strayhorn, Joseph 804
Streight 774
Stribling, A. 758
  C. C. 771, 772, 775
  J. T. 758
  Amelia A. 886
  Andrew H. 886
  Christopher C. 886
  Cornelius K. 886
  Edward L. 845
  Emma I. 886
  Fannie K. 845
  James H. 845
  James L. 844
  John 757, 886
  Mary 844
  Mary A. 845
  Mary Frances 810
  Mary J. 845
  Monetta L. 886
  Obadiah T. 844
  Obediah 757
  Pattie S. 886
  Rachel 886
  Robert Lee 845
  Rose E. 845
  Sarah E. 886
  Thomas H. 886
Strickland 751
Stricklin, Polly Ann 906
Stringham 751
Stubblefield, Elizabeth M. 864
  Peter 864
  Sallie 864
  Stephen 771
Sullivan, John 750
  Martha 818, 831
Surrett, James 764
Sutton, K. I, 797
  James B. 781
Swanzy, Nancy 915
Swinton, Sam 757
Sykes, W. H. 749
  Eliza 815
  Elizabeth 845
  James 815, 845
  Jennie P. 845
  Maggie J. 815
  Mollie E. 818
  Sarah T. 815
  William H. 845

Talby, John 750
Tally 754
Tankersley, Rachel 876
Tanner, Wiley 779
Tarkington, J. O. 752
  J. W. 753
  John G. 791
Tarpley, Alexander 845
  Benjamin M. 845
  Catherine D. 845
  Charles C. 845
  Elizabeth 845
  Elizabeth Agnes 845
  Helen M. 845
  John C. 845
  John R. 845
  Leonidas J. 845
  Mary V. 845
  Sarah P. 845
  Temperance M. 845
  Thomas D. 845
  William A. 845
Tarrant, James 807
  Samuel L. 806
Tate, Alvin 906
  Lemuel 906
  Millie Elizabeth 901
  Nellie 906
  Polly Ann 906
Tatom, Susan 908
Tatum, John 791
Taylor, J. C. 858
  J. W. 786
  Z. 760
  Betsey 906
  Charity 812
  Jesse 783, 784, 906
  John 783
  John M. 794
  Laura A. 865
  Louisa 865
  Mary 906
  Mary A. 907
  Melissa 865, 866
  Viola A. 858
  William 906
  William H. 865
Teas, Chas. 767, 771
  James 750
  Joseph 750
Terrell, Joseph 757
Terry, Eliza Elizabeth 900
  Jason 900
  Sallie 853
Thomas, E. W. 759
  R. M. 783
  Chas. 756
  James H. 794
  Nathaniel 766
  Priscilla 823
  Samuel 750, 808
  Temperance 809
  Verlinda 808
  William 750
Thompson 772, 773, 776
  A. T. 796
  E. G. 794, 796
  G. W. 859
  W. D. 793
  W. J. 798
  Allen 796
  Asa 921
  Asberry 775
  Catherine 921
  Ebenezer 750
  Elisha G. 921
  Elizabeth 882
  Fannie 921
  H. Clagett 921
  Jackson 850
  Jesse 764
  John 757
  Lillie A. 850

Thompson, Cont.
　Lucy 921
　Mary 850, 921
　Naomi Elizabeth 916
Thornton, Mary 824
Thrasher, Elias 775
Tidwell, C. D. 846
　Andrew J. 846
　Calloway H. 846
　Charles W. 846
　Darling M. 846
　Emma L. 846
　Frances L. 846
　James C. 846
　John V. 846
　Lulu 846
　Mary J. 846
　Nancy D. 846
　Phoebe 846
　Phoebe E. 846
　Robert E. L. 846
　Roxanna W. 846
　Sarah M. 834
　Thomas M. 846
　Vincent 846
　Wiley N. 846
　William J. 846
Tinnon, Carns M. 886
　Elizabeth B. 870
　Jane 886
　John 886
　John A. 844
Tinsley, Spencer 790
Tipton, W. E. 751
Todd, Malinda C. 843
Toll, Jonathan 790
Tracy, John 779, 780
Travis, W. E. 889
Trimble, J. M. 800
Trotty, Barnett 795
　Lewis P. 795
　Zachariah 795
True, T. K. 846
　Carrie E. 809
　David H. 846
　Ellen 846
　Sarah A. 809
　Shiloh 809
Tucker, E. 760
　G. H. 773
　Enoch 751, 757
　Jesse 751
　Joseph 779
　William 751
Tulley, Wm. F. 798
Tumbo, Hugh 868
　Louisa J. 868
　Mary 868
Turnbow, S. H. 888
　Ambrose M. 888
　Della 888
　Jacob 751
　James W. 888
　John 888
　Martha 888
　Mary 888
　William 888
Turman 867
　E. V. 775
　Benjamin 888
　Benjamin D. 887
　Camilla 887
　Dorothy A. 882, 888
　Ione 887
　James 888
　John 882, 887, 888
　John C. 887
　Lizzie 888
　Mary A. 887
　Nancy D. 874
　Sarah 887
　William 887
　William B. 887

Turner, J. B. 759
　John 779
　Wm. K. 794
Tutnell 751
　Needham 753
Twilla, Anna 907
　Catherine 907
　Elizabeth 907
　James W. 907
　John H. 907
　Lucinda 907
　Sarah E. 907
　Thomas B. 907
　William F. 907
Tyree, Cyrus 771
Vandiveer, John H. 805
Vaughan, John L. 907
　Martha 907
　Melissa 907
　Minnie A. 907
　Myrtle Estelle 907
　Sallie M. 907
　William 907
Vaughn, Araminta T. 847
　Elizabeth 838
　Mary A. 819, 847
　Mary E. 901
　Theodore D. 847
　Thomas 819, 847
　William 901
Venable, Bryson B. 802
　Hugh B. 803, 804, 805
　Wm. 767
Winyard, William 795
Voorhees, Daniel 764
　David 803
　John 750
Voorhies, Aaron 912
　Angeline 912
　David 879, 912
　Elizabeth 879
　Jane 879
　Jasper Newton 912
　John 912
　Margaret Malissa 912
　Martha 912
　Mary 912
　Mary Jane 912
　Melissa 812
　Rebecca 912
　Robert 912
Voss, James 803
　John 750
　Levi 809
　Lou 809
　Sarah 809
　Wm. 750
Wade, Robert 790
Waggoner, Lewis C. 783
Waites, Amelia A. 886
Walker 751, 776
　G. T. 773
　J. C. 769, 794
　J. P. 764
　J. W. 760
　T. J. 793
　W. B. 764
　Elijah 769, 794
　Eliza A. 851
　Elizabeth 764
　George 851
　James 772, 921
　James P. 764
　Joel 792, 796
　John F. 796
　John T. 796, 921
　Mary E. 922
　Mary J. 880, 922
　Mollie E. 919
　Polly 871
　Pleasant 793
　Samuel 790
　William 807

Walker, Cont.
　William B. 764
　Wm. 772
　Wm. B. 765
Wallace, Hugh 790
Ward 795
　J. C. 797
　Hillary 794
　John 790
　Malissa C. 909
　Nathan 779
　William 779
Wardard, Elizabeth 849
Warner, I. 771
Warren 771
　A. W. 794
　D. B. 793
　J. T. 791
　T. F. 772
　Charles 790
　John 754
Warrington, Wesley 765
Wasson, Elizabeth C. 831
　Wm. 754
Watson, John 764
Wayland, Miss M. E. 826
　S. H. 827
　Simeon H. 759
Wayne, Anthony 765
Weams, Joseph 795
Weatherford, Sarah 851
Weatherly, A. W. 806
　S. Q. 805
Webb 898
　J. L. 782
　W. C. 782, 783, 786
　Elizabeth 907
　John 779, 907
　John L. 783, 784, 907, 918
　Martha A. 908
　Nancy J. 897
　Polly A. 907
　William C. 907, 908
Weber, Margaret 898
Weems, W. T. 784
　Augustus 908
　Ella Eugenie 908
　George F. 908
　Jesse A. 908
　Mary J. 908
　Susan 908
　William T. 908
Welch 754'
　J. W. 848
　Albert S. 848
　Ben T. 848
　Elizabeth 847
　Ella J. 848
　Elroy E. 848
　Fannie E. 848
　George K. 848
　Georgia A. 848
　Henry 762
　James 751, 755, 850
　James A. 848
　John 750, 756, 764
　John A. 848
　John L. 847
　John W. 847
　Josephine R. 848
　Kate E. 848
　Leonard G. 848
　Maggie E. 848
　Malinda 837
　Martha E. 848
　Mary J. 820, 848
　Maude E. 848
　Nicholas 779
　Rachel 847
　Rachel J. 848
　Senith 850
　Thomas 751, 752, 755
　Wm. 783

Welker, Elijah 751
Wellington, Henry 750
Wells, G. P. 773
  Mary 819
Welsh, Lucy 836
West, Rebecca H. 915
  Wm. 770
Westmore, Mary A. 819
  Thomas J. 757
Westmoreland, Martha A. 823
Wharton 751, 754
Whitaker, Betsey 874
  Delphia 851, 874
  James 850
  James C. 874
  John 874
  Martha C. 850
  Sallie A. 874
Whitby 770
White 754
  B. C. 796
  G. O. 753
  J. M. 760
  Augustus J. 848
  Carrie May Cleveland 849
  George O. W. 848
  John 755
  Lena Gertrude 849
  Lena J. 849
  Lyndal Warren 849
  Mary A. 848
  Mary Isabella 899
Whitehead, P. 771
  T. D. 774
Whiteside 879
  Samuel 806
Whitesides, Samuel A. 805
Whitfield, J. W. 794
  T. J. 796
  John W. 794
  Mary 911
  Theodosia C. 911
  Wilkes 911
Whitley, S. D. 771
Whitsides, Charles 796
Whitson 796
  R. M. 795
  Jennie 905
  Robert 795
  Samuel 793, 794
Whittaker, Ada 871
  John C. 871
  Susan 871
Whitton, J. C. 768
Whitwell, P. 784
  W. H. 786
  James Lomax 779
  John 779
  Malissa C. 909
  Margaret 908
  Pleasant 908, 909
  Samuel 779
  Thomas 779, 781, 784, 908
Wilburn, Mary 895
  Nancy 896
  Noami 905
Wiley, C. T. 784
Wilkes, Mary 891
Wilkey, Nancy 892
Wilkins, James 779
Willeford, Hardy 820
  Mary O. 820
  Nancy 820
Williams, 781
  A. M. 796
  J. J. 794, 795
  S. G. 791
  S. H. 794, 796, 917
  Amanda J. 823
  Andrew 888
  Cordelia 917
  Daniel 751
  Jane E. 888

Williams, Cont.
  Joseph R. 888
  Lovick R. Bell 888
  Margaret C. 917
  Moses 751
  Samuel H. 758, 861
  Thomas A. 888
  Violet A. 888
  William 764, 888
  Wm. 750
Williamson, Susan A. 890
Willis, R. D. 759
Wilson, G. W. 759
  Adam 790
  Estelle 922
  Eunice 922
  Fannie 922
  James 793
  Jordan 922
  Mary 822
  Mary T. 922
  Rebecca 817
  Roffie 922
  S. McE. 794, 796, 797, 922
  Samuel B. 922
  Thomas 922
  Tillissee 922
  Ursely 924
  William 792, 924
Wimberly, Malachi 771, 772, 765
Wims, John 780
Wisdom 751, 754
  A. B. 773
  Margaret 873
  Pollard 751, 752, 755, 756
  Wm. 755
Wood, Betsey 906
  West 780, 781, 782, 783
Woodard, Eliza 849
  Solomon 849
Woods, W. H. 870
  Martha E. 870, 871
  Mary E. 870, 871
  William 871
Wooten, Martha N. 816
Worten, Wm. 750
Wright 775
  J. 772
  Anna 910
  Simeon C. 910
Yarbrough, Nancy 836
Yates, James 779, 780, 781
Yaw, Jane 868
Yeager, Elizabeth A. 840
Young, H. J. 783
  T. G. 901
  Docia 898
  Elizabeth 909
  Evan 772
  Henry 790
  James Walker 909
  John 779
  John Brownlow 909
  John M. 909
  Robert T. 909
  Samuel 898, 909
  Samuel G. 909
  Sarah A. E. 901
  Sarah E. 909
  Thomas 771
  William H. 909
Youngblood, Edith 883
  Edith M. C. 883
  John William 889
  J(oseph) 888, 889
  Josiah 883
  Margaret 889
  Mary 883
  M(atthew) 888, 889
  M. Elizabeth 883
  William 883
Zeigler, Christina 840
Zollicoffer 821

Zollicoffer, Cont.
  F. K. 833
  Felicia 833

www.ingramcontent.com/pod-product-compliance
Lightning Source LLC
Chambersburg PA
CBHW051431290426
44109CB00016B/1517